De-democratization Processes in Poland in 2015–23

The crisis of liberal democracy is clearly visible today, manifesting itself, *inter alia*, in the declining interest of citizens in participating in elections; the disappearance, or at least weakening, of the traditional axis of social conflict between labour and capital; the growing importance of populism; attacks on democratic institutions; and the efforts of leaders in many countries to centralize power. Across the globe, anti-establishment, anti-system, anti-elite and populist sentiments are on the rise, accompanied by the increasing prominence of anti-democratic parties. This volume aims to identify universal mechanisms of de-democratization using the example of Poland, by searching for reliable indicators of these processes. The authors examine and analyse the weakening of democratic institutions, the limitation of civil liberties, and the growth of authoritarian tendencies and political polarization, seeking out indicators of de-democratization phenomena in the legal-institutional, political-social and economic spheres, while also looking into actions that strengthen and protect de-democratization, which take place in the symbolic, social, political and economic domains.

The authors thus seek to expand the existing analyses of de-democratization processes in a volume which will be of great use to those researching and studying democracy, the rule of law, contemporary politics and de-democratization in Poland and beyond.

Grzegorz Foryś is a sociologist, political scientist and professor at the Institute of Law, Economics, and Administration of the University of the National Education Commission in Kraków, Poland. He specializes in the sociology of social change, the sociology of politics, the sociology of social movements and democracy. His works include *The Dynamics of Contention: Farmers' Protests in the Third Polish Republic* (2008), *Agritourism Farms and Associations in Poland: In Search of a Social Movement* (2017), *Politics, Society, and the Economy in Contemporary Poland* (2016) and *Development as a Social Movement* (2023). He has also published numerous articles in Polish and international journals.

Europa Country Perspectives

The Europa Country Perspectives series, from Routledge, examines a wide range of contemporary political, economic, developmental and social issues from areas around the world. Complementing the *Europa Regional Surveys of the World* series, *Europa Country Perspectives* is a valuable resource for academics, students, researchers, policymakers, business people and anyone with an interest in current world affairs.

While the *Europa World Year Book* and its associated Regional Surveys inform on and analyse contemporary economic, political and social developments at the national and regional level, *Country Perspectives* provide in-depth, country-specific volumes written or edited by specialists in their field, delving into a country's particular situation. Volumes in the series are not constrained by any particular template, but may explore a country's recent political, economic, international relations, social, defence, or other issues in order to increase understanding.

Electoral Politics in Sri Lanka: Presidential Elections, Manipulation and Democracy
S. I. Keethaponcalan

Global India: The Pursuit of Influence and Status
Edited by Chris Ogden

Portugal Since the 2008 Economic Crisis: Resilience and Change
Edited by António Costa Pinto

Austalia's Refugee Politics in the 21st Century: STOP THE BOATS!
Kim Huynh

Cyprus 1974: Anatomy of an Invasion
Vassilis K. Fouskas and William D. E. Mallinson

Why Do Peace Negotiations Fail? The Case of Sri Lanka
S. I. Keethaponcalan

De-democratization Processes in Poland in 2015–23: Legal, Economic and Socio-political Dimensions
Edited by Grzegorz Foryś

For more information about this series, please visit: www.routledge.com/Europa-Country-Perspectives/book-series/ECP

De-democratization Processes in Poland in 2015–23

Legal, Economic and Socio-political Dimensions

Edited by
Grzegorz Foryś

Routledge
Taylor & Francis Group
LONDON AND NEW YORK

Designed cover image: Shutterstock

First published 2027
by Routledge
4 Park Square, Milton Park, Abingdon, Oxon OX14 4RN

and by Routledge
605 Third Avenue, New York, NY 10158

Routledge is an imprint of the Taylor & Francis Group, an informa business

British Library Cataloguing in Publication Data
A catalogue record for this book is available from the British Library

ISBN: 9781041363125 (hbk)
ISBN: 9781041363149 (pbk)
ISBN: 9781042002030 (ebk)

DOI: 10.4324/9781042002030

Typeset in Times New Roman
by Taylor & Francis Books

Contents

Illustrations

Figures

Tables

Contributors

Grzegorz Foryś is a sociologist, political scientist, and professor at the Institute of Law, Economics, and Administration at the University of the National Education Commission in Kraków, Poland. He specializes in the sociology of social change, the sociology of politics, the sociology of social movements, and democracy. His works include *The Dynamics of Contention: Farmers' Protests in the Third Polish Republic* (Scholar Publishing House, 2008), *Agritourism Farms and Associations in Poland: In Search of a Social Movement* (Scholar Publishing House, 2017), *Politics, Society, and the Economy in Contemporary Poland* (Scholar Publishing House, 2016), and *Development as a Social Movement* (Scholar Publishing House, 2023). He has also published numerous articles in Polish and international journals, and he has participated in research projects as a member of Polish and international research teams in the United States and Europe.

Bogusław Balza is an assistant professor in the Faculty of Law, Economics and Administration at the University of the National Education Commission. He holds doctorates in both economics and law. His academic work focuses on the intersection of legal and economic systems, and he specializes in tax law, civil law, immigration law, and public finance. He is the author of numerous scientific articles and monographs addressing issues related to taxation and the relationship between legal frameworks and national economies in both the Polish and international contexts. Dr Balza actively participates in numerous international and national academic conferences, where he contributes to scholarly debates on law and economics. He also delivers guest lectures at several Polish universities.

Dawid Chaba holds a PhD in legal sciences and is an assistant professor in the Department of Administrative Law and Civil Society at the University of the National Education Commission. He previously served for many years as a public administration officer. He currently heads the Audit and Internal Control Team at the Voivodeship Fund for Environmental Protection and Water Management in Kraków. Additionally, Chaba is the scientific supervisor at the Law Clinic of the University of the National Education Commission. He is the laureate of numerous awards for his scientific activity and has participated in many research grants and projects. He was awarded the Professor Michał Kulesza prize for the best PhD thesis on local government. He has authored numerous research publications, including monographs, book chapters and journal articles. His research interests encompass local government law, administrative law, audit and control, public employment law, and technology law.

Agnieszka Faron holds a PhD in management science and is an assistant professor in the Faculty of Business and International Relations at Vistula University in Wrocław, Poland. Her research interests include strategic management, the SME sector, and entrepreneurial ecosystems. She is the author and co-author of numerous research papers in the fields of management and economics. She actively participates in international conferences and delivers guest lectures at European universities. She continues her professional development through national and international training courses, thereby enhancing both her academic knowledge and teaching skills. She is currently engaged in academia-industry collaboration focused on the practical applications of research.

Anna Jastrzębiec-Witowska earned a PhD in sociology from the Jagiellonian University in Kraków and a master's degree in European Studies from the University of Exeter, UK. Her research interests focus on food security and the resilience of food systems in times of crisis. She works at the University of Opole, Poland. She previously served on the Dąbrowa County Council (2014–18), and was a municipal official and consultant for the international non-governmental organization Food & Water Watch.

Małgorzata Kmak holds a PhD in humanities, and is a political scientist, lecturer, and trainer. She is a graduate of the Faculty of Political Science at the KEN Pedagogical University in Kraków. Her research interests include local government, public administration in Poland and Europe, regional policy, sustainable development, human resources management, leadership and social impact, and promotion and territorial marketing.

Anna Magdalena Kosińska is a graduate of the art history programme run by the Faculty of Humanities at the John Paul II Catholic University of Lublin, a habilitated doctor of law and a professor at the University of Szczecin. She is a co-founder of the MIGRA–TEAM research group at the Rule of Law Institute, and served from 2015 to 2023 as head of the Research Centre on European Migration Law and Policy at the Catholic University of Lublin, where the book series Law and Migration Policy was inaugurated. She coordinates the Department of Foreigners in the Law Clinic at the University of Szczecin and leads numerous projects dedicated to the assistance and integration of migrants, including Support for Voluntary Returns in the Lublin Region I and II co-financed by the European Return Fund. She is the author of monographs and articles on migration and refugee law and has coordinated NCN-funded projects, including the Ombudsman as a Guarantee of the Protection of Migrants' Fundamental Rights. She is head of the MIGRA-Szczecin research team in the Faculty of Law and Administration at the University of Szczecin, and the creator and organizer of summer migration law schools and winter human rights schools, also in the Faculty of Law and Administration at the University of Szczecin.

Grzegorz Krawiec has a PhD in legal sciences and is a professor at the University of the National Education Commission. He is a long-time employee of public administration, currently working as a legal expert in the Office of the Territorial Plenipotentiary of the Ombudsman in Katowice. He is the author of publications on European administrative law, administrative procedure, substantive administrative law, among others. He has lectured at universities in Lithuania, the Czech Republic (Czechia), and Slovakia. In addition, he is a commentator for the media, including the legal information portal prawo.pl.

Wojciech Maciejewski, PhD, is an assistant professor in the Chair of Entrepreneurship and Social Innovations at the University of the National Education Commission. He is a board member of the Naooka Association. His research interests include entrepreneurship, entrepreneurial features, decision-making and factors influencing the success of business ventures. He is the author of many scientific publications and the co-author of books. As part of the Erasmus programme, he has taught in Türkiye (formerly Turkey), Finland, the Czech Republic, Italy, and Hungary. In 2010 he completed a semester-long internship at the American University in Washington, DC, USA. From 2018–20 he coordinated the 'Entrepreneurial and Socially Responsible Citizen' project. He also participates in national and international research projects in the field of entrepreneurship and social entrepreneurship.

Dorota Pietrzyk-Reeves is Professor of Political Philosophy and Political Science at the Jagiellonian University in Kraków. Her research interests include normative political theory, democratic theory, civil society, and democratization in Central and Eastern Europe, republicanism and political education. She has published in journals including *Politics, Acta Politica, Education, Citizenship and Social Justice*, the *Cambridge Review of International Affairs, East European Politics and Societies, Communist and Post-Communist Studies*, and the *Journal of Civil Society.* Her recent books include *Activism in Hard Times in Central and Eastern Europe: People Power* (Routledge, 2024) and *Polish Republican Discourse in the Sixteenth Century* (Cambridge University Press, 2020). Recently she has been the principal investigator on the international research project 'The Conditions of Civil Society in Central and Eastern Europe Thirty Years After: A Comparative Perspective', funded by the National Science Centre in Poland.

Joanna Podgórska-Rykała is Professor of Political Science and Administration. She has and holds degrees in law (2019), political science (2011), and administration (2011). She is a Doctor of Social Sciences (2016), and was habilitated in Political Science and Administration (2024). She works at the University of the National Education Commission and serves as the coordinator of the research and analysis department at the Foundation in Support of Local Democracy. She has been a Visiting Scholar at Trinity College Dublin (the internship lasted 12 months, throughout the entire year 2025), a Jean Monnet Fellow at the European University Institute in Florence (2022–23), and a Fellow at the Silesian University in Opava (2020). She was awarded the Scholarship of the Polish Minister of Science for Outstanding Young Scientists (2022–25). Her research focuses on citizen participation, with a specialization in democratic innovation. Beyond advanced research on citizen assemblies, she studies a wide range of participatory tools in Poland and other European countries. She is the author of over 130 publications, including single-author monographs, such as *Deliberative Democracy, Public Policy, and Local Government* (Routledge, 2024) and *Deliberative Innovation according to the Decision-Makers: A Clash between Perceptions and Reality* (Brill, 2025).

Agnieszka Ziółkowska, PhD, is an associate professor in the Faculty of Law and Administration at the University of Silesia, Poland. She is a specialist in administrative law, administrative proceedings, and administrative court proceedings, with a research focus on the protection of human rights in legal sphere. She is also an attorney-at-law and serves on the Disciplinary Committee for the Responsibility of Academic Teachers at the Main Council of Science and Higher Education, and on the disciplinary committee of the Ministry of Science.

Abbreviations

AFSJ	Area of Freedom, Security and Justice
BGK	Bank Gospodarstwa Krajowego (Polish Development Bank)
BGŻ	Bank Gospodarki Żywnościowej (Bank of the Agricultural Economy)
C/I	Cost-to-Income
CDD	Committee for the Defence of Democracy (Komitet Obrony Demokracji)
CEDR	Committee on the Elimination of Racial Discrimination
CFS	Commission for Financial Supervision (Komisja Nadzoru Finansowego)
CJEU	Court of Justice of the European Union
COVID-19	Coronavirus Disease of 2019
CR-5	Concentration Ratio
CSO	Civil Society Organization
CT	Constitutional Tribunal (Trybunał Konstytucyjny)
EC	European Commission
ECHR	European Convention on Human Rights
ECJ	European Court of Justice
ECP	Employee Capital Plan (Pracownicze Plany Kapitałowe)
ECtHR	European Court of Human Rights
EP	Employers of Poland (Pracodawcy RP)
EU	European Union
GDP	Gross Domestic Product
IDA	Industrial Development Agency (Agencja Rozwoju Przemysłu)
KUKE	Korporacja Ubezpieczeń Kredytów Eksportowych (Export Credit Insurance Corporation)
LGBTQ+	Lesbian, Gay, Bisexual, Transgender, Queer
MP	Member of Parliament
NATO	North Atlantic Treaty Organization
NBP	Narodowy Bank Polski (National Bank of Poland)
NCJ	National Council of the Judiciary (Krajowa Rada Sądownictwa)

NCP	National Council of Prosecutors (Krajowa Rada Prokuratury)
NGO	Non-Governmental Organization
NHF	National Health Fund (Narodowy Fundusz Zdrowia)
NIF-CDCS	National Institute of Freedom – Centre for the Development of Civil Society (Narodowy Instytut Wolności – Centrum Rozwoju Społeczeństwa Obywatelskiego)
NIT	National Institute of Technology
NRP	National Recovery Plan (Krajowy Plan Odbudowy)
OECD	Organisation for Economic Co-operation and Development
OSCE	Organization for Security and Co-operation in Europe
PARP	Polska Agencja Rozwoju Przedsiębiorczości (Polish Agency for Enterprise Development)
PBR	Polish Business Roundtable (Polska Rada Biznesu)
PCC	Polish Chamber of Commerce (Krajowa Izba Gospodarcza)
PCL	Polish Confederation Lewiatan (Konfederacja Lewiatan)
PDF	Polish Development Fund (Polski Fundusz Rozwoju)
PGE	Polska Grupa Energetyczna (Polish Energy Group)
PGNiG	Polskie Górnictwo Naftowe i Gazownictwo (Polish Oil and Gas Company)
PID	Polish Investments for Development (Polskie Inwestycje Rozwojowe)
PISA	Programme for International Student Assessment
PIT	Personal Income Tax
PITA	Polish Investment and Trade Agency (Polska Agencja Inwestycji i Handlu)
PKO BP	Powszechna Kasa Oszczędności Bank Polski (Polish Bank for General Savings)
PKP	Polskie Koleje Państwowe (Polish State Railways)
PLN	Polish National Currency
PZU	Polski Zakład Ubezpieczeń (Universal Insurance Company of Poland)
ROA	Return on Assets
SAC	Supreme Administrative Court (Naczelny Sąd Administracyjny)
SAF	State Agricultural Farms (Państwowe Gospodarstwa Rolne)
SAO	Supreme Audit Office (Najwyższa Izba Kontroli)
SC	Supreme Court (Sąd Najwyższy)
SOE	State-Owned Enterprises (Spółki Skarbu Państwa)
SRD	Strategy for Responsible Development (Strategia na Rzecz Odpowiedzialnego Rozwoju)
ST	State Tribunal (Trybunał Stanu)
TEU	Treaty on European Union
TFEU	Treaty on the Functioning of the European Union
TVP	Telewizja Polska (Polish Television)
UN	United Nations

Introduction

The birth and decline of democracy in Central Europe

Grzegorz Foryś

Introduction

A rare, but potentially recurring, moment in history seems to be unfolding on a global scale, as certain countries in Europe and beyond appear to be moving away from democracy. This phenomenon has motivated the authors of this volume to analyse it in juxtaposition with democratization. Just as waves of democratization can be observed and examined, so too is it possible to recognize waves of democracy renouncement, particularly in its liberal form. The phenomenon of de-democratization is neither new nor without historical antecedents, but now its first, general symptoms are becoming visible again. The unique character of contemporary de-democratization processes means that the questioning and backsliding of democracy do not only occur in countries with a relatively short history of democracy and problems with its consolidation. Negative tendencies within Western democracies with stable political systems can also be observed. Hungary may serve as an example here, as well as Poland under the governance of the Zjednoczona Prawica (United Right), which lost power in October 2023 resulting in some retreat from de-democratization processes. However, the erosion of democracy in consolidated democratic systems may prove to be only a matter of time, contingent upon circumstances and the determination of those who oppose liberal democracy. The authors of this volume agree with the widespread diagnosis of weak democratic consolidation in Central Eastern Europe and are willing to acknowledge the specific pattern of this consolidation, described as '"illiberal consolidation" built on an accommodation between technocratic, economistic liberalism and forces of rent-seeking and cultural conservatism' (Dawson and Hanley 2016, 20).

However, this pattern may not be permanent and some particular, non-standard paths taken to reach the model of liberal democracy should not be precluded. Moreover, attempts to explain the failure of democratization in Central Europe solely in terms of the region's historical background and relatively short and limited experience of democracy are overly simplistic and indicate fatalism. The authors of this volume argue that, although the Polish and Hungarian democracies may be viewed as inadequately consolidated and

DOI: 10.4324/9781042002030-1

thus susceptible to de-democratization, other countries should not assume that the risk of de-democratization will never apply to them. The near future might bring de-democratization processes to countries whose commitment to democracy has never been questioned. Regional factors play a role here, particularly the length and duration of the democratic experience, but categorical statements highlighting a single cause of democratization and de-democratization paths in Eastern Europe remain inadequate and biased. In retrospect, the opinions of experts who downplayed concerns regarding the end of the politics of liberal consensus in the countries of Central and Eastern Europe as benign due to the lack of any ideological alternative (Krastev 2007, 58) appear to be premature and misguided. Nonetheless, an ideological alternative manifested itself in Poland from 2015 to 2023. To paraphrase Krastev, the streets of Budapest (Hungary) and Warsaw (Poland) are slowly being appropriated by paramilitary formations that currently seek power and may, in the near future, be ready to pursue more dramatic, if not final, solutions.

Furthermore, such tendencies can also be observed in Western countries, thereby unmasking the errors of analyses conducted in the first decade of the 21st century on the state of democracy in Central and Eastern Europe. This observation suggests that, while the level of democracy consolidation is meaningful for analyses of de-democratization processes, it is not a decisive factor. Therefore, general explanations should not be based on specific local cases, although one should remember that local and regional factors constitute an important part of people's social and political lives and thus warrant consideration.

This volume does not seek to downplay the symptoms of de-democratization by treating them as 'turns' or 'deviations' from democracy, as suggested by some authors (Bustikova and Guasti 2017). Instead, it focuses on de-democratization in various stages of advancement in particular countries, including those with stable democratic systems. Contemporary de-democratization is slowly unveiling its multiple possible forms. In some cases, it entails a shift from a democratic or hybrid system to a non-democratic one; in others, it involves the loss of democratic quality or a halt to democratic changes in non-democratic countries (Szymański and Ufel 2018, 594). Therefore, the processes of de-democratization are more universal than might generally be expected. It remains to be seen whether these developments constitute a historical regularity of cyclical character or a dramatic introduction to the third democratic transformation, in which the existing paradigm of democracy may no longer be applicable. Could new, better forms of this political system be expected in the future, built on the ruins of representative democracy? At this point, such a question might be premature, as de-democratization processes with their economic, legislative, political, and social aspects must be studied in greater depth to provide answers. The goal of this volume is to distinguish between those characteristics that are indicative of the universality of de-democratization processes and their more specific features connected with particular cases. The author of this chapter considers the general logic of the de-democratization process as universal, but is aware that variations of this process could exist within particular political systems. In other words, there are many ways in which democratic backsliding may occur.

Theoretical contexts of de-democratization and the research context

De-democratization does not constitute a simple reversal of democratization, as the two processes have different dynamics, scope, and consequences. Democratization does not occur in a vacuum and it requires a well-prepared foundation, based on stable economic, social and political conditions, which take many decades to build. De-democratization may emerge suddenly and may take place rapidly. It usually stems from the reaction of government authorities concerned about their political situation, which they perceive as a crisis threatening the maintenance of their political power. It is of secondary importance whether such a crisis diagnosis is accurate or not, as de-democratization can often be initiated on the basis of a misperceived crisis.

As noted earlier, democratization and de-democratization processes are permanent features of contemporary political systems. What can be observed with the emergence of nation-states and the completion of the second democratic transformation promoting the dominant paradigm of representative democracy is the ongoing movement of political systems towards and away from democracy. Over the past two centuries, however, the contexts of democratization and de-democratization processes have been changing. Previous classical drivers of change in political systems, such as modernization, economic development, transformations of social structure and empowerment of the people, were then exposed to conditions which tested the endurance of state institutions and democratic systems. Other factors that are widely recognized as having influenced democracy in a variety of ways include economic crises, growing social inequalities, increased social unrest, the weakening of civil society, and soaring populism. These factors do not, however, exhaust the list of influences on democracy and new phenomena must be taken into account. Among them are globalization, neoliberalism, the digital revolution, environmental threats, demographic changes, a plummeting sense of security, and organized interference by authoritarian powers hoping and working for the decline of liberal democracy. All these changes contribute to a rather hostile and not very supportive context for contemporary democratic political systems.

Analyses of democratization and de-democratization may be approached in two ways. They may involve detailed descriptions of all the causative factors related to democratization and de-democratization leading to a broad spectrum of conditions facilitating these processes. The classic works of Martin Lipset (1959) and Samuel Huntington (1965, 1991) may serve as pertinent examples here, as they focus on economic actors and more broadly conceived developmental processes. It is also possible to reflect on democratization and de-democratization in a more general way, pointing to broader tendencies or even 'a golden principle' that determines these two processes. This more general perspective is reflected in the works of authors such as Reinhard Bendix (1964), Barringon Moore (1966), or Thomas H. Marshall (1992) who searched for agents of democracy-related change among the different social classes, including the peasantry, the working class, and the middle class. Contemporary concepts stressing the role of collective mobilization and human empowerment in confrontation with the state apparatus are formulated in a similar manner (Foweraker 1989; Tarrow 1995; McAdam et al. 2001).

The concept of de-democratization proposed by Charles Tilly (2007) is of primary importance for the authors of this volume as it combines the advantages of the two approaches described earlier. Tilly viewed de-democratization processes in a general sense, namely as an interplay of relations between the state and the nation. He conceptualized the latter as society and its citizens. According to Tilly, the balance of power between the state and the nation determines whether democratization or de-democratization prevail. Democratization could be connected to the dominance of the will of the people, while de-democratization meant that this dominance was weakening while the state disconnected itself from citizens' control. However, this simplified – but not untrue – vision of the relationship between the state and the nation could be made more specific if the checklist of de-democratization indicators was applied. Much like indicators of democratization, which include changes in social structures, levels of economic development and changes in legal systems, these should not be viewed as a simple continuum between the two processes. Rather, within the relationship between the state and the nation, each of the discussed indicators has the potential to change the power dynamics between rivals, namely the state and the nation. Consequently, any list of de-democratization indicators cannot be either precise or exhaustive. While this may be considered a weakness, it also constitutes an opportunity. The set of canonical qualities of democracy may serve as a point of reference for the trajectory of democratic backsliding as these qualities are damaged in the processes of de-democratization. In this respect, Tilly's proposal, owing to its flexibility in selecting de-democratization indicators, is well suited to an analysis of specific case studies and provides a strong argument for a closer examination of Poland. Discussions about the crisis of democracy in Poland, Europe or globally only make sense if there is a reference point of a well-defined 'ideal type' of contemporary democracy such as liberal democracy (Ossowski 2008, 100).

Furthermore, Tilly's proposal, unlike some other analytical perspectives on democratization and de-democratization, did not pigeonhole countries on the basis of their histories, past experiences with democracy or specific characteristics of their societies and culture (Lorenz and Anders 2021). In other words, he was far from suggesting that the countries of Central and Eastern

Europe were unable to establish or maintain durable democracies due to their unique communist heritage and specific (perhaps not final) transitions from authoritarian rule to democracy. It should be emphasized that, at present, de-democratization processes can also be observed in contemporary Western states such as Germany, the United Kingdom, and the United States, but they may take quite different forms than the processes occurring in Central and Eastern Europe (Porritt 2019; Przeworski 2019). While the specifics of particular countries or groups of countries merit careful consideration, one should not ignore the fact that similar effects can be achieved through various paths of de-democratization.

Rationale for case selection

Why does Poland appear to be a suitable field for research? First, the authors of this volume find Poland to be representative of other countries in the region in terms of its historical background and experiences of the past century shared across Central Europe, with the notable exception of Germany. These states enjoyed the restoration of independence after World War I and the formation of modern nation-states, but only had a very short time to develop democracy, which faced crises in the 1930s. All these states had to deal with the atrocities of World War II, followed by the period of Soviet dominance that lasted until 1989, after which they started along the path of democratization culminating in membership of the North Atlantic Treaty Organization (NATO) and accession to the European Union. This commonality of fate among these countries also continued when their governments opted to engage, to a greater or lesser degree, in de-democratization processes (Hungary, Poland, Slovakia, and, more recently, the Czech Republic). In the cases of Poland and Hungary, the emerging crises of democracy, freedom and the rule of law have attracted the attention of and reactions from European institutions. Poland, in particular, has experienced a significant decline in its democratic ranking. According to the Democracy Index published by the Economist Intelligence Unit, Poland's democratic system before 2015 qualified as a full democracy with only minor flaws and the country scored 7.47 on a 10-point scale. By 2019, this score had declined to 6.62, resulting in a 'flawed democracy' classification (Economist Intelligence Unit 2015, 2019, 2022). This reflects a rather significant deterioration in Poland's democracy status, moving it from a minimally flawed system towards a seriously flawed or even a hybrid regime. A similar tendency was observed in a report published by the V-Dem Institute in collaboration with the University of Gothenburg, which noted that between 2010 and 2020 the Liberal Democracy Index in Poland declined from 0.83 to 0.49, indicating Poland's transition from a liberal democracy to an electoral democracy (V-Dem Institute 2020).

It should be stressed that Poland's population size and economic potential are of key importance for the region and Europe as a whole, and this justifies its selection as a case study. Without undermining the role of the other Central and Eastern European countries mentioned above it is noticeable that, geopolitically, the Polish case carries more weight than the interplay of symptoms of de-democratization in the Central European context. Finally, Polish democracy exemplifies a system that is not highly consolidated and this makes it representative of the group of Central European countries, while the specifics of de-democratization in Poland merit an in-depth analysis.

Outline of the book's structure

This book is organized into four parts. Chapters 1 and 2 provide the theoretical foundation for the entire work, extending far beyond this brief introduction. The authors highlight those characteristics of democracy that may be considered controversial, leading to questions about their meaning and the way in which they undermine or even negate democracy as a political system. This analysis stems from the conviction that democracy enjoys an overwhelmingly positive reputation, reflected in the extensive scholarly literature and in the popular opinions of the rational majority of Europeans. Therefore, repeating the arguments supporting the thesis that democracy is the most desired political system, despite its imperfections, seems redundant. Instead, focusing on the weaknesses of democracy appears to be more appropriate for the purposes of discussing the theoretical aspects of de-democratization, as conceptualized by Charles Tilly. Such an approach to defining de-democratization processes gives priority to their indicators, which is reflected in Chapter 1. The crucial features of the Polish political system as well as the initiatives taken by the state to strengthen its position in relation to its citizens during the period under study, from 2015 to 2023, are explained in Chapter 2. The authors of this chapter present a sequence of legislative, economic, and socio-political endeavours that are symptomatic of de-democratization processes in Poland.

In Part II, the changes that occurred in Poland under the governance of the United Right are examined in Chapters 3, 4 and 5, with particular emphasis on the crucial role played by transformation of the judiciary and measures affecting the Trybunał Konstytucyjny (Constitutional Tribunal – CT) and judicial independence. These developments led to the partial subordination of the judiciary to the state authorities, reduced the autonomy of judges and created the conditions conducive for concealing the possible failures of state authorities at the legislative level due to the overpowering of the CT. For the authors, changes in the judiciary are of fundamental importance in de-democratization processes, as they are the most obvious indicators of democratic backsliding.

Part III of this volume comprises Chapters 6, 7, and 8. In it, the authors focus on key issues such as the centralization, nationalization and monopolization of the Polish economy. The section reconstructs the process through which the state becomes increasingly detached from the will of the people. The economic and financial independence of the state may constitute not only an element of state sovereignty but also an instrument of increased control over citizens. State control of financial assets allowed it to pursue policies from 2015 to 2023 that were beneficial for citizens, but even more so for the authorities, particularly as it allowed them to finance their political activities and build a competitive advantage over their political opponents. They rewarded loyalty and 'paid' citizens for their political support through financial transfers of dedicated social programmes, regardless of the consequences for the economy and the state budget. Such practices support the argument that de-democratization may have an economic foundation, often obscured by economic policies ostensibly pursued by the state to benefit the citizenry. Whenever this has been the case in Poland and elsewhere, de-democratization has occurred through a hidden agenda that only emerges upon a closer examination of the economic policies that in reality marked a departure from democracy.

In Part IV of this volume, comprising Chapters 9–13, attention is given to issues pertaining to civil rights and civil society, which complement the overall reflection on de-democratization. Tilly's line of thought has a strong presence in this chapter, particularly with regard to the power struggle between the state and the *demos*. The dominance of the citizenry shows that democracy is thriving, while the increasingly competitive advantage of the state may necessitate an assessment of the extent to which a particular system is moving away from democracy. This process is presented from two angles. The first is a legal perspective, which points out civil rights restrictions and violations. The second is the political science approach, which emphasizes the erosion of empowerment in local communities, as well as the shrinking of civil society while also showing the attempts of the right-wing state authorities to construct an alternative 'civil society' of their own.

Part IV begins with an outline of the essential aspects of de-democratization processes and subsequently turns to the specific features of the Polish case, illustrating key milestones in the country's democratic backsliding. Comprehensive analyses of de-democratization processes include the description of the power struggle between the state and its citizens, who emerge as supporters and defenders of democracy and its core values.

References

Bendix, Reinhard. 1964. *Nation Building and Citizenship*. New York: Wiley and Sons.

Bustikova, Lenka and Petra Guasti. 2017. 'The Illiberal Turn or Swerve in Central Europe?' *Politics and Governance* 5(4): 166–176.

Dawson, James and Sean Hanley. 2016. 'What's Wrong with East-Central Europe? The Fading Mirage of the "Liberal Consensus"'. *Journal of Democracy* 27(1): 20–34.

Economist Intelligence Unit. 2015. *Democracy Index 2015. Democracy in an Age of Anxiety*. https://web.archive.org/web/20210203051256/https://www.yabiladi.com/img/content/EIU-Democracy-Index-2015.pdf (accessed 21October 2024).

Economist Intelligence Unit. 2019. *Democracy Index 2019. A Year of Democratic Setbacks and Popular Protest*. https://web.archive.org/web/20201201160911/https://www.in.gr/wp-content/uploads/2020/01/Democracy-Index-2019.pdf (accessed 21 October 2024).

Economist Intelligence Unit. 2022. *Democracy Index 2022. Frontline Democracy and the Battle for Ukraine.* Chrome-extension://efaidnbmnnnibpcajpcglclefindmkaj/https://www.eiu.com/n/wp-content/uploads/2023/02/Democracy-Index-2022_FV2.pdf (accessed 21 October 2024).

Foweraker, Joseph. 1989. *Making Democracy in Spain: Grassroots Struggle in the South 1955–1975*. Cambridge: Cambridge University Press.

Huntington, Samuel. 1965. *Political Order in Changing Societies.* New Haven, CT: Yale University Press.

Huntington, Samuel. 1991. *Third Wave. Democratization in the Late Twentieth Century.* Norman: University of Oklahoma Press.

Krastev, Iwan. 2007. 'The Strange Death of the Liberal Consensus'. *Journal of Democracy* 18(Oct.): 56–63.

Lipset, Seymour M. 1959. 'Some Social Requisites to Democracy: Economic Development and Political Legitimacy'. *American Political Science Review* 55: 69–105.

Lorenz, Astrid and Lisa H. Anders (eds). 2021. *Illiberal Trends and Anti-EU Politics in East Central Europe.* Cham: Palgrave Macmillan.

Marshall, Thomas H. 1992. 'Citizenship and Social Class'. In Thomas H. Marshall and Tom Bottomore (eds), *Citizenship and Social Class.* London: Pluto Press, pp. 3–51.

McAdam, Doug, Sidney Tarrow, and Charles Tilly. 2001. *Dynamics of Contention.* New York: Cambridge University Press.

Moore, Barrington. 1966. *Social Origins of Dictatorship and Democracy: Lord and Peasant in the Making of the Modern World.* Boston, MA: Beacon Press.

Ossowski, Szymon. 2008. 'Kryzys liberalnej demokracji w Polsce na tle innych państw członkowskich Unii Europejskiej'. *Studia polityczne* 2: 99–114.

Porritt, Luisa. 2019. *Britain's Democratic Gap: It's Ironic the British Government Insists EU Is 'Undemocratic' as It Loses Sight of Its Own Values.* Politico. https://www.politico.eu/article/britain-democracy-gap-brexit-mepeu-uk-liberaldemocrats-boris-johnson/ (accessed 27 September 2025).

Przeworski, Adam. 2019. *Crises of Democracy.* Cambridge: Cambridge University Press.

Szymański Adam and Wojciech Ufel. 2018. 'Beyond Vote Rigging: Common Patterns in Electoral Malpractices in De-Democratizing Regimes'. *Polish Political Science Yearbook* 47(7): 593–617.

Tarrow, Sidney. 1995. 'Mass Mobilization and Regime Change: Pacts, Reform and Popular Power in Italy (1918–1922) and Spain (1975–1978)'. In Richard Gunther, P. Nikiforos Diamandours, and Hans-Juergen Puhle (eds), *Democratic Consolidation in Southern Europe.* Baltimore, MD: Johns Hopkins University Press, pp. 204–230.

Tilly, Charles. 2007. *Democracy.* Cambridge: Cambridge University Press.

V-Dem Institute. 2020. *Autocratization Surges – Resistance Grows. Democracy Report 2020*. https://v-dem.net/documents/14/dr_2020_dqumD5e.pdf.

1 De-democratization

The Essence of the Process

Grzegorz Foryś

Introduction

Democratic political systems are widely regarded as the most desirable form of governance globally, as democracy provides political stability, favourable conditions for societal and economic development, and predictability in international relations. However, democracy should not be taken for granted. Political actors and societies within democratic countries must ensure the continuity of democracy through their everyday practices. This notion is encapsulated in the thesis advanced by Francis Fukuyama (1992), according to which the demise of communism marked the 'end of history', with Western-style liberal democracy and the free market emerging as the universal forms of political and economic organization, respectively. An apparent crisis of liberal democracy is manifesting itself in various ways, including declining citizen participation in elections, the blurring of traditional lines of social conflict between labour and capital, the increasing power of populism, attacks on democratic institutions, and leaders' pursuit of authority centralization. Democracy, despite its obvious and undeniable strengths, such as citizens' influence on governing processes and, to some extent, the exercise of power, also exhibits weaknesses that democratic theorists tend to regard as controversial. These weaknesses fuel the arguments advanced by critics and, more often, by outspoken opponents of democracy. In this volume, democracy is defined as a form of governance and is discussed as a political system. This understanding takes precedence over other manifestations of democracy that may be identified, including democracy as a social condition (social democracy; see de Tocqueville 2002); democracy as a network (local democracy; see Sartori 1987); as well as economic democracy and industrial democracy.

This chapter aims to address issues that are essential to understanding and analysing processes of de-democratization. What comes to mind here are democracy-related controversies of a normative and procedural character, including the boundary conditions that a political system must meet to be considered democratic, as well as the nature and indicators of de-democratization processes. Accordingly, reflections on democracy are the primary focus

DOI: 10.4324/9781042002030-2

of this chapter, as an understanding of the core features of democracy and of the controversies surrounding this political system facilitate comprehension of the phenomenon of de-democratization. This also provides some insight into the arguments made by the opponents of democracy and their actions against democracy. Consideration is given not only to the universal findings of leading authors specializing in the subject, but also to particular characteristics of the analysed processes that stem from individual and unique cases.

Why does democracy face problems of legitimacy?

A reflection on the legitimacy of democracy should start by examining these dimensions of democracy, that are controversial and might be used to undermine this political system. Two critical approaches to democracy can be distinguished here. The first approach is grounded in political theory that is researched by scholars specializing in the study of this political system. It attaches fundamental value to democracy and our way of thinking about this political system and its arguments are far more constructive for democracy than those highlighted by the critics of a more liberal version of democracy. This type of criticism represents the second approach and it is often articulated by theorists in periodicals or by political actors, who often justify their anti-democratic activities as necessary to restore what they perceive as 'real' democracy. In reality, such endeavours tend to result in varying degrees of authoritarian rule.

The critical perspective on democracy grounded in political theory, on the one hand, reveals the weaknesses of this political system but, on the other hand, it increases awareness that democracy is not ideal – at least in its empirical form – beyond the normative framework. A brief review of the academic debate within the first critical approach to democracy, regarding its core principles, shows that it is limited to a handful of its essential characteristics. The background for such a debate might be shaped either by realism through the concept of real, pure politics, based on authority and not values, as popularized by authors such as Nicolo Machiavelli, Gaetano Mosca, Vilfredo Pareto, and Joseph A. Schumpeter, or by idealism, which situates politics in humanistic values, often deemed by critics to be unrealistic or naïve. In other words, realists perceive the foundational premises of democracy as unrealistic and largely inapplicable in social practice. They contribute to the broadest stream of criticism towards democracy that regards its values and principles, such as majority rule and the sovereignty of *demos*, as overly idealistic. Giovanni Sartori mocked this seemingly fundamental dispute as artificial and argued that examining arguments for and against democracy through its lens might be inadequate. He wrote:

> Historically, the realistic and the democratic schools of politics have long clashed. It is a fact, that is, that the realists generally sneer at 'democratic

> idealism' and that, conversely, the democratic persuasion looks on realism as an incongenial, if not antidemocratic, approach.
>
> (Sartori 1987, 43)

For Sartori, this contention stems from flawed premises within both schools of thought, portraying realists as fundamentally hostile to democracy and entertaining the idea of politics without ideals. In reality, however, these two extremes, although rare, can pose an equal threat to democratic political systems. In politics, facts and values cannot be ignored. Advocates of such extremes usually turn out to be the harshest critics of democracy, if not its ardent opponents.

One of the key controversies grounded in the theory of democracy pertains to the idea of *demos*. While the scope of this term is not questioned here, the focus lies on the extent of the authority exercised by the people. Emancipation processes occurring over the centuries (i.e. political rights for previously excluded social groups, such as townspeople, peasants and women) led to the more inclusive definition of *demos*, which now applies to a vast aggregation of citizens. However, the actual exercise of popular rule is a multifaceted phenomenon, and thus warrants further consideration. Democracy, although recognized as rule by the majority, must not ignore minority rights. If it does, the ruling majority may exploit its privileged position to maintain authority indefinitely, which, in fact, would mean the end of democracy. The need for a somewhat limited majority rule is sometimes met with a lack of understanding from the masses who may seek to absolutize their power. Analogously, some politicians may justify their decisions by appealing to the majority in a monolithic, absolutist manner, after gaining its temporary support.

Another dimension of the empowerment of the *demos* concerns its nominal power, which should be distinguished from the power actually exercised by the people. This issue has been discussed by scholars such as Gaetano Mosca, Vilfredo Pareto, and Robert Michels, whose works examine the principles that constitute the core of democracy and, at the same time, lay the groundwork for a more critical approach to democracy. For example, Mosca argued that actual majority rule is impossible to achieve due to the genetic characteristics of social organizations, which renders the majority passive and paves the way for a well-organized minority. Pareto used even stronger language, treating democracy as a certain kind of political religion, whose symbolic layers could provide tools for manipulating the masses. A similar point was reflected in the concept formulated by Michels, known as the 'iron law of oligarchy', asserting that every social organization, regardless of how democratic they are initially, will, sooner rather than later, become an oligarchy. Some interpretations of this democracy dilemma can be seen in the works of political realists, who proposed a more narrow definition of democracy, reducing it to the act of voting, as reflected in Schumpeter's concept of procedural democracy. Other democratic theorists, such as

Sartori, defined democracy as rule by the minority chosen by the will of the people to govern, while Robert Dahl presented polyarchy as an imperfect form of democracy.

Critics of democracy often highlight these characteristics, which can readily generate controversy about this political system. In practice, this can lead to the absolutization of the will of the majority under the pretext of promoting what they call 'real' democracy. Such arguments were employed in the early 19th century by Bolsheviks, who referred directly to the will of people and they continue to be used today by staunch opponents of democracy, who ignore minority rights. Contemporary examples of such practices can be observed in Hungary under Viktor Orbán and in Poland under the governance of the Zjednoczona Prawica (United Right) alliance from 2025 to 2023.

In the context of representation, another dimension of the will of the people concerns the quality of the institutions tasked with ensuring democratic representation. Critics of the idea of representation often overlap with proponents of direct democracy, who stress that specialized institutions representing citizens' interests often exhibit ossifying tendencies, generally resisting the regular replacement of representatives. Not only does this obviously weaken the quality of representation but it also creates the conditions for eroding democracy to, at best, a procedural function with uncertain prospects for its long-term survival. If power remains in the hands of the same majority for a long time, the temptation to forego regular mandate renewal through election may arise. Such a hypothetical situation bears some resemblance to Schumpeter's (1976) vision of corporatism, a model to which post-war Japan adapted its institutions. From the mid-1950s, Japan's Liberal Democratic Party was continuously in power for several decades. Assuming that during this time frame the political system should experience at least two exchanges of ruling elites from opposing political camps in order to be deemed democratic, then according to this criterion, Japan had not fulfilled the norms of a democratic state for a long time.

The reality of citizens' representation in democratic systems is closely connected with two further issues. The first relates to the principle of 'one person, one vote' and the second to the role of civic activism in democracy. The first issue puts citizenship competence (i.e. the ability to act as responsible citizens and to fully participate in civic and social life) in the spotlight, raising concerns about whether treating all votes in democratic systems as equal to each other truly serves justice. In this context, the votes of citizens who decide on crucial matters, while not being engaged in public matters and perhaps not understanding their complexities, might be undermined. This argument is prevalent among the critics of representative democracy and proponents of other forms of democracy, such as direct participation by well-informed and engaged citizens, who have contribute to decision-making processes. Civic activism is generally valued in democracy but is treated with some ambivalence (della Porta and Diani 1999). Populist critics of democracy often encourage civic activism, while those who favour statism may view its excesses as threatening to democracy. Not all types of activism are created equal and only those forms of activism based on knowledge and competence strengthen democracy, rather than turning it into the rule of the unrefined masses prone to demagogy and willing to support the authoritarian tendencies of the ruling class.

Reflections on citizenship competence and activism should emphasize the role of democracy as a decision-making agenda, with citizens exercising control over it, as envisioned by Robert Dahl (1989). In this context, the flow of information through pluralist media and the aforementioned citizenship competence become crucial. Today, with the rise of new media, the decision-making agenda is subject to manipulation and attempts to exert control by actors who do not respect democratic principles.

The list of democracy-related controversies or flashpoints has by no means been exhausted. There also exists a critical perspective on liberal democracy – though not discussed here in detail – that points to its insufficiency. While this critique does not occupy a significant position within the theory of democracy, it has an impact on democratic practices, as it is often used by populist actors. Among these controversies are (1) the ideological neutrality of democracy, which places diverse worldviews and opinions on an equal footing, including those that may be destructive for the political community and cultural identity (a conservative critique); (2) the aforementioned actual rule of minority elites, who may be prone to closing the political system and isolating it from citizens (a populist critique); and (3) the inability of democracy to elaborate a concept of the common good (a communitarian critique).

Democracy, although widely recognized as the best possible political system, is not a perfect form of governance. Critical perspectives notwithstanding, there are also concepts aimed at renewing and improving democracy, and among them are ideas for direct, participatory, and empowered democracy (Fung and Wright 2003). Such solutions are, to some extent, treated as a form of compensation for the imperfections of representative democracy and are cast in the role of reviving contemporary democracy, which is facing multiple crises. Examples include citizens' budgets and social consultations that local authorities are employing more and more frequently. These initiatives seek to revive democracy and to remedy deficiencies, potentially leading to the so-called third democratic transformation (with Athenian democracy being the first transformation and representative democracy emerging as an outcome of the second), the precise shape and form of which remain unknown. This optimistic augury is often overshadowed by de-democratization processes, which usually affect political systems that lack deep-rooted democratic traditions. These processes will be analysed later in the chapter.

When does democracy stop being democracy?

In order to investigate processes of de-democratization, one must fully understand what constitutes the core features of democracy and how they can be threatened. This, in turn, requires the identification of those areas of democracy in which backsliding of this political system has already been initiated.

The contemporary understanding of democracy can be credited to the great thinkers of the French Enlightenment, such as Jean-Jacques Rousseau and Montesquieu. The former proposed the idea of popular sovereignty and the latter the separation of government authority into three distinct branches: legislative, executive and judicial. The enactment of these ideas was made possible in the 19th century, when representative democracy was introduced to political and social life by the United States, France, and Great Britain. Its three fundamental principles included freedom (allowing citizens to express their opinions on matters connected with the state), equality, and the principle of majority (the majority rule). The emergence of this political system required the reformulation of its social, structural and institutional settings (Bielecka 2012, 43–44) in a variety of ways. First, the concept of 'the people' was expanded in terms of inclusion in power sharing, thanks to election participation and through the emancipation of numerous social categories, which resulted in a broad change in thinking about *demos*. Today, the term 'civil society' is often preferred to 'the people'. Second, the structure of the state also underwent changes resulting in several centres of power (legislative, executive and judicial) at different levels (central versus local authority). Third, the legitimation of power is less reliant on customs and tradition and more on statutory law. Fourth, the development of mass media has given citizens far greater engagement in public matters, preparing the ground for wide public debate and enriching it with new content. The results of such a transformation must clearly be reflected in the debate about the set of characteristics that a political system should possess in order to be recognized as democratic.

To maintain a concise and orderly discussion of what constitutes democracy, it is useful to mention the work of Charles Tilly (2007, 7–9), who, having familiarized himself with the work of democracy theorists, delineated four approaches to defining the democratic political system. First, the constitutional approach focuses on laws governing political activity as enacted by the regime. However, the fact that some principles of the political system are included in a country's constitution does not necessarily mean that democratic practices will follow. In other words, a system may be formally recognized as democratic on the basis of its constitutional provisions but may have little to do with democracy. Second, the substantive approach focuses on the conditions of social and political life fostered by a given regime. Does the system truly lead to the realization of democratic values, such as general welfare, individual freedom, security and social equality? Third, the procedural approach defines democracy in terms of government practices related to election processes and the possibility of regular alternations in governmental elites and policies. Within this approach, the risk of a 'facade democracy' becomes especially apparent . Finally, the fourth approach takes procedural definitions further by describing the set of processes that need to take place within the political system for it to be considered democratic. In this process-oriented approach, Tilly builds and improves upon Robert Dahl's vision of polyarchy. At this point, it is appropriate to address Dahl's ideas before moving onto Tilly's criteria of democracy in the next chapter, as they complement early work.

Dahl described modern democratic systems as polyarchies and identified the following characteristics: political pluralism; freedom of speech and information; voting equality; the active participation of citizens in the political process; citizens' access to information and the development of an enlightened understanding enabling conscious decision-making; citizens' control of the political agenda; and an inclusive approach to all members of society (Dahl 1989, 108–14). In his earlier writings, Dahl also emphasized citizens' eligibility for public offices in elections; the right to vote; the right of political leaders to compete for the support of both the *demos* and the electorate; and the emergence of institutions that make government policies dependent on citizen's votes (Dahl 1971, 3) This wide array of characteristics, deeply rooted in debates on democracy, constitutes a set of indicators for assessing whether a given political system can rightly be called a democracy.

Tilly did not hesitate to follow in Dahl's footsteps in constructing the indicators of de-democratization processes and this led him to identify the canonical features of democracy, elaborated on the basis of a process-oriented approach. Nevertheless, the other approaches discussed above should not be disregarded because once de-democratization occurs it has far-reaching consequences for the quality of democracy. The effects of de-democratization are likely to affect the entire political system regardless of which criteria are used to define democracy. Democratic backsliding may manifest as constitutional changes that eliminate democratic solutions in order to preserve the rule of anti-democratic elites. Within the substantive approach, one might see a deficit of certain democratic values, such as individual freedom, justice or social equality. Problems with the democratic system may also appear in the procedural approach to democracy through a lack of fair political competition between the ruling party and the opposition. Actors seeking to abandon democratic principles usually do so to maintain power indefinitely but tend to conceal their intentions from the public, both domestically and internationally. In such cases, the constitutional, substantive and procedural criteria applied to define and evaluate democracy could possibly become misleading. The strongest impulse for abandoning democracy stems from the desire to cling onto power much longer than voters and the opposition are willing to accept. To achieve this, actions must be taken in various areas such as legal solutions, changes in economic policy, limiting citizens' rights and freedoms, and subordination of the judicial branch. Such changes and their destructive consequences are obvious regardless of the definition of democracy employed. While definitions of democracy may vary in their evaluation of democratic qualities, all facilitate a precise diagnosis of democratic decline.

Tilly's strategy, based on perfecting the process-oriented approach, deserves further attention and appreciation. His set of indicators of de-democratization seem so universal that they could be applied to any democratic system. However, they only allow for partial success in identifying de-democratization attempts and processes. On the one hand, general principles of democracy should be considered in any evaluation of its quality but, on the other hand, some attention to detail is needed in order to note the specifics of each case under study. Tilly was aware of the usefulness of these two angles within the process-oriented approach, and this volume accepts and applies his methods of analysis.

So far, this chapter has outlined a relatively broad catalogue of the characteristics of the democratic system. It began with an analysis of the most general traits of democracy and was enhanced by more concrete and tangible examples of its qualities. Collectively, they lay the foundation for the study of democracy, offering practical indices of traits suitable for monitoring political systems. However, such positions will not be explored in depth in this volume, as the number and type of indicators of democracy can vary considerably. One may begin with early indices that list various aspects of democracy (Coppedge 2012), their relative weight, hierarchies of importance, and the impact of particular indicators on the quality of the political system (Bollen and Paxton 1998). This can be followed by a rather broad set of measurement indicators of democracy (Andreev and Schuman 2005) that includes 21 criteria, and finally, the Democracy Index published by the Economist Intelligence Unit, comprising 60 indicators of democracy. In this volume, emphasis will be placed on two issues that will also be considered in the selection of de-democratization processes. First, in defining democracy and how to research it, a concrete concept of democracy should come to mind (Coppedge 2012, 12). Here, the broadly understood concept proposed by Dahl is used, as it closely resembles representative democracy. Second, Dahl's definition is also the starting point for Charles Tilly's reflections on de-democratization, which in turn constitute a major source of inspiration for us. It is worth taking a closer look at the process-oriented model of democracy perfected by Tilly.

The nature of de-democratization and problems with the indicators of this process

The concept of de-democratization proposed by Tilly allows for a certain level of generality and universalism without losing the required precision. It can also be adapted for analyses of a particular political system rooted in a certain tradition and affected by a variety of conditions. Tilly's reference to the concept of democracy as proposed by Dahl provides fertile ground for creative improvement of the methods needed for researching de-democratization processes. Let us take a closer look at the logic of Tilly's reflection and establish how it can be useful as an analytic tool.

As de-democratization cannot be discussed productively outside of certain theoretical traditions, such discussions should not ignore the existing research output on de-democratization. Democratization and de-democratization are ongoing processes within a political system, each manifesting with varying intensity over time. According to Tilly,

> democratization and de-democratization do not work in strict symmetry. On the whole, de-democratization occurs in the course of rulers' and elites' responses to what they experience as regime crises, most obviously represented by threats to their own power. Democratization usually occurs in state response (however reluctant) to popular demands, after crises have eased. As a result, de-democratization generally occurs more rapidly, and with much greater central direction, than democratization.
>
> (Tilly 2007, 58)

Following periods of consolidation, democracy may be either strengthened or weakened, and de-democratization processes can also occur. At the core of both democratization and de-democratization lies the relationship between the central authority and the will of the nation. Democratization is characterized by the increasing dominance of the will of the nation, while de-democratization diminishes its importance and increases the power of the state, which frees itself from citizens' control. So long as citizens retain agency, democracy functions – sometimes effectively and sometimes less so. However, if the state frees itself from the will and expectations of the nation and does not have to follow the demands of the people, it becomes a self-sufficient being, independent of its citizens. The preservation of such a status quo is in the interest of ruling elites. Assuming that, in the broadest sense, democracy is understood as the rule of the people, then in this scenario the people have very little say and democracy is effectively absent. De-democratization can manifest in numerous ways. In some cases, it involves a transition from a democratic or hybrid political system to a non-democratic one. In other cases, it means a decline in democratic quality or the cessation of democratic changes in non-democratic states (Szymański and Ufel 2018, 594).

The key mechanism that sets the process of democratization and/or de-democratization in motion is the power relationship that exists between the state and its subordinate citizens. This relationship should not be viewed as static; rather, it is a fluid process, in which power is an attribute of this dynamic relationship (Elias 1978, 116) and its sources have various social origins, not all of which are economic.

> Based on this understanding of the concept of power, the direction of processes of democratization indicates the growing distribution of all available power resources between all members of a society. On the contrary, processes of de-democratization could gain the upper hand if the power resources in a society become increasingly monopolized by a

> specific 'sector' and institution or group of influential individuals. Both of these processes occur simultaneously in all societies.
>
> (Alikhani 2017, 192–93)

This general description of de-democratization explains the core of the process but lacks an empirical footing and must be bolstered with concrete examples. Analysing the relationship between citizens and the state, Tilly identifies three dimensions for the potential destruction of democracy. Deficiencies in any of these areas may harm democracy. The first dimension consists of trust networks, in which citizens are willing to risk their valuable resources. In politics, trust networks may be formed between citizens and political parties. Such trust usually arises between people who share similar political preferences and, to for democracy to function effectively, private trust networks must be welded to politics. The second dimension of relations described by Tilly is categorical inequality. It is evident that social life might be described as an interplay of diversity and inequalities (i.e. sex, gender, social upbringing, faith, and values). So long as these differences result in different rights and different duties, democracy will not be present. The third and final dimension is the emergence of autonomous power centres that may become detached from public policy and remain outside citizen influence, leading to de-democratization.

In sum, democracy is not possible without including the trust networks in public policy and without making public policies independent from categorical inequalities. Finally, democracy requires the elimination of autonomous power centres. If these three conditions are not met in democratic systems, they are prone to de-democratization. If the state does not need citizens' approval and does not have to treat their needs and opinions with consideration, democracy will not prevail. The dynamic between these three dimensions can also be understood as a trajectory along which political systems move, either towards democratization or towards de-democratization.

Consistent with the above discussion, Tilly's (1997, 25) proposal for binding consultations, in which citizens can express their preferences regarding the politics of the state, makes the most important democratic process pivotal to maintaining democracy. These binding consultations require broad and equal citizenship as well as effective protections against arbitrary power and commitments. Therefore, the most democratic political systems are those in which the category of citizenship is not conditional upon ethnicity and is the most inclusive, giving extensive rights to citizens. In such a system, all citizens are equal before the law and the ruling class fulfils the obligations it pledged during binding consultations. As Tilly argues, 'de-democratization occurs chiefly as a consequence of withdrawal by privileged, powerful political actors from whatever mutually binding consultation exists' (2007, 195). In recent years, this process has been observed in Poland under the governance of the United Right alliance and is currently evident in Hungary under Orbán's government and in Slovakia. This list of examples is not exhaustive.

De-democratization usually occurs under the umbrella of criticism towards liberal democracy, focused on its weaknesses in solving the contemporary problems of citizens and highlighting its impossibilities. Reactions that stem from such criticism involve attempts to strengthen the state at the expense of the rule of law, as well as citizens' rights and liberties. At least three processes can initiate democratic backsliding, including (1) disconnecting trust networks from public policies, along with economic centralization and economic autonomy of the state from the will of citizens; (2) the immersion of new categorical inequalities into public policies that are manifested in inequality before the law, and the symbolic exclusion of selected social categories, such as people with dissenting political views or sexual minorities; and (3) the emergence of new autonomous centres of political power that remain outside citizen control, such as the position of party leader Jarosław Kaczyński and his inner circle, who lacked formal state authority when the Prawo i Sprawiedliwość (Law and Justice Party) held power.

Conclusion: which indicators of de-democratization processes in Poland should be applied for research purposes?

Given that de-democratization processes constitute the main theme of this volume, their empirical manifestations in Poland from 2015–23, when the United Right alliance was in power, warrant particular attention. During that period, government activities that could be interpreted as attacks on democracy were met with strong reactions from international institutions such as the European Commission and the Court of Justice of the European Union. As noted earlier, indicators of de-democratization, particularly those of a universal character, have been the subject of numerous discussions among academics. Accordingly, Tilly's proposal should be regarded as a recommendation for pinpointing suitable indicators, rather than a definitive set of instructions. Nevertheless, Tilly strongly advises monitoring changes in the relations between citizens and the state, which he views as indicative of de-democratization processes (Tilly 2007, 60), with particular consideration to changes in the breadth and equality of citizenship, protection from arbitrary power, or alterations in respecting mutually binding consultations. Their manifestations might be quite particular, reflected in relations between the citizens and officials and in governments' treatment of political opponents.

While following the path mapped out by Tilly and drawing on some of his indicators, this volume also offers some novel ones stemming from the author's conviction that de-democratization and democracy are only partially universal processes. The authors of this volume seek to describe and explain the universal patterns and rules that shape social and political processes; however, these processes are, to some extent, determined locally, with the countries under study being particular cases. The conditions for democracy are determined by a set of specific characteristics of the social, political and economic system in a particular state, as well as the historical background and a large array of political, social, cultural and economic circumstances that create the conditions for a variety of processes to unfold, including negative ones such as de-democratization. The destruction of democracy is, to a large extent, driven by a certain contingent of political elites within a given state. Moreover, democratic backsliding frequently occurs in a variety of ways, with each trajectory reflecting the specific features of individual states and their respective elites.

This volume follows Tilly's assertion that de-democratization processes are three- dimensional, bringing changes to the judicial system, the economic system and local governance. The judicial system can be viewed as the backbone of a democratic system and matters of equality, justice and civil rights that are tied to it. A strike against the judicial system results in its subordination to political actors. Its dismantling leads to the destruction of mutually binding consultations and undermines the principles of the rule of law and equality before the law, without which democracy ceases to exist. The economic dimension is quite difficult to assess in the context of democratic backsliding and should be perceived differently from the usual academic reflections on the relationship between the economy and democracy or democratization (e.g. Lipset and Rokkan 1967; Huntington 1991; Przeworski 1991). Economic development and transformations of the social structure that accompany it, combined with the emergence of a strong middle class, are generally conducive to democracy. However, turning away from democracy may not necessarily lead to economic collapse. The Polish economy recorded a period of growth when the United Right alliance was in power, with some small dips resulting from the COVID-19 pandemic, which could possibly imply a positive role played by economic growth in strengthening democracy. For that reason, within the framework of de-democratization the economy should be conceptualized differently than in analyses of democratization processes, as it may become a tool in the hands of political actors. On the one hand, the ruling class becomes independent from the will of people and the state becomes self-sufficient in an economic sense but, on the other hand, when the distribution of economic resources is conducted by the state, society can become dependent on the state and this dependence allows for certain forms of bribery. Social categories that are crucial to the ruling elite receive profits in exchange for turning a blind eye to lawbreaking and infringements on civil rights. In Poland, the establishment of monopolies was supposed to achieve this goal, particularly in strategic sectors of the economy, such as energy and banking, as their functioning was no longer connected with economic rationality but instead was tied to political calculations. Finally, the dimension of local governance warrants closer examination. Reformed in 1998, local governments have remained the stronghold of democracy and development. The agency of local governments ensured adjustments in the developmental trajectories to meet the needs of ordinary people, who were able to participate in these processes and take part in decision-making. This not only enhanced citizens' empowerment and increased their engagement in matters concerning the local community, while strengthening their identities, but also laid the groundwork for the natural development of democracy. Independence and local governance became obvious obstacles to some political elites in their anti-democratic actions. For that reason, the processes of limiting the governance, independence and agency at the local level were introduced in Poland from 2015 to 2023, while state centralism was advanced.

In Poland, the indicators of de-democratization, as well as their empirical manifestations, were evident in all three areas discussed above. In the judiciary, legislative changes limited judges' independence and breached constitutional norms. In the economic sphere, there were changes in ownership encouraging re-Polonization, with the state and its concerns taking control of local and regional media. At the level of local governments, financial resources were reduced and competences transferred to central authorities. Signs of de-democratization could also be seen during anti-government protests, when political opponents were treated with hostility. Newly introduced regulations curtailed civil rights and freedoms. Indicators may also be connected with the state's 'soft' power in the symbolic realm, which, on the one hand, intensified existing social conflicts (religious or cultural in nature) while, on the other, symbolically excluded certain parties in the conflict from the *demos*. The symbols associated with groups and categories who did not follow the government's political line and ideology became unwelcome in the public space. The list of indicators presented in this volume is not exhaustive, but in the author's view, it is sufficient to demonstrate the mechanism of de-democratization observed in Poland from 2015 to 2023. Before presenting a detailed description of the indicators, it is helpful to follow the chain of events bearing the hallmarks of de-democratization. This will provide a factual description of these processes and allow the author to capture the mechanisms used by the ruling elites to consolidate their power in an anti-democratic manner.

References

Alikhani, Behrouz. 2017. 'Post-Democracy or Processes of De-Democratization? United States Case Study'. *Historical Social Research/Historische Sozialforschung* 42(4): 189–206.

Andreev, Svetlozar. 2005. 'Conceptual Definitions and Measurement Indicators of the Quality of Democracy: An Overview'. EUI Working Papers, vol. 5. Florence: European University Institute, pp. 1–16.

Bielecka, Małgorzata. 2012. 'Nowoczesna koncepcja demokracji w Europie'. *Civitas Hominibus: Rocznik filozoficzno-społeczny* 7: 41–49.

Bollen, Kenneth A. and Pamela M. Paxton. 1998. 'Detection and Determinants of Bias in Subjective Measures'. *American Sociological Review* 63(3): 465–478.

Coppedge, Michael. 2012. 'Research Methods and Democratization'. In *Democratization and Research Methods*. Cambridge: Cambridge University Press.

Dahl, Robert A. 1971. *Polyarchy: Participation and Opposition*. New Haven, CT: Yale University Press.

Dahl, Robert A. 1989. *Democracy and Its Critics*. New Haven, CT: Yale University Press.

De Tocqueville, Alexis. [1835] 2002. *Democracy in America*. Chicago: Chicago University Press.

Della Porta, Donatella and Mario Diani. 1999. *Social Movements. An Introduction*. Oxford: Blackwell.

Elias, Norbert. 1978. *What is Sociology?*London: Hutchinson and New York: Columbia University Press.

Fukuyama, Francis. 1992. *The End of History and the Last Man*. London: Hamish Hamilton.

Fung, Archon and Eric O. Wright. 2003. *Deepening Democracy. Institutional Innovations in Empowered Participatory Governance*. London and New York: Verso.

Huntington, Samuel P. 1991. *The Third Wave: Democratization in the Late Twentieth Century*. Norman: Oklahoma University Press.

Lipset, Seymour M. and Stein Rokkan. 1967. 'Cleavage Structures, Party Systems, and Voter Alignments'. In Seymour M. Lipset and Strin Rokkan (eds), *Party Systems and Voters Alignments: Cross-National Perspectives*. New York: Free Press, pp. 1–66.

Michels, Robert. 1911. *Zur Soziologie des Parteiwesens in der modernen Demokratie: Untersuchungen über die oligarchischen Tendenzen des Gruppenlebens*. Leipzig: Verlag von Dr Werner Klinkhardt.

Przeworski, Adam. 1991. *Democracy and the Market*. New York: Cambridge University Press.

Sartori, Giovanni. 1987. *The Theory of Democracy. Revisited*. Chatham, NJ: Chatham House.

Schumpeter, Joseph A. 1976. *Capitalism, Socialism and Democracy*. London and New York: Routledge.

Szymański, Adam and Wojciech Ufel. 2018. 'Beyond Vote Rigging: Common Patterns in Electoral Malpractices in De-Democratizing Regimes'. *Polish Political Science Yearbook* 47(7): 593–617.

Tilly, Charles. 1997. *Rewolucje europejskie 1492–1992* (*European Revolutions, 1492–1992*). Warsaw: Wydawnictwo Krąg, Oficyna Wydawnicza Volumen.

Tilly, Charles. 2007. *Democracy*. Cambridge: Cambridge University Press.

2 State and Elites as Subjects of De-democratization

The Case of Poland

Grzegorz Foryś and Anna Jastrzębiec-Witowska

Introduction

Poland was one of the first countries in the Soviet bloc to begin the modernization process in 1989. Its long-term goals can be summed up as threefold: the establishment of a democratic political system, the creation of a free market economy and the rebuilding of civil society. Several key milestones can be noted in the whole process. The first became known as the Polish Round Table Talks organized in early 1989 between the government and the opposition, which included the leaders connected with the then-banned Solidarity trade union. The talks resulted in partially free elections on 4 June 1989, initiating a sequence of transformations that culminated in the contemporary social and economic system in Poland. The next milestone was marked on 2 April 1997 by the adoption of a new democratic Constitution providing the foundation for a modern, democratic state following the rule of law and respecting human and civil rights. A little over a year later, administrative reforms were conducted, aiming at empowering local governments and preparing them for the allocation of external financing in anticipation of membership of the European Union (EU). In 2003, Poles participated in a nationwide referendum expressing their willingness to join the EU. Accession was granted on 1 May 2004 and three years later, in December 2007, Poland became a member of the Schengen Area.

The milestones outlined above had lasting effects on the achievement of democratic governance, a robust civil society and a functioning free market economy. Clearly, they do not capture the full complexity of the processes of radical change that unfolded over a quarter of a century in Poland, nor the huge effort that Polish society made to achieve full democratization and free market reforms. It is also noteworthy that the ruling elites of the time had to work diligently and in solidarity. For readers from Western countries, democracy and the free market may appear to self-evident and something that can be taken for granted as they have little experience of political systems other than democracy, or economic systems other than capitalism. For Poles, and for the inhabitants of other Central and Eastern European countries, democracy and free markets historically represented a challenge and a goal that they ultimately succeeded in attaining.

DOI: 10.4324/9781042002030-3

This chapter examines in close detail the political system and the de-democratization processes that took place from 2015 to 2023. However, in the preceding quarter of a century, prior to this period of transformation, Poland built and consolidated its democratic institutions and adapted to a free market economy. The constitutional approach to defining democracy shows that the democratic achievements of 1989 and the subsequent years were distinctly confirmed in the Konstytucja Rzeczypospolitej Polskiej z dnia 2 kwietnia 1997 r. (Constitution of the Republic of Poland of 2 April 1997). Two caveats are worth noting. First, what is written in the Constitution does not necessarily becomes reality and, for that reason, evaluation of the political system based on the content of the Constitution is insufficient. Second, processes of de-democratization, which effectively constitute democratic backsliding, may in extreme cases lead to anti-democratic constitutional changes. However, the de-democratization indicators described in this volume will be consistent with the interruption of the process-oriented democracy as proposed and defined by Charles Tilly (2007) and as discussed in the previous chapter.

The chapter begins with a factual, general presentation of the sequence of events that took place in Poland when the Zjednoczona Prawica (United Right) was in power from 2015 to 2023, and that are considered anti-democratic in nature, followed by a more detailed analysis of the legal, socio-political, and economic changes indicative of de-democratization.

What happened in Poland? The Polish political system and the chronology of de-democratization

The presentation of some key characteristics of the Polish political system will allow readers to understand its specifics in order to identify the de-democratization processes that it have taken place. In a general sense, democratic systems are similar to each other, having shared values and foundations in common, but they differ in terms of institutional solutions. This provides a useful point of departure for analysing the changes that have occurred in Poland's legal and political systems in recent years and for assessing the direction of these transformations. Identifying and evaluating these changes should be the first task of this chapter.

Legal experts agree that the primary purpose of a country's constitution, as the supreme law, is to define its political system. According to the Constitution of the Republic of Poland, the country is a parliamentary republic and, as stated in Article 2, a democratic state governed by the rule of law and observing the principle of social justice. This formulation, together with a series of legal guarantees and references to core values, is typical of democratic systems. The principles declared in the Polish Constitution include sovereignty of the nation and the state; independence; separation of three powers (administrative, executive, and judicial); the rule of law; pluralism; a market economy; civil society; and human dignity. Other principles that more directly describe the Polish political system as a democracy include a parliamentary form of governance; the active role of the president, who is the head of the state but who has limited authority; judicial independence; decentralization of public authority with established local governments; and representative democracy complemented by well-established elements of direct democracy (Grzybowski 2017). Also of importance is the ideological and religious impartiality of the public authorities, as well as the equal rights and freedoms of churches. All these principles are directly connected with the democratic political system, particularly the principle of the democratic state governed by the rule of law. Additional principles, such as equality before the law, the social justice proportionality principle, the right to a fair trial, and the protection of acquired rights, stem from the rule of law. This principle is central to this volume, as it applies to all institutions of public authority, which are required to act within the legal framework without crossing its boundaries.

The concrete constitutional framework that underpins the Polish political system reflects a tripartite separation of powers: legislative, executive, and judicial. The relationship between the legislative and executive entities in Poland indicates a parliamentary cabinet system, in which the prime minister and the government (cabinet) are selected and appointed by parliament in cooperation with the president, who provides formal countersigned approval. While both the government and the president hold executive authority, the bulk of power rests with the government.

The formal position of the president is regulated by Article 126 of the Constitution, which designates the president as the highest representative of the Republic of Poland and the guarantor of state continuity. He or she is responsible for safeguarding the Constitution and overseeing its observance. The government, in turn, is responsible for domestic and foreign affairs and all public policies of the state, except those reserved for other state institutions or local governments. Despite the dualism of executive power, the real and presumed competences related to state policy are vested in the Council of Ministers. The president, however, is able to influence the government's foreign policy and, to a lesser extent, domestic affairs by signing laws, initiating legislation, vetoing or referring legislation to the Trybunał Konstytucyjny (Constitutional Tribunal – CT) (in order to review their constitutionality). Additionally, the president serves as the supreme commander of the armed forces and appoints heads of the senior judiciary, judges and members of many central institutions. This type of cohabitation between the president and the cabinet may have positive or negative consequences, It is likely that the authors of the Constitution intended the president to serve as a 'buffer' between the government and the nation, thereby allowing the president to control the government's endeavours and to prevent actions that could weaken democratic principles through veto power. Conversely, these safeguards may fail if the president refrains from exercising his or her powers to protect democratic principles to satisfy a political constituency, as was the case with President Andrzej Duda and the Prawo i Sprawiedliwość (Law and Justice Party). In other words, the Polish political system has built-in mechanisms for democracy protection, but they are not always effective in practice.

Legislative power in Poland rests with the parliament, which consists of two chambers: the Sejm (Assembly), the lower chamber and the Senat (Senate), the upper chamber, with the Sejm occupying a leading role. Members of both chambers are elected to four-year terms in general elections that are universal, direct, equal and proportional, although elections to the Senate are conducted under a majority vote system. Voting is conducted by secret ballot. The legislative initiative is not limited to the Sejm and the Senate but is also vested in the president, the Council of Ministers, and a group of at least 100,000 citizens eligible to vote in elections to the Sejm.

Judicial power constitutes the third branch in Poland's tripartite system of separated powers and is exercised by an independent system of courts and tribunals, with the Sąd Najwyższy (Supreme Court – SC) serving as the highest court in the land and as the head of the judiciary. It includes common, administrative and military courts, as well as the CT and the Trybunał Stanu (State Tribunal – ST). The scopes of jurisdiction for both the CT and ST are defined in the Constitution. The competences of the CT include reviewing abstract and concrete norms by adjudicating on the conformity of lower-ranking normative acts to higher-ranking ones and eliminating provisions adjudicated as unconstitutional from the body of law; settling disputes over authority between the central constitutional state organs; assessing whether the purposes or activities of political parties conform to the Constitution; and determining the existence of a temporary impediment to the exercise of the president's office. The ST rules on the constitutional liability of those holding the highest state offices. It examines cases concerning the infringement of the Constitution or laws enacted by the president while in office, the overstepping of presidential powers, and the commission of common or tax-related crimes.

During the period in which the United Right held power in Poland (2015–23), several significant developments occurred that indicated democratic backsliding. Some of them may be viewed as minor departures from democratic norms, while others signalled democratic backsliding, but in a wider context. First, the changes occurring in the judicial system should be considered as those having most directly led to the weakening of the separation of powers and potentially laying the groundwork for exempting the executive from judicial oversight and legal accountability.

In order to examine the most important incidents illustrating the process of de-democratization, it is useful to group them into three categories. The first, and the most important category, deals with incidents in the legal dimension, that is, the judicial system and the Constitution. The second category encompasses incidents involving political and sociocultural issues connected with civil rights and the symbolic realm of de-democratization processes. The third category pertains to incidents in the economic dimension, as de-democratization transforms the economy into a resource base for the state and makes it independent from the will of the people. All three categories will be analysed in turn here and in the chapters that follow.

Legal changes as a framework for the process of moving away from democracy

The United Right alliance won the 2015 parliamentary election with 37.6% of the vote. This initial success was enhanced by the premium for the winner resulting from the application of the d'Hondt method for allocating seats in the Sejm. The Law and Justice Party secured 235 seats out of 460 in the Sejm and 61 seats out of 100 in the Senate. The latter vote was conducted in single-member districts. Shortly after the election, during the first session of the Sejm in November 2015, the law on the CT was amended. As a consequence, the Sejm annulled the nominations of five judges to the CT made by the previous Sejm and replaced them with five new judges nominated by the current Sejm. This was made possible with the support of President Andrzej Duda, who swore in four of these judges during the night of 2–3 December 2015. As a result, some judicial positions were duplicated, and the President of the CT, Andrzej Rzepliński, did not allow the new judges to hear cases until his term finished in mid-December 2016. The measures concerning the CT were adopted largely within a single day and without consultations or any input from legal experts. Matters were further complicated by the March 2016 ruling of the CT, which found the 2015 amendment to be unconstitutional. To avoid the legal consequences of that ruling, Prime Minister Beata Szydło did not publish it in *Dzienniku Ustaw* (*Journal of Laws of the Republic of Poland*), thus rendering it formally non-binding. However, the failure to publish the ruling constituted a violation of the law. Political commentators described these manoeuvres around the CT as a founding charter of the new order that initiated a series of unconstitutional activities aimed at securing the independence of the judicial branch and of the autonomy the courts (Podemski 2020, 116).

Subsequent operations subjecting the judicial branch to the whims of political actors occurred in 2017. These were made possible by amendments to the law on the Krajowa Rada Sądownictwa (National Council of the Judiciary – NCJ), which effectively deprived judges of their representation at the national level. Members of the NCJ, who had previously been elected by the judges themselves, were now to be nominated by political actors. As a result, these actors gained the right to nominate judges at the expense of judicial self-government, with judges' nominees replaced by those aligned with the United Right. Changes related to the SC appeared to follow a similar trajectory. At first, proposals made by the United Right were vetoed by President Andrzej Duda; however, in December 2017 the new law on the SC was adopted and took effect in 2018. One of the key intentions of the

United Right was to remove certain judges from their posts, as the Act lowered the retirement age from 70 to 65 years, unless the head of state allowed them to remain in office. The structure of the SC also changed through the creation of two new chambers: the Disciplinary Chamber and the Extraordinary Control and Public Affairs Chamber. Further changes were introduced in 2019 when the Common Court system and the Supreme Court Act were implemented, which raised further concerns about judicial independence, the autonomy of judicial self-governance and the protection of individual rights.

These changes were criticized by legal experts and generated numerous protests in defence of the Constitution, the judiciary, and the judicial branch in general, and these protests began in mid-2017 and continued until late 2023. International institutions, such as the Venice Commission, were not indifferent to the situation in Poland and issued two opinions, first in 2016 and then in 2017. The first pertained to the CT and the so-called surveillance law, and the second reflected on the legal amendments affecting the NCJ and the SC. Both opinions were unfavourable but the Polish government questioned their validity. The European Commission voiced concerns on numerous occasions regarding the changes to the judicial system in Poland and even initiated infringement proceedings in 2020. All these statements and proceedings were unfavourable but the Polish government found them to be lacking in diligence and objectivity. The interactions between the Polish government and international institutions were peculiar, especially in the context of the 2019 law on the system of ordinary courts, often referred to as the 'muzzle law', which (1) limited the participation of judges and their self-government in decisions on the functioning of the courts; (2) established the Disciplinary Board in the SC, which could be seen as a move against judicial independence, as they were not allowed to question the status of other judges appointed after the changes to the legal system that were not fully compliant with the Polish Constitution, and could be disciplined for attempting to protect the legal system from the illegal interventions of other authorities; (3) banned the application of EU laws in light of the 2019 ruling of the Court of Justice of the EU (CJEU), which found that Poland had failed to fulfil its obligations under Article 19 of the Treaty on European Union (TEU) by lowering the retirement age of judges and establishing differentiated retirement ages for male and female judges. In 2023, the CJEU made another ruling stating that the changes applied to laws on the CT and the system of the ordinary courts and certain other laws did not guarantee judicial independence and impartiality, and that Poland had once again failed to comply with Article 19 of the TEU.

Two additional legal issues that emerged when the United Right was in power merit consideration. The first deals with the treatment of Adam Bodnar, the National Ombudsman (known in Poland as the Commissioner for Human Rights), who disagreed with the legislative changes introduced by the United Right to the justice system, particularly those affecting civil and human rights. Retaliatory efforts included accusations of excessive focus on the rights of sexual minorities and budget cuts for the ombudsman's office during Bodnar's term. The second issue had to do with the reversal of the 2009 reform which had separated the roles of the Minister of Justice and the Prosecutor General. Under the 2016 law on the Public Prosecutor's Office, the two positions were merged again, giving the Minister of Justice formal control over a significant part of the judicial system. By 2020, thanks to the legislative changes described above, the entire justice system had become dependent on the political leadership of the ruling party, making it possible to control the Public Prosecutor's Office and to remove judges deemed superfluous, overly independent or uncooperative from their posts.

The adoption of changes to the judicial system had multiple consequences in terms of de-democratization, two of which stand out. First, the ruling party gained control of both society and the opposition. This was exemplified by various accusations made towards political opponents, often pursued on a commission basis. The government authorities ignored legal violations if they involved their own political circle and enjoyed a certain level of impunity, which they willingly used. In sum, the rule of law was negated, as well as the principle of equality before the law. This could be seen as a foundation of the state organized by the United Right, paving the way to abuses of power in the public realm and violations of civil rights.

Why do civil rights matter?

Civil rights was another area that fell under the excessive state control, causing concern among institutions monitoring the protection of human rights in Poland. As several legislative initiatives negatively impacted civil rights, the Institute of Public Policies prepared a 2023 report entitled *Polityka państwa wobec społeczeństwa obywatelskiego 2015–2023* (*State Policy Towards Civil Society 2015–2023*). In 2025, the Batory Foundation addressed these issues in a publication entitled *Demokracja obywateli. Mobilizacje społeczne w latach 2015–2023* (*Citizens' Democracy: Social Mobilization 2015–2023*). The Public Ombudsman Office likewise produced numerous analyses signalling as early as 2016 inadequate protection of the right to legal defence and human rights concerns linked to the CT crisis.

One of the earliest examples of human rights violations emerged as a by-product of the law on the provision of electronic services, which gave the authorities the ability to conduct surveillance of citizens without a court order. Prior to the adoption of the new law, such solutions could only be applied to the operators of telecommunication services and were based on phone records. The new law was to expand these abilities to internet providers. The bill was heavily criticized by the Office of Public Ombudsman, the Personal Data Protection Office, the NCJ, the Office of Analysis of the Sejm, and the Helsinki Foundation. The Digitalization Council, operating under the auspices of the Minister of Digital Affairs, did not support the bill and suggested numerous changes, but none of them were implemented by the legislator.

The anti-terrorist law of June 2016 had similar consequences, undermining civil rights, particularly in terms of free speech, personal freedoms, personal security and the right to privacy. The Polish state gained the right to block websites, ban or dismiss public gatherings and mass events, conduct surveillance of foreigners without a court order, collect and store biometric data on foreigners, and arrest and detain foreign suspects for 14 days if recommended by the Internal Security Agency. This law was met with strong criticism from legal experts and non-governmental organizations (NGOs) alike. The Panoptykon Foundation, known for its advocacy for freedom and privacy in the realm of new technologies, submitted a protest to the Speaker of the Sejm, which had been signed by 40 NGOs and approximately 9,000 citizens.

In 2017, the Polish authorities purchased the Pegasus spy system, which in itself would not be unusual had it been intended solely for use against criminal organizations. In practice, however, this acquisition reflected heightened interest by state authorities in monitoring and checking on citizens, particularly members of the opposition. A notable example is the surveillance of member of parliament Krzysztof Brejza, who led the 2019 election campaign for Platforma Obywatelska (Civic Platform). Brejza was not the only individual placed under surveillance. The matter provoked outrage from the Chief of the Najwyższa Izba Kontroli (Supreme Audit Office), who warned that Pegasus posed a serious threat to democracy. Intensive explanations were needed, including the establishment of a parliamentary inquiry committee.

Public media became a key instrument through which the authorities of the ruling United Right could gain an advantage over political competitors and increase their influence over society. Its importance for the conservative government was confirmed in December 2015 with the preparation and introduction of amendments to the Broadcasting Act of 1992. These transferred the power to appoint or dismiss the management and supervisory boards of public radio and television from the National Broadcasting Council to the Ministry of the Treasury. A new television board was established and the controversial right-wing politician Jacek Kurski was appointed President of Polish Public Television. This initiated a 'cleansing' process among employees, while the public media, now known as the national media, became a symbol of the control that the authorities had regained for both themselves and the Polish people. The directors of regional radio and television channels were replaced. A further strike on freedom of speech and pluralism of information occurred in 2020 when the state took control of local media, mostly press outlets. This task was completed thanks to the financial assets of the state-owned energy giant PKN Orlen, which had purchased Polska Press, the owner of 20 regional daily newspapers. Increased state control over the media was clearly affecting freedom of speech as well as the pluralism of information sources, and it also impacted the citizens' agenda and increased control over it. According to Sartori (1987, 87), 'we say that the people must be sovereign. But an empty sovereign who has nothing to say, without opinions of his own, is a mere ratifier, a sovereign of nothing'.

For full sovereignty, citizens need access to various sources of information to shape their knowledge and consciousness and enable them to make independent decisions. From 2015 to 2023, the state made it harder for Poles to exercise such sovereignty. It should be added here that some attempts to limit the pluralism of information were unsuccessful. This was the case with the proposed 2021 media law which President Andrzej Duda vetoed. The bill was meant to prevent foreign companies (from outside the European Economic Area) with shared capital (direct or indirect) exceeding 49% from applying for broadcasting licenses. The official narrative was that such a move was needed to protect the media from hostile takeovers by unwanted companies, especially those connected to the Russian government. In practice, the law was widely regarded as an attempt to eliminate TVN, a television station funded using US capital and openly critical of the Polish United Right.

In 2016, the amendment to the Law on Assemblies represented another step towards restricting civil rights. The law gave precedence to cyclical assemblies over other types of assemblies. In practice, the authorities used the new provision of cyclical assemblies to organize regular public ceremonies and to protect them from the presence of political opponents, as other demonstrations could not take place at the same time and location. In this case, the United Right received support from the CT (already legally defective), which recognized the amended Law on Assemblies as constitutional, despite numerous protests from Polish and international NGOs, including Amnesty International, the Centre for Civic Initiatives, the Civil Society Development Foundation, the Batory Foundation, and the Helsinki Foundation for Human Rights. Adam Bodnar, the Polish Public Ombudsman at the time, unequivocally stated that the amendment to the Law on Assemblies did not meet the standards of a democratic state, as well as constitutional and international standards on freedom of assemblies (Rzecznik Praw Obywatelskich 2018, 56).

Civil rights and freedoms were also violated in other ways. The state became quite diligent in pressing criminal charges against organizers of protests, severely restricting access to legal abortions, and harassing doctors providing lawful pregnancy terminations, as well as engaging in 'pushbacks' of illegal immigrants at the eastern border. Additional measures involved financial cuts for NGOs whose agendas did not align with that of the government, combined with increased funding for organizations that were supportive of the United Right, including newly emerging organizations. In 2017, the Narodowy Instytut Wolności – Centrum Rozwoju Społeczeństwa Obywatelskiego (National Freedom Institute – Centre for Civil Society Development) was established and tasked with centrally financing NGOs. In practice, the institute was set up to control and eliminate independent organizations with different world views than that promoted by the government, which made it harder for organizations representing LGBTQ+ people to access funding. This strategy was coupled with a propaganda campaign presenting certain NGOs as enemies of society and agents of foreign states. This strategy resembled the method used in Putin's Russian Federation. The rights of LGBTQ+ people were not respected, while anti-LGBTQ+ propaganda intensified, most notably during the 2020 presidential campaign, which could be interpreted as the dehumanization of those who did not identify as heterosexual or who did not conform to traditional gender categories.

Taken together, these examples of human rights infringements reflect the logic of an oppressive state, that sought to increase control over citizens' activities. Two mechanisms of such control can be distinguished: the surveillance of citizens and the regulation of freedom of speech.

State and economy: nationalization as a basis for de-democratization

Economic indicators of de-democratization are not always straightforward. Countries conduct their economic policies in a variety of ways, choosing liberalization or centralization, while mapping out developmental goals linked to public policies. In the case of Poland, the interpretation of selected economic processes as leading to de-democratization is only possible when considered in the specific contexts in which they occurred and in relation to the goals they were intended to serve.

The first noticeable change during the tenure of the United Right in Poland was a departure from some market reforms that started in 1989. This was a natural consequence of the United Right's enduring narrative highlighting the real or perceived negative effects of these reforms. The image of Poland in ruins was the recurring theme of several election campaigns before 2015. To some extent, this rhetoric reflected a way of thinking associated with the 1990s, the decade during which Polish society experienced the worst hardships of the systemic transformation. The most visible signs of such policy had to do with limiting economic freedom on the one hand, and intensifying efforts to renationalize a large part of the Polish economy on the other. The latter was legitimized by arguments invoking economic security. Time has shown that such a policy was reasonable, especially in the context of Russia's full-scale war on Ukraine, but prior to 2020, there were no indicators supporting the direction of renationalization. It was conducted to a great extent, and promoted with determination, as providing financial security, as well as other types of security in terms of energy, food and transport. During the United Right's first term in office, this was manifested through an increase in the number of state companies of strategic significance, from 22 to 33, giving the state special prerogatives related to ownership.

The process of renationalization was particularly noticeable among the largest companies and banks. Major state-owned companies, such as fuel giant Orlen, SA (formerly PKN Orlen) Powszechna Kasa Oszczędności Bank Polski (PKO BP – Polish Bank for General Savings), Polski Zakład Ubezpieczeń (PZU – Universal Insurance Company of Poland), Polska Grupa Energetyczna (Polish Energy Group) and Narodowy Bank Polski (National

Bank of Poland), were targeted for renationalization. What can be interpreted as the first step to renationalization involved identifying and strengthening a group of strategic companies, which later were supposed to finance the state's acquisition of other entities in various economic sectors. In this way, some previously privatized companies, including railway companies such as PGE Energetyka Kolejowa, Polskie Koleje Linowe (Polish State Railways), the regional press company Polska Press, Stocznia Gdańska (Gdańsk Shipyard), as well as a significant portion of the banking sector (e.g. Alior Bank, Bank PEKAO SA, Grupa Nordea, Meritum Bank, Bank BPH), were returned to state ownership. The State Treasury also directly acquired partial assets of state companies, such as energy companies' coal holdings. The banking, energy and transport sectors were most affected, with over 50% of their assets placed under the control of the State Treasury. As noted earlier, state security was used to justify this policy, but some of its effects indicated the potential for monopolization of the Polish economy. It is entirely possible that this was the unstated goal of the state economic policy, at least during the United Right's first term in office. A pertinent example of this approach was the merger of Poland's two largest energy concerns, namely PKN Orlen, a fuel giant with 80 subsidiaries, with the gas company Polskie Górnictwo Naftowe i Gazownictwo (PGNiG) and Grupa Lotos SA, another major player in the energy and fuel market. The consequences of these endeavours, as well as the intentions of the authorities, became clear in the run-up to the 2023 parliamentary election. PKN Orlen, for instance, reportedly leveraged its position to manipulate gas prices, lowering them by 20% in order to ensure a favourable voter reaction to the United Right. Following the election, gas prices went up, suggesting market manipulation, given the situation on the international market, which had lower prices. Such manoeuvres can give some indication of the sense of the economic policy conducted by the state from 2015 to 2023. To use the language of Charles Tilly, the authorities were trying to maintain a balance between the state and society, which could liberate the ruling class from the will of the people and consequently guarantee victories in subsequent elections. Following Tilly's line of thought, it can be argued that a foundation for building a strong state with an undemocratic political system was being prepared at that time. Of course, the goal was still very distant but the extent of changes, particularly the legislative ones, justified such an interpretation.

The expansion of the state had a significant effect on social policy thanks to the introduction of the Family 500+ programme that provided monthly payments of 500 złoty (equivalent to €120) per child in April 2016. The benefit was increased to 800 złoty in January 2024 and is now called the Family 800+ programme. This was the most important social programme of the United Right and it warrants a positive reaction for many reasons. As a result of the programme, the number of children at risk of poverty fell from 26% in 2015 to slightly above 16% in 2022. Therefore, the programme can be viewed as addressing a gap in Poland's social policy after 1989. Finally, the state was sharing the benefits of a successful transformation with its citizens. Nevertheless, the programme did not achieve its primary objective, namely an increase in the birth rate, which remained well below the replacement rate. The programme had no impact on the risk of extreme poverty, which remained at around 7% between 2015 and 2023. In some ways, it contributed to a decline in the number of women in the workforce. In the 21st century, women were more likely than ever to choose to stay at home over going to work, a trend that was reflected in official statistics.

Encouraged by citizens' favourable response to the Family 500/800+ programmes, the authorities extended significant financial support to other social groups, with little apparent concern for creating an extra burden on the state budget. Seniors received additional payments to their pensions – the 13th and 14th instalments within one year – while minimal salaries rose, as well as hourly rates for contract workers. In 2016, the minimum salary was raised to the equivalent of 45% of the average salary, and in 2020 it was raised again to the equivalent of 55% of the average salary. Families with the lowest incomes were eligible to receive co-financing of their gas and energy bills. While these measures can be regarded as justified instruments of social policy, their impact on the state budget cannot be overlooked. Under the Law and Justice Party, Polish public debt increased by almost 70%, approaching the constitutionally capped level of 60% of gross domestic product. The official level of the budget deficit did not initially raise concern, but it remained hidden from public view thanks to the practice of moving finances outside the budget. The government created and then used various earmarked funds. This obscured the real state of the budget and made it almost impossible for parliament to control government spending. It was not accidental that attempts to align the budget with actual needs caused a sudden and unexpected spike in the deficit from approximately 85,000,000,000 złoty in 2023 to an officially planned deficit of 156,000,000,000 złoty in 2025, although the actual deficit may have been double that amount.

Within the major trends of state economic policy from 2015 to 2023, efforts to strengthen the state were most apparent, but they were combined with 'buying off' social favour that in the long term increased societal dependence on state politics. Such manoeuvres were reinforced by rhetoric claiming that only the ruling United Right could guarantee the continuation of social programmes and social transfers. The interdependence of the politics-economy-media triangle in contemporary Polish society took the form of relentless shaping of public opinion through political propaganda. Within the legal system, the mechanism of subjecting the judiciary to political interests appeared to have had a lasting effect.

Conclusion: towards an omnipotent state

The changes described above concerning the rule of law, civil rights and economic policy, which were orchestrated by the Law and Justice Party, were crucial for initiating de-democratization processes in Poland. The government's practices extended beyond sociotechnical manoeuvres aimed at increasing the governing party's chance of re-election. In this chapter, the actions of the United Right were compared to the characteristics of de-democratization processes as described by Charles Tilly.

First, it should be highlighted that citizens contested certain actions of the state, such as changes to the judiciary and the CT, restrictions on the freedom of public media and violations of civil rights. Street protests became a frequent mode of citizen's engagement in public matters, but the state responded with repression towards protest organizers and increased brutality in police interventions, with physical force being used against protesters. There were even reported cases of police violence towards members of the opposition, who were protected by parliamentary immunity. The scale of the state's involvement in suppressing civil disobedience was the most intense since the transformation of the late 1980s. The state authorities used the provisions of the new law on gatherings, effectively curtailing the right of protesters to engage in collective action.

Second, civic contestation quickly intensified in the relationship between citizens and the state. The limitation, if not elimination, of certain channels of social influence led to the professionalization and radicalization of a non-institutional repertoire of citizens' involvement. It was applied when the law was being violated, which happened often. Citizens' protests and acts of civil disobedience became cyclical, and even permanent in some cases.

The third indicator of state democratic backsliding relates to the disruption of mutually binding consultations, particularly with regard to their equality and inclusiveness. The authorities' narrative was aimed at producing symbolic exclusion from the national community of various social categories which did not agree with certain state practices or the worldview promoted by the United Right. This exclusion affected supporters of the opposition, people with left-of-centre political sympathies and sexual minorities. Not only was this phenomenon present in the public realm but it also penetrated everyday life, even its more private aspects. Manifestations of worldviews, critique of the government in the workplace or in public institutions could lead to mistreatment, including job loss. In the public media, employees who did not conform to the party line were dismissed from their posts and replaced with compliant journalists. Similarly, in the educational system, at universities and in public administration, independent thinkers were treated unfairly. Disregard for the rule of the law could potentially limit or even suspend the principle of equality before the law, even in the absence of formal criteria of categorical inequalities differentiating political rights and obligations according to social categories.

The fourth indicator of de-democratization involved the extent of changes introduced by the state which had only been subjected to citizens' consultations to a minimal extent. The range of subjects on which citizens were consulted narrowed significantly and the consultation process itself became corrupted and deceptive. Consultations characteristic of participatory democracy were not taking place. Selected public policies were implemented with hidden agendas, while the official narrative justified these measures in the name of the common good. The state authorities ignored experts' opinions and manipulated public opinion.

The fifth problem was unmistakable, as it represented the accumulated consequences of the changes presented above, leading to the centralization of power which, according to the United Right-led government, was aimed at overcoming the perceived limitations of the previous administration and of liberal democracy more broadly. This was accompanied by another indicator of de-democracy, namely the emergence of an autonomous centre of power outside of the legal framework and public space. This centre was located at the headquarters of the Law and Justice Party on Nowogrodzka Street in Warsaw, where key decisions were made under the authority of party leader Jarosław Kaczyński. It did not matter that for much of the time period analysed in this chapter he did not hold any official decision-making role or function, and served merely as a member of the Sejm. His ambiguous yet distinctive status indicated that democracy in Poland started to assume a facade, whereby informal factors exercised power at the expense of legal and respected institutions.

The chapters that follow will provide a more detailed examination of the processes presented above. The analysis will address the legal, economic and socio-political aspects of de-democratization in Poland.

References

Grzybowski, Marian. 2017. 'Konstytucyjne zasady ustrojowe Rzeczpospolitej Polskiej'. In Jerzy Posłuszny, Wiesław Skrzydło, and Krzysztof Eckhardt (eds), *Ustrój polityczny Rzeczpospolitej Polskiej*. Rzeszów: WSPiA Rzeszowska Szkoła Wyższa, pp. 46–77.

Marczewski, Paweł. 2025. *Demokracja obywateli: Mobilizacje społeczne w latach 2015–2023*. Warsaw: Fundacja im. Stefana Batorego.

Podemski K. (2020). 'Proces de-demokratyzacji systemu politycznego a demokratyzacyjne ruchy społeczne: Przypadek Polski 2015–2018'. In Jacek Kołtan and Grzegorz Piotrowski (eds), *Kontrrewolucja u bram*. Gdańsk: Europejskie Centrum Solidarności, pp. 115–141.

Rzecznik Praw Obywatelskich. 2018. *Wolność Zgromadzeń w Polsce w latach 2016–2018: Raport Rzecznika Praw Obywatelskich*. Warsaw: Biuro RPO.

Sartori, Giovanni. 1987. *The Theory of Democracy Revisited*. Chatham, NJ: Chatham House.

Szpak, Konrad and Anna Biloboka (eds). 2023. *Polityka państwa wobec społeczeństwa obywatelskiego 2015–2023*. Kraków: Fundacja Instytut Polityk Publicznych.

Tilly, Charles. 2007. *Democracy*. Cambridge: Cambridge University Press.

3 Procedures for Appointing Constitutional Tribunal Judges as a Means for the De-democratization of Poland's Political System

Dawid Chaba

Introduction

An independent constitutional judicial system is a fundamental component of contemporary liberal democracies, founded on the principle of the rule of law (Sadurski 2019, 268). Constitutional tribunals of liberal democracies serve a dual purpose. On the one hand, they safeguard the ultimate constitutional standards and fundamental rights. On the other hand, they control the expansion of political power by enforcing the hierarchy of sources of law. Their legitimation emerges from procedural credibility, notably apolitical appointment procedures. The tribunals' capability to pursue their purposes both effectively and objectively is inherently related to their institutional and judicial independence. Therefore, the procedures for appointing constitutional court judges are among the most vulnerable and critical points of every constitutional system (Landau 2013, 209–10). The comparative literature considers constitutional courts a soft target for illiberal governments. When 'hijacked', they can protect the majority against constitutional review and facilitate further sequential changes in the legal and political system (Bugarič 2019, 597–616; Castillo-Ortiz 2019, 48–72).

The chapter proposes that the distortion of the procedures for appointing judges to the Trybunał Konstytucyjny (Constitutional Tribunal – CT) in Poland after 2015 formed part of a strategy of planned autocratic incrementalism, understood as a process of creeping undermining of checks and balances (Ginsburg and Huq 2018, 78–169). The primary research problem concerns the way in which CT judicial appointment procedures were instrumentalized to neutralize the institution's guardian function. The chapter argues that the sequence of legislative mechanisms and political practices, from resolutions rendering judicial elections null and void, the selective promulgation of judgments, to alternative interpretations of the role of the President of the Republic of Poland in the oath-taking procedure, has permanently undermined the independence of the CT. This paved the way for successive anti-liberal reforms and the conversion of the CT into a body furthering the agenda of the legislative majority. The research methods include analysis of legal acts, case law, appointment practices, and relevant

DOI: 10.4324/9781042002030-4

European documents to situate the case study within the context of the theory of autocratic legalism.

Democratic decline is defined as the erosion of internal systems of checks and balances caused by elected actors leveraging the law and institutions (Bermeo 2016, 6–7; Levitsky and Ziblatt 2018). Contemporary illiberal governments prefer to pursue 'legal revolutions', understood as formal changes that erode the democratic substance while maintaining the facade of the rule of law. Kim Scheppele refers to this process as 'autocratic legalism', whereas Ozan Varol uses the term 'stealth authoritarianism' to describe a strategy of using the law to dismantle the rule of law, while controlling political costs. The mechanism involves introducing seemingly neutral rules that redistribute institutional powers and hinder checks on the majority, particularly on the part of the constitutional courts (Scheppele 2018, 547; Varol 2015, 1673–97). One of its important components is a strategy of polarization. It places the conflict along a binary us–them axis and delegitimizes opponents, wearing down the constitutional consensus. Polarization reinforces the electorate's acceptance of 'exceptional' actions towards accountability institutions, normalizing practices leading to the capture of the justice system (McCoy and Somer 2021, 7–14). Owing to its concentric role in the checks and balances system, the constitutional court becomes the primary target in these circumstances, as its paralysis affords long-term legislative flexibility and a safe path for further transformations (Solska 2025, 210).

The 2015 constitutional crisis in Poland has become a stress test for the Polish constitutional order, revealing the system's fundamental vulnerabilities (Sadurski 2019, 58). These included disproportionate confidence in the country's political culture and the goodwill of political actors, rather than the incorporation of solid and formal safeguards against political pressure into the system (Scheppele 2018, 549). The CT judicial appointment system has functioned effectively for years based on a tacit assumption that public actors will respect norms and exercise constitutional restraint. However, when a political force willing to ignore these norms and to interpret its authority to the largest possible extent came to power, the construct's frugality became apparent (Antoszewski 2023, 137; Drinóczi and Bień-Kacała 2019, 1140–66). Therefore, the crisis was a political fiasco as well as a failure of the constitutional order, whose resilience was insufficient to survive the rule of a majority determined to test its limits in a systematic manner.

Disassembly through procedures: the erosion of constitutional norms and appointment practices in Poland after 2015

To provide a comprehensive account of the gravity and nature of the changes set in motion in 2015, it is necessary to precisely outline the status of the CT and the procedures for judicial appointments prior to the crisis. The analysis of the status quo ante identifies both the functional components of the system and its covert structural vulnerabilities, which were later leveraged to undermine its independence. According to the Konstytucja Rzeczypospolitej Polskiej z dnia 2 kwietnia 1997 r. (Constitution of the Republic of Poland of 2 April 1997), the CT is a central judiciary body critical to the separation and balance of powers. Its position in the legal system of Poland, specified in Chapter VIII of the Constitution, makes the tribunal a guardian of the primacy of the Constitution and a fundamental component of a democratic state operating under the rule of law.

The architecture of the constitutional system provides for the tribunal to consist of 15 judges elected by the Sejm (the lower house of the Polish parliament) for single nine-year terms (Constitution of the Republic of Poland of 2 April 1997, Article 190 and Article 194). Article 195 of the Polish Constitution guarantees the independence of tribunal judges by stating that they shall be subject only to the Constitution in the exercise of their office. The required qualifications and procedures for submitting candidates are specified in statutes and Rules of Procedure of the Sejm. The president receives their oath of office in a conventional ceremony that marks the culmination of the procedure. The temporal overlapping of the terms is intended to ensure pluralism within the judiciary and to maintain judicial continuity, while the length of term reduces the dependence of judges on the parliamentary majority that elected them. Until 2015, the general practice was to accept nominations across political divisions, albeit that they were openly politically motivated (Sadurski 2018, 1–38). This was due to the fact that the right to propose candidates was confined to a small number of strictly political entities: the Praesidium of the Sejm or a group of at least 50 deputies. This regulation barred other bodies or juridical circles from proposing candidates.

One structural weakness of this model was the use of an ordinary majority vote, in contrast to practices in many consensus democracies. For example, judges of the German Federal Constitutional Court are elected by the Bundestag (the federal parliament) and the Bundesrat (the federal council representing the Länder) by a two-thirds' majority, which forces the main political powers to seek a common candidate. In such systems, qualified majorities are required, so that parties have to find a middle ground (cf. Zalasiński 2015). In the case of Poland, any stable legislative majority could elect judges unilaterally, while ignoring the opposition (Antoszewski 2023, 137–38). The role of the President of the Republic of Poland was limited to receiving the oath of office from by the individual elected by the Sejm, and until 2015, this function was considered a purely ceremonial act. The Sejm's monopoly over judicial appointments, not countered by compensation mechanisms, created an opportunity for a cohesive parliamentary majority to fill vacancies in a short space of time, particularly when multiple terms of office expired concurrently. Thus, the system appeared to have been founded on an unwritten agreement to exercise political restraint and to respect constitutional culture, which has proven insufficient.

In 2015, during the seventh term of the Sejm, in which a majority was held by Platforma Obywatelska (Civic Platform) and the Polskie Stronnictwo

Ludowe (Polish People's Party), a new Act on the CT was enacted, including a transitional arrangement to address five imminent vacancies. In October, five new judges were duly elected, with two of them set to start their terms in December, during the next term of the Sejm. Following the parliamentary elections, the new majority, namely the Prawo i Sprawiedliwość (Law and Justice Party), enacted an amended Act on the CT, the purpose of which was to render the previous election of judges null and void and allow them to fill all the vacancies anew on 19 November. On 25 November, during its eighth term of office, the Sejm adopted resolutions 'on ascertaining the lack of the legal effect' of the resolutions of 8 October allowing for the election of the five judges. Subsequently, on 2 December, the Sejm elected five new CT judges in a hasty procedure. Julia Przyłębska and Piotr Pszczółkowski filled the two vacancies (from December). Henryk Cioch, Lech Morawski, and Mariusz Muszyński were elected to the three positions that had lawfully been filled in October during the eighth term of the Sejm. These three judges are commonly referred to in public discourse as 'double judges' as they were elected to posts that were not vacant, according to the law and a judgment of the CT. President Andrzej Duda received the oaths of office from four new judges on the night of 2–3 December 2015. The fifth judge took the oath a few days later. This unprecedented haste was part of a *fait accompli* tactic to forestall any legal response (e.g. Act of 25 June 2015 on the Constitutional Tribunal; Act of 22 December 2015 amending the Act on the Constitutional Tribunal; Act of 30 November 2016 on the Organization and Procedures before the Constitutional Tribunal; Act of 30 November 2016 on the Status of Constitutional Tribunal Judges). These activities were deliberately designed to introduce legal chaos. The legislative majority created profound legal uncertainty by enacting mutually contradictory laws and establishing two groups of judges: those legally elected but not yet sworn in, and those illegally elected but sworn in. The chaos was orchestrated to delegitimize the institution in the public perception and paralyse its effective functioning, thereby paving the way for the instalment of loyal actors in the court (Antoszewski 2023, 138).

Having introduced loyal judges to the tribunal, the new majority proceeded to enact a series of amendments to the Act on the CT, referred to as 'remedial acts', that were intended to bring the tribunal to a gridlock. The Act of 22 December 2015 drastically changed the way in which the CT operated. It increased the minimum number of judges required to adjudicate *en banc* to 13, introduced the requirement of a two-thirds' majority for adjudicating *en banc*, and enforced a chronological order of case examination (Sadurski 2019, 73–79).

The tribunal decided a series of disputes in three fundamental judgments. On 3 December 2015 (CT Judgment K 34/15), it confirmed the legality of the election of the three judges whose terms ended in November and found no basis for electing the two whose terms ended in December. On 9 December 2015 (CT Judgment K 35/15), the tribunal contested the 19 November amendment regarding the legality of new elections and the reduction of the tribunal board members' terms. On 9 March 2016 (CT Judgment K 47/15), it declared the 'remedial act' of 22 December 2015 unconstitutional (CT Judgment K 6/21). The critical issue in this case was the refusal to promulgate the judgment of 9 March 2016 in violation of Article 190(2) of the Constitution, leading to a legal dualism of the constitutional order and governmental practice (cf. Commissioner for Human Rights, Poland, n.d.a, n.d.b). The refusal to promulgate judgments and the introduction of night-time oath-taking shifted the dispute from the framework of interpretation to the domain of actual control over the CT. Consequently, the parties attempted to settle the dispute through political means rather than judicial decisions. The amended procedures (including the prioritization of cases and the requirement for 13 judges for *en banc* adjudication) served to slow down and selectively block the adjudication process in 2016. The accumulation of these measures, including the problem of 'double judges', a redefined role for the president, selective promulgation, and the reorganization of internal rules of conduct, all contributed to the emergence of institutional capture, whereby legal principles became a function of political calculation (Antoszewski 2023, 131–44).

It should be noted that, although multiple judges were occasionally appointed on a single day in previous years due to expiring terms, these incidents never led to controversies comparable to those of 2015. For example, the Sejm adopted a resolution on electing CT judges on 27 October 2006 and then did the same for another vacancy on 17 November. These were standardized appointment resolutions promulgated in *Monitor Polski* and the appointments were not contested (see Resolution of the Sejm of the Republic of Poland of 27 October 2006 on Appointing Constitutional Tribunal Judges 2006). Similarly, the Sejm appointed three CT judges on 26 November 2010 (Stanisław Rymar, Piotr Tuleja, and Marek Zubik) (see Resolution of the Sejm of the Republic of Poland of 26 November 2010 on Appointing Constitutional Tribunal Judges 2010). Despite subsequent accusations of 'bloc appointment', official opinions, including those of the Krajowa Rada Sądownictwa (National Council of the Judiciary – NJC) and the Sejm, indicated that the appointments had been made for individual persons and conformed to Article 194(1) of the Constitution. Additionally, the wording of the resolution correctly specified the beginning of each term. This practice did not bring about a constitutional crisis. Accordingly, previous cases of appointing three judges on a single day were incidental and occurred on a scale incomparable with the consequences of the developments of 2015.

Instrumentalization of the Constitutional Tribunal

Following the reorganization of the judiciary in December 2016 and the appointment of loyal judges as the tribunal's officers, the CT ceased to serve as a check on legislation regarding matters relevant to the state. The takeover of political control over the CT has led to a pivot in its role within the political system. Rather than operating as an independent guardian of the Constitution, it has become a means for legitimizing actions taken by the legislative majority (Pacześniak 2022, 43–44). This was accompanied by a decline in the tribunal's judicial activities and a tendency towards dismissing critical cases. Past judgments against the 'remedial acts' were removed from public databases of judgments. Their promulgations were delayed or sometimes blocked. At the same time, the Sejm enacted acts to redefine the NJC and the Sąd Najwyższy (Supreme Court) using the 'defence gap' left by the weak CT, which no longer served as a guardian of the Constitution (Roszkiewicz 2019, 128–29).

After the term of the President of the CT Andrzej Rzepliński ended in late 2016, the parliamentary majority passed more laws to elect a new president (Julia Przyłębska), bypassing the opinion of the General Assembly of CT Judges and involving the 'double judges' in the process. At this point, the tribunal was under the complete political control of the Sejm majority. Its ensuing judgments, particularly those questioning the primacy of European Union (EU) law over the Constitution of the Republic of Poland and undermining the authority of the European Court of Human Rights (ECtHR), confirmed the metamorphosis of the independent constitutional court into a body for legitimizing the actions of politicians in power (Drinóczi and Bień-Kacała 2019, 1146–47).

The modus operandi involved arbitrary decision-making with respect to the CT's judgments. Some were ignored, while others were used to legitimize resolutions favoured by the government, including in disputes over authority. In general, the strategy was to bring about a certain situation or status quo and then retroactively legalize it through acts or judgments. Such 'autocratic instrumentalization' does not require a single constitutional overturn. Instead, it is instituted through a series of seemingly small steps that alter the systemic vector towards a illiberal structure without formally abolishing democracy (Antoszewski 2023, 139).

European institutions have verified the consequences of Poland's CT crisis. On 7 May 2021, the ECtHR, in *Xero Flor* w Polsce sp. *z o.o.* v. *Poland*, concluded that a CT panel including a person elected to a non-vacant office was not a 'court established by law' under Article 6 of the European Convention on Human Rights (ECHR), which violated the right to a fair hearing (application 4907/18 2021 and application 1469/20 2022). This final and unambiguous judgment delegitimized the effects of rulings made by the 'double judges' under ECHR standards and initiated an obligation to remedy the structural cause of the violation. Nevertheless, in an attempt to deny any domestic effects of the ECHR judgment, the CT ruled on 24 November 2021 (CT Judgment K 6/21) that Article 6(1) of the ECHR was at variance with the Constitution of the Republic of Poland insofar as it defines the CT as a 'court'. The ECHR's approach was confirmed on 15 March 2022 in *Advance Pharma* sp. *z o.o.* v. *Poland*, where another violation of Article 6 was found to have been caused by improperly appointed judges on the CT bench (ECHR Judgment 1469/20 2022). In the meantime, the Committee of Ministers of the Council of Europe called for a systemic solution to the problem. The consequences were both symbolic and practical, affecting the validity of judgments and confidence in the judiciary. Rulings of the Court of Justice of the European Union (CJEU) on cases regarding judicial reforms in Poland (such as Case C-204/21) have underscored the obligation to provide effective court protection and independence standards, and advocates general have highlighted the risk of recognizing the decisions of bodies that do not satisfy 'court' criteria under EU law (CJEU Judgment C-204/21 2023). Although the CJEU disputes mainly concerned the SC and the NJC, their systemic impact directly affects the CT. The lack of an independent constitutional court diminishes treaty protection, complicates judicial dialogue, and paves the way for conflicts between national and European standards.

It should also be noted that, in the context of dispersed constitutional control in Poland after 2015, President Andrzej Duda played a significant auxiliary role. By signing laws and actively supporting the appointment of 'double judges' to the CT, he further legitimized the CT's controversial actions against the Constitution. Consequently, he failed to fulfil his role as the guardian of the Constitution as envisioned by its framers, thereby indirectly contributing to the weakening of effective constitutional review and exacerbating the political polarization of the judiciary. Such presidential conduct facilitated the further delegitimization of the CT by other state bodies and reinforced dispersed constitutional control mechanisms exercised by common and administrative courts, which increasingly resorted directly to the Constitution.

Systemic results: from the neutralization of constitutional control to a 'dual state of the judiciary'

The capture of the CT has blurred the boundary between what is legal and what is not. Although a formal institutional facade has been maintained, the CT is controlled by the majority. The dissonance between the declared legality and political agency of the executive and the legislative branches draws many parallels with the concept of a 'dual state', where normative and prerogative orders coexist. The CT's check function has been undermined, paving the way for extensive changes in the SC and the NJC and resulting in scattered and fragmented standards of judicial independence.

As a side effect, the tribunal's judicial activities have declined while legal uncertainty has increased. Selective promulgation or disregard for judgments, the dismissal of cases involving 'double judges', and instrumental decisions in disputes over judicial authority have undermined public perception of the CT as an impartial arbiter. International assessments (V-Dem Institute, Freedom House) have reported deteriorating rule of law scores for Poland after 2015, regarding the capture of the CT as a cornerstone of broader democratic backsliding. Confidence in constitutional judgments has been replaced by political calculations, which is a repercussion of a persistent crisis (V-Dem Institute 2021, 6–35; Freedom House 2021, 12).

The decline of trust in the CT was symbolically evident in the actions of other authorities such as the Ombudsman, who withdrew their petitions from the CT in light of the presence of unauthorized judges on the bench. Distributed constitutional review emerged in Poland as a response to the passive stance or bias of the CT. Some common and administrative courts started to apply the Constitution directly without the CT's mediation if they believed that the tribunal was unable to guarantee effective review. For example, in June 2018, the Voivodeship Administrative Court in Warsaw ruled that a 'double judge' (Mariusz Muszyński) was not authorized to pass judgments in the CT and questioned the validity of the CT judgment invoked by an administrative body (Antoszewski 2023, 136–39).

The crisis of the Constitutional Tribunal: a case study in de-democratization

The capture of the CT was not an end in itself but a strategic first step towards much more extensive judicial 'reforms' targeting the SC and the NJC. With full control over the tribunal, the government could ensure that no measures seeking to dismantle the independence of the judiciary would be effectively opposed. This has led to a domino effect initiated by the instrumentalization of the procedure for appointing CT judges. Neutralization of this single body was key to an all-out attack on the rule of law in Poland (Pech and Scheppele 2017, 5–19). The CT's capture set a precedent and created the conditions for further controversial reforms by Law and Justice Party. The CT can be considered the 'first casualty' of de-democratization, followed by the NJC, the SC, the common courts, the public media, the civil service, etc.

The appointment crisis and dispute concerning the promulgation of CT judgements (especially judgement K 47/15 of 9 March 2016) sparked a meaningful response from the public and civic mobilization. Several thousand people marched in Warsaw on 12 December 2015 to 'defend democracy', while another rally by the Democracy Defence Committee took place on 19 December 2015. Demonstrations and pickets were also held in front of the CT building (on 3 December 2015, for example). The mobilization was largely peaceful. The participants called for defending the Constitution and the rule of law. It was one of the first mass protests against the operations of the legislative majority in 2015–16 (TVN24 2015).

The political reorganization following the 2023 elections in Poland brought the issue of restoring judicial standards to the fore. Recommendations from the Venice Commission and the domestic debate proposed multiple options, including reconsideration of defective nominations, a compromise to shorten the terms of office for 'double judges', and legislative mechanisms to redefine the procedure for electing judges through a qualified majority vote. Still, presidential obstruction and disputes over authority a risk undermining these efforts, such that the cure could compromise the very principles it seeks to restore. The challenge of restoring judicial standards without undermining judicial principles follows the logic of the crisis: the struggle once again centres on procedural principles (Venice Commission 2016, 1–28).

Researchers argue that even legal reforms require consensus among the elites and reduced polarization to effect any repairs. This approach emphasizes that the rule of law is founded on an unspoken agreement between political and legal elites regarding the division of roles. Continued polarization after a new party rises to power can hinder the restitution of standards, even if legality is formally restored (Solska 2025, 211). In this way, the CT controversy tested the system's capability for procedural regeneration, not only in a legislative sense, but also in a cultural sense.

Conclusion

The 2015 events concerning the Polish CT transcend the boundaries of a regular political conflict. They are a model example of democracy erosion processes analysed in both constitutional law and the political science literature. With a proper theoretical framework, the Polish crisis can be situated within a wider global context, enabling researchers to move beyond a recapitulation of events and provide a scientific explanation. The notion of de-democratization regards the gradual, often creeping, undermining and dismantling of democratic institutions from the inside out by legally elected governments. Unlike classic coups, de-democratization maintains the facade of democratic procedures, such as elections. Still, it involves systemic elimination of checks and balances, restrictions on citizens' rights, and subjugation of independent institutions to the executive (Levitsky and Ziblatt 2018).

The case under study shows how procedures for appointing CT judges, which to citizens are inconspicuous and seemingly technical, may become a central instrument of de-democratization. The events after 2015 are consistent with the patterns of autocratic legalism. Staff control, redefined adjudication principles, arbitrary promulgation, and biased attitudes towards judgments all lead to the neutralization of constitutional review. Judgments by the ECtHR and the CJEU confirmed that the problem extends beyond the domestic context, as it concerns European standards of minimal court protection and the principle of a 'court established by law'. Its restoration requires simultaneous normative and cultural adjustments. Consensual barriers (such as a qualified majority vote and a nomination procedure involving all political parties), a legalistic solution for the 'double judges' problem, and restoration of the practice of complete and immediate promulgation of judgments are needed. Still, even the best laws cannot guarantee long-term resilience without the de-escalation of polarization and the renewal of the unspoken consent to self-limitation by the elites. The micro-mechanisms of regression brought to light by the CT dispute demonstrate that when political actors colonize judicial procedures, democracy itself is eroded.

The CT was neutralized through regulatory capture, a form of systemic political corruption, whereby particular interests significantly affect state-level decision-making to pursue their own interests at the expense of the public interest. This process involves several critical mechanisms identified in the literature: loyalty-based nominations and the debased purpose of the institution. The appointment of judges by a single political power, including the introduction of 'double judges' in contradiction to with the CT's judgments, is a clear example of this mechanism in practice (Pacześniak 2022, 46). The dismantling of the CT marked the starting point for a broader systemic transformation of the judiciary in Poland, which also encompassed the NJC, judicial independence, and the SC.

Currently, Polish democracy faces the challenge of restoring the authority and independence of the CT. Following the change in the legislative majority in 2023, efforts were made to alleviate the situation and restore the tribunal's constitutional role. The proposed changes aim to manage the impact of the crisis and introduce safeguards for the future. The critical proposed reforms include addressing the status of 'double judges', introducing the requirement of a qualified three-fifths' majority vote when electing judges in the Sejm, establishing a grace period for political actors, and improving transparency through public hearings of candidates. These propositions are intended to strengthen systemic guarantees for the CT's independence.

The analysis demonstrates that the 2015 CT appointment controversy was not merely an interpretative dispute, but a watershed moment in the process of de-democratization. The boundary between formal legality and political agency was blurred, and the Constitutional Court ceased to function as an effective check on the majority. Unlike the previous instances of incidental accumulation of appointments, the scale and consequences of the manipulations after 2015 were systemic and amplified by the refusal to promulgate judgements, combined with night-time oath-taking. The case of Poland confirms the hypothesis of autocratic legalism, whereby minor and seemingly technical procedural devices, aggregated over time, facilitate the permanent capture of constitutional control and shift the systemic vector beyond the standards of liberal democracy.

References

Antoszewski, Andrzej. 2023. 'Erozja demokracji liberalnej w Polsce po 2015 roku'. *Wrocławskie Studia Politologiczne* 33: 131–144.

Bermeo, Nancy. 2016. 'On Democratic Backsliding'. *Journal of Democracy* 27(1): 5–19.

Bugarič, Bojan. 2019. 'Central Europe's Descent into Autocracy: A Constitutional Analysis of Authoritarian Populism'. *International Journal of Constitutional Law (I- CON)* 17(2): 597–616.

Castillo-Ortiz, Pablo J. 2019. 'The Illiberal Abuse of Constitutional Courts in Europe'. *European Constitutional Law Review* 15(1): 48–73.

Commissioner for Human Rights, Poland (Biuro Rzecznika Praw Obywatelskich – BRPO). n.d.a. 'RPO publikuje usunięte z serwisu Trybunału Konstytucyjnego jego wyroki: w sprawach K 47/15, K 39/16, K 44/16'. https://bip.brpo.gov.pl/pl/content/rpo-publikuje-usuniete-z-serwisu-trybunału-konstytucyjnego-wyroki-w-sprawach-k-4715-k-3916-k–4416.

Commissioner for Human Rights, Poland (Biuro Rzecznika Praw Obywatelskich – BRPO). n.d.b. 'Stanowisko RPO w sprawie sytuacji w KOZZD w Gostyninie'. https://bip.brpo.gov.pl/pl/content/stanowisko-RPO-w-sprawie-sytuacji-w-kozzd-w-gostyninie.

Commissioner for Human Rights, Poland (Biuro Rzecznika Praw Obywatelskich – BRPO). 2016. 'Ombudsman's Address to the Prime Minister Regarding the Promulgation of CT Judgments, 24 March 2016.' https://bip.brpo.gov.pl/pl/content/stanowisko-RPO-w-sprawie-sytuacji-w-kozzd-w-gostyninie (accessed 11 September 2025).

Commissioner for Human Rights, Poland (Biuro Rzecznika Praw Obywatelskich – BRPO). 2023. 'Ombudsman Publishes Constitutional Tribunal's Judgments Removed from its Website Regarding Cases K 47/15, K 39/16, K 44/16.' https://bip.brpo.gov.pl/pl/content/rpo-publikuje-usuniete-z-serwisu-trybuna%C5%82u-konstytucyjnego-wyroki-w-sprawach-k-4715-k-3916-k–4416 (accessed 11 September 2025).

Demagog. 2017. 'Niemiecki system wyboru sędziów?' https://demagog.org.pl/wypowiedzi/niemiecki-system-wyboru-sedziow/ (accessed 10 September 2025).

Demagog. 2022. 'Wybór sędziów w Polsce, Niemczech i Hiszpanii: Czy porównania są zasadne?' https://demagog.org.pl/wypowiedzi/wybor-sedziow-w-polsce-niemczech-i-hiszpanii-czy-porownania-sa-zasadne/ (accessed 10 September 2025).

Drinóczi, Tímera and Agnieszka Bień-Kacała. 2019. 'Illiberal Constitutionalism: The Case of Hungary and Poland'. *German Law Journal* 20(8): 1140–1166.

Freedom House. 2021. *Nations in Transit 2021 – Poland*. Washington, DC: Freedom House.

Ginsburg, Tom and Aziz Z. Huq, 2018. 'How to Lose a Constitutional Democracy'. *UCLA Law Review* 65: 78–169.

Helsinki Foundation for Human Rights (HFPC). 2023. *Wyroki TK wydane w nieprawidłowych składach: Raport* (*CT Judgments Passed by Defective Panels: Report*). https://hfhr.pl/upload/2023/07/raport-wyroki-tk-wydane-w-nieprawidlowych-skladach.pdf. https://tvn24.pl/polska/marsz-obywateli-dla-demokracji-przeszedl-ulicami-warszawy-ra602423-ls3320647 (accessed 7 November 2025).

Venice Commission. 2016. *Opinion on the Act on the Constitutional Tribunal, CDL-AD(2016)026*. Strasbourg: Council of Europe.

Landau, David. 2013. 'Abusive Constitutionalism'. *U.C. Davis Law Review* 47(1): 189–260.

Levitsky, Steven and Daniel Ziblatt. 2018. *How Democracies Die*. New York: Crown.

Levitsky, Steven and Daniel Ziblatt. 2018. *Tak umierają demokracje*. Łódź: Wydawnictwo JK.

McCoy, Jennifer and Murat Somer. 2021. 'Overcoming Polarization'. *Journal of Democracy* 32(1): 6–21.

Pacześniak, Andrzej. 2022. 'Zawłaszczanie państwa przez partię rządzącą jako konsekwencja demontażu demokracji liberalnej w Polsce'. *Studia Socjologiczno-Polityczne. Seria Nowa* 2(17): 41–52.

Pech, Laurent and Kim L. Scheppele. 2017. 'Illiberalism Within: Rule of Law Backsliding in the EU'. *Cambridge Yearbook of European Legal Studies* 19: 3–47.

Roszkiewicz, Janusz. 2019. 'Spór o Trybunał Konstytucyjny – geneza i przebieg kryzysu'. *Studia Iuridica* 77: 119–138.

Sadurski, Wojciech. 2018. 'How Democracy Dies (in Poland)'. *Sydney Law School Research Paper*, no. 18/01.
Sadurski, Wojciech. 2019. *Poland's Constitutional Breakdown*. Oxford: Oxford University Press.
Scheppele, Kim L. 2018. 'Autocratic Legalism'. *University of Chicago Law Review* 85 (2): 545–583.
Solska, Magdalena. 2025. 'Polarization and Rule of Law Crisis: Insights from Poland'. *Zeitschrift für Vergleichende Politikwissenschaft* 19: 201–216.
TVN24. 2015. '"To Warszawa, nie Budapeszt!". Przez stolicę przeszło 50 tysięcy manifestantów'. 13 December. https://tvn24.pl/polska/marsz-obywateli-dla-demokracji-przeszedl-ulicami-warszawy-ra602423-ls3320647.
Varol, Ozan O. 2015. 'Stealth Authoritarianism'. *Iowa Law Review* 100: 1673–1742.
V-Dem Institute. 2021. *Democracy Report 2021: Autocratization Turns Viral*. Gothenburg: University of Gothenburg.
Zalasiński, Sławomir. 2015. 'Zasady wyłaniania kandydatów na sędziów TK'. *INPRIS*. https://demagog.org.pl/wypowiedzi/niemiecki-system-wyboru-sedziow/; https://demagog.org.pl/wypowiedzi/wybor-sedziow-w-polsce-niemczech-i-hiszpanii-czy-porownania-sa-zasadne/.

Primary Legal Sources

Act of 22 December 2015 amending the Act on the Constitutional Tribunal, *Dziennik Ustaw* (*Journal of Laws*) 2015, item 2217.
Act of 25 June 2015 on the Constitutional Tribunal, *Dziennik Ustaw* (*Journal of Laws*) 2015, item 1064.
Act of 30 November 2016 on the Organization and Procedures before the Constitutional Tribunal, *Polish Journal of Laws*2016, item 2072.
Act of 30 November 2016*on the status of Constitutional Tribunal judges*, *Dziennik Ustaw* (*Journal of Laws*) 2016, item 2073.
Constitution of the Republic of Poland of 2 April 1997, *Dziennik Ustaw* (*Journal of Laws*) 1997, no. 78, item 483 as amended.
Constitutional Tribunal, judgment of 3 December 2015, K 34/15.
Constitutional Tribunal, judgment of 9 December 2015, K 35/15.
Constitutional Tribunal, judgment of 9 March 2016, K 47/15.
Constitutional Tribunal, judgment of 24 November 2021, K 6/21.
Court of Justice of the European Union, judgment of 5 June 2023, C-204/21 *Commission* v. *Poland* (interim measures and judiciary independence).
European Court of Human Rights, judgment of 7 May 2021, *Xero Flor w Polsce sp. z o.o.* v. *Poland*, application 4907/18.
European Court of Human Rights, judgment of 15 March 2022, *Advance Pharma sp. z o.o.* v. *Poland*, application 1469/20.
Resolution of the Sejm of the Republic of Poland of 27 October 2006 *on Appointing Constitutional Tribunal judges*, *Monitor Polski* 2006, no. 80, item 792.
Resolution of the Sejm of the Republic of Poland of 26 November 2010 *on Appointing Constitutional Tribunal judges*, *Monitor Polski* 2010, no. 93, item 1067.

4 The Process of De-democratization of the Judiciary in Poland in 2015–23 in the Context of the National Council of the Judiciary

Agnieszka Ziółkowska

Introduction

The Polish legal system incorporates Montesquieu's principle of the separation of powers in Article 10 of the Konstytucja Rzeczypospolitej Polskiej z dnia 2 kwietnia 1997 r. (Constitution of the Republic of Poland of 2 April 1997. Forming the core of modern constitutionalism, the principle assumes the separation of powers as well as a system of checks and balances between the legislative, executive, and judicial branches. The separation of powers aims to serve as an effective tool for blocking authoritarian tendencies. The principle of separation, or even isolation, features in the judgments of the Trybunał Konstytucyjny (Constitutional Tribunal – CT) of 21 November 1994, K 6/94, of 14 April 1999, K 8/99, and of 19 November 2005, P 16/04; Sokolewicz 1999. Article 173 of the Constitution of the Republic of Poland further develops this principle in relation to the judiciary, stating explicitly that courts and tribunals are separate and independent from other bodies, both in organizational and functional terms. This principle is the foundation of a democratic state ruled by law, a reference point for the interpretation of state bodies' competences, and a guarantee of individual rights (see Garlicki 2003; Monteskiusz 1957; Sarnecki 2002). The case law of the CT confirms this position (see the judgment of 19 July 2005, K 28/04). Independence from executive and political influences means that courts hear cases solely based on law (see Lautenbach 2013). However, this independence does not exclude inter-authority connections, which in the case of the judiciary manifest in the executive power's influence that has the form of the presidential appointment of judges (see Rynkun-Werner 2023) or the Minister of Justice's administrative supervision of the courts (see Chmielarz 2024; Olszanowski 2025; judgment of the CT of 9 November 1993, K 11/93, judgment of the CT of 15 January 2009, K 45/07). In turn, the influence of the legislative branch on the judiciary (see Wasilewski 1998; Dąbrowski 2009) primarily involves statutory regulation of the courts' functioning. Following the reform resulting from the Act of 8 December 2017 amending the Act on the National Council of the Judiciary (hereafter Act on the NCJ) and certain other acts, it also includes the election of 15 members of the Krajowa Rada Sądownictwa (National

DOI: 10.4324/9781042002030-5

Council of the Judiciary – NCJ). Consequently, the legislative and executive branches may influence the composition of this body and its functioning, but only to the extent expressly provided for in the Constitution of the Republic of Poland (see Article 187(1)(1), final part, and paragraphs 3–4). Disrupting the balance between the branches of power threatens the rule of law and citizens' fundamental rights, in a system in which the nation acts as the sovereign. Importantly, it was the will of the so-called sovereign that justified the need to democratize the judiciary.

The role of the National Council of the Judiciary in a democratic state of law

The legal doctrine on judicial governance indicates that the presence of a judicial council in the constitutional system of public authority is neither necessary nor typical of a modern state (see Garlicki 2005). In Europe, the oldest such councils have been operating since 1946 and 1947 in France and Italy, respectively. Other countries, including Germany, Austria, Finland, the Czech Republic, and Luxembourg, do not have equivalents of the NCJ (see Borkowski and Michalczewski 2017).

The Polish government established the NCJ by the Act of 7 April 1989, which amended the Constitution of the Polish People's Republic (*Dziennik Ustaw – Journal of Laws –* 1989, no. 119, item 101; Article 60, sections 1 and 3). The first piece of relevant legislation was the Act of 20 December 1989 on the NCJ (*Journal of Laws* 1989, no. 73, item 435, as amended). The Act was relatively concise, comprising only 14 articles, which defined the shape, powers, and procedures for establishing the composition of the NCJ, as well as its operation. Article 4 of the Act clearly indicated the mixed composition of the Council, including representatives of all three branches of government, with a numerical predominance of judiciary representatives (at least 18 to 26 members in the total composition). The Constitution of the Republic of Poland of 1997 and subsequent Acts on the NCJ (particularly those of 2001 and 2011) maintained the NCJ's role as the body responsible for safeguarding the independence of courts and judges (Article 186 of the Constitution). This measure ensures that the legal system is free from threats to judicial independence (see the judgments of the CT of 28 November 2007, K 39/07, and of 16 April 2008, K 40/07). The NCJ's competences encompass both counteracting violations of the independence of courts and judges and ensuring the body's participation in the decision-making process concerning the judiciary, including through exercising the right to present candidates for judicial positions to the president (Article 179 of the Constitution). Moreover, the body has active legitimacy to initiate proceedings before the CT regarding the constitutionality of normative Acts concerning the independence of courts and judges (Article 186, paragraph 2 of the Constitution), thereby preventing potential violations. The institutional independence of the judiciary depends mainly on the role of the Council as a central institution maintaining appropriate relations with the legislative and executive authorities (for more information, see Thomas 2009). This body should balance the competences traditionally vested in the executive power (see Ereciński 1994). For this reason, the body should be independent of the executive and legislative authorities, and even more so of any political authority. In their activities, judges are subject only to the Constitution and statutes, while judges of the CT are subject only to the Constitution, which establishes the special role of the judiciary and its independence.

Scholars do not share a uniform understanding of the Council's position in the system. The sole undisputed fact is that it functions as a constitutional and collegial state body (see Ereciński et al. 2002). In the literature and official documents, it is either classified as a judicial authority in a broad sense (see Gudowski 1994) or denied such status (see the judgment of 19 July 2005, K 28/04). According to some arguments, it is a specific, independent, and central state body with functional links to the judiciary (CT judgments of 15 December 1999 in case no. 6/99, 18 July 2007, K 25/07, 27 May 2008, SK 57/06), while both its functions and legal means of operation do not allow to identify the NCJ with courts and tribunals.

Furthermore, the Council's structural position between the state authorities underscores its dual role: as a mechanism for upholding the constitutional principle of balance among the three branches of government and as a platform for cooperation and balance among these authorities (see CT judgment of 20 June 2017, K 5/17). On occasion, the NCJ functions as an independent, extra-judicial body of the judiciary (see Banaszak 2001), or as a sui generis body operating in the broadly understood sphere of public administration (see Sarnecki 2002). Although the NCJ is not a body of judicial self-government (see CT judgment of 18 February 2004, K 12/03; see too Wasilewski 1998), some scholars in the doctrine describe it as a representative of the judiciary vis-à-vis other branches of government (Safjan 2009).

The essence of the NCJ is determined by its composition (see Tuleja 2010), which is not uniform in terms of quantity. The Council comprises 25 members and has a mixed character, creating links between the judicial community and other state bodies, which delegate members to the Council in proportions specified in the Constitution. At the same time, judges have an advantage in the Council's composition over individuals appointed by the president and parliament. Article 187(1)(2) of the Constitution governs the principle for electing judges to the NCJ, without specifying any additional characteristics that would condition their membership in the Council. The Constitution does not favour specific courts when electing judges to the NCJ, meaning that all judges have the same electoral status (see Kostyk 2015). The same provision of the Constitution does not prejudge the desired model for electing judges to the NCJ by specifying the electoral entity (see Mikuli 2014). Hence, in its judgment of 20 June 2017 (K 5/17), the CT indicated that the Constitution does not require that judges elected by other judges should be members of the NCJ. Such an interpretation is contrary to fundamental constitutional principles, including the doctrine of the separation of powers and the protective function of the NCJ, but also contrary to point 27 of Recommendation CM/Rec (2010)12 of the Committee of Ministers of the Council of Europe on judges and their independence, responsibility, and efficiency, adopted on 17 November 2010, according to which no less than half of all members of the NCJ should be judges elected by their representatives from among judges at all levels of the judiciary (see Gajewski 2018). In this respect, the Tribunal's case law is also different (see CT judgment of 18 July 2007, K 25/07). Furthermore, the functioning of the Council finds its validation in European standards (see the European Commission's Recommendation of 20 December 2017 regarding the rule of law in Poland, C(2017)9050, point 34).

Reforms of the National Council of the Judiciary that simulate judicial democracy

The currently applicable Act of 12 May 2011 on the NCJ broadly defines the scope of its powers in the provisions of Article 3, sections 1 and 2. These powers include tasks related to the appointment and career progression of judges, judicial training, and the protection of the public image of the justice system (see Zawiślak 2012), as well as providing opinions on legal acts concerning the judiciary, judges, and assessors, and submitting motions in this regard. The body adopts resolutions regarding applications to the CT for an examination of the conformity of normative acts with the Constitution of the Republic of Poland insofar as they concern the independence of courts and judges, adopting a set of principles of professional ethics for judges and assessors and ensuring their compliance, and overseeing the processing of personal data by the CT, the Trybunał Stanu (State Tribunal – ST), the Sąd Najwyższy (Supreme Court – SC), the Naczelny Sąd Administracyjny (Supreme Administrative Court – SAC), and appellate courts in the course of their proceedings.

Even before the period covered by this report, there were voices in public debate that society has little influence over the appointment of judges and judicial authority, emphasizing its corporate (closed) nature. Nevertheless, this threat to judicial independence should be assessed as incidental, not systemic. The Act of 8 December 2017 introduced fundamental changes of a de-democratizing nature by amending the Act on the NCJ and certain other acts (*Journal of Laws* 2018, item 3). The authors of the reforms adopted an overly broad scope of judicial independence as the starting point for judicial reforms and the NCJ, which the will of the sovereign (i.e. the nation) does not legitimize.

The changes introduced primarily concerned the principles of appointing Council members by the Sejm (Assembly; see Article 9a of Act of 8 December 2017), including specifying that the joint term of office of new Council members elected from among judges should commence the day after their election. Consequently, the authorities repealed Article 11, which they had previously amended, successively limiting the ability of their community to elect judges to the NCJ. The first amendment in 2017 (*Journal of Laws* 2017, item 1183, as amended) restricted the role of the General Assembly of Judges of the SAC in electing members jointly with representatives of the general assemblies of provincial administrative courts, appellate court judges, and district judges. The authorities also repealed Article 12, which regulated the election of electors of provincial administrative courts, and Article 13, which regulated the election of electors of appellate court judges and district judges. The 2017 Act added provisions in Articles 11a–11e specifying the procedure for nominating candidates to the Council. On 6 March 2018, in a single vote and with a three-fifths' majority, the Sejm elected 15 judges as new members of the NCJ. Ultimately, the latest election mechanism resulted in authorities other than the judiciary appointing 23 of the 25 members. As a result of these normative changes, the ruling authorities in Poland took a further significant step in 2018 by dissolving the Council during its term. The Sejm then appointed its new composition, replacing the previous system in which assemblies of courts of various types and instances elected the judges. These actions became possible thanks to the judgment of the CT of 20 June 2017, K 5/17. Incidentally, questions remain regarding the normative value of the CT's rulings (see Radziewicz 2018; European Court of Human Rights (ECtHR) judgment of 7 May 2021, *Xero Flor* v. *Poland*, application no. 4907/18). In the judgment, the CT indicates that the Polish Constitution does not provide a term of office for a body such as the NCJ. The fact that most NCJ members assume a four-year term does not make the entire Council a term-limited body. The term of office applies not to the body itself, but to specific individuals (groups of members) constituting it, and the four-year term guarantees for elected NCJ members are not absolute. As a result of the Sejm's election, the NCJ included 13 district court judges, one regional court judge, and one provincial administrative court judge. Judges of appeal courts, the SC, and military courts lacked their representatives. Simultaneously, serious doubts arose regarding the support lists for NCJ candidates, which were classified by the Speaker of the Sejm. The lists remained secret during the elections of new Council members and for nearly two years thereafter. The SAC's judgment of 28 June 2019 (I OSK 4282/18) changed this situation.

As a result of the 2017 reform, the judiciary lost its right to elect judges to the NCJ. Moreover, the legislative and executive branches (the parliamentary political majority) gained decisive influence over the composition of the NCJ. The changes, together with amendments to other judicial acts, also curtailed the judiciary's influence over the selection of candidates presented to the president for appointment as judges of common courts, military courts, the SC, and administrative courts. Society began to refer to the reconstituted Council as the 'neo-National Council of the Judiciary'. Supporters of the changes argue that the adopted model enables opposition clubs to the parliamentary majority to select at least six candidates with their support, which they view as a more democratic solution compared with the previous system, in which a large portion of judges – particularly those from district courts, the largest group in the Polish judiciary – were excluded from the process, and the elections themselves were deemed 'undemocratic curial elections' (Kancelaria Prezesa Rady Ministrów 2018, 55). The exclusion of some judges aimed to deprive them of any real influence on the NCJ's composition, which in turn was a source of undesirable phenomena, such as nepotism or a focus on personal interests at the expense of the interests of citizens. Consequently, this situation created a public image of a closed, extraordinary professional corporation that does not serve society but places itself above it (see Kancelaria Prezesa Rady Ministrów 2018, 58, 60). Following its election, the Council itself remains independent of both parliament and other bodies, which essentially means a return to the concept of independence as understood in the Polish People's Republic, i.e. its reduction to functional (judicial) independence (this is the opinion of the 'Lex Super Omnia' Association). Commentators also emphasize that the

> democratization of the NCJ is necessary for society (through the Sejm) to have some influence on how the judiciary is formed – but this influence ends with the appointment of a judge to the office and the receipt of the guarantees of independence enshrined in the Constitution and statutes.
>
> (Kancelaria Prezesa Rady Ministrów 2018, 72)

Among numerous arguments, opponents of the changes raise the need to democratize the election process to the NCJ with a significant participation of the civic factor, including the nomination of candidates to the Council by citizens and a public hearing of the candidates (see the Association of Polish Judges 'Iustitia' project, Bojarski 2023, 2017). In response to the Compendium of the White Paper on the reform of the Polish justice system presented by the Government of the Republic of Poland to the European Commission, 'Iustitia' emphasizes that the alleged greater influence of district judges on the composition of the NCJ does not strengthen the reform, as the judicial community can no longer elect members of the Council.[1]

The Act of 20 December 2019, amending the law on the system of common courts, the Act on the SC, and other acts (*Journal of Laws* 2020, item 190) added Article 45a to Article 45c. The provision of Article 45a refers to the inadmissibility of the name of the consideration of a case related to the concluded application to the President of the Republic of Poland regarding the appointment to the position of judge or an application for appointment to the position of assistant judge in a common court. Article 45b provides for the discontinuation of proceedings regarding an appeal against a resolution of the NCJ in an individual case concerning the appointment to office in that position, insofar as it concerns a resolution containing a proposal for appointment to that position in a situation where the president has appointed an individual to the office of judge. Article 45c regulates the inadmissibility of reopening proceedings before the NCJ or repealing a resolution containing a motion to appoint an individual to the office of judge, if the individual presented to the president meets, on the adoption date of the resolution by the Council, the formal conditions required to hold office, as specified in the Constitution. In this regard, the amendment's objective was to protect the justice system. In the opinion of the bill's authors, challenging the act of appointment could undermine the very foundations of this judicial power, raising concerns about chaos and the uncertainty of court decisions. In this context, the above-mentioned findings regarding the NCJ's composition, which nominates candidates for the office of judge, remain valid. It is becoming clear that the solutions adopted in Article 45a–Article 45c intend to prevent anybody from challenging an appointment made pursuant to the resolution of the new NCJ, even though the nomination procedure adhered to provisions that raise doubts regarding its compliance with EU law and the constitutionality of the composition of the NCJ itself. The inability to challenge judicial appointments resulting from a flawed nomination procedure violates the right to legal protection (Article 19(1)(2), TEU, Article 6 ECHR, Article 47 CFR EU). In this context, the ECtHR's judgment in *Guðmundur Andri Ástráðsson* v. *Iceland* (application no. 26374/18) is also significant. The judgment stated that the judicial appointment process should inspire public confidence in the justice system and be based on a normative act that meets the standards of a democratic state ruled by law.

Article 12, section 1 of the 2020 Amending Act is also crucial because it makes Article 45c of the amended Act applicable to proceedings and resolutions that the NCJ adopted before the Act entered into force. Similarly, Article 12, section 2 reads:

> A decision to grant security issued before the date of entry into force of this Act in proceedings following an appeal against a resolution of the National Council of the Judiciary regarding appointment to the office of a judge shall have no legal effect and shall not affect the effectiveness of the appointment by the President of the Republic of Poland to the office of a judge, even if the appointment occurred before this Act's date of entry into force.

This regulation aims to legalize the flaws in earlier nomination proceedings.

Finally, the Act of 28 July 2023, amending the Civil Code and certain other acts (*Journal of Laws* 2023, item 1615) repealed Article 6 of the Act on the NCJ. The original draft of the Act did not propose this change. The addition of the change occurred during parliamentary proceedings. Notably, the change in the procedure for electing the disciplinary spokesperson and their deputies (see Article 112 of the Act on the System of Common Courts) occurred earlier, on 3 April 2018, by the Act of 8 December 2017 on the SC (*Journal of Laws* 2018, item 5). Prior to the amendment, the election of the disciplinary spokesperson and their deputies was essentially the responsibility of the judicial self-government. General assemblies of judges from individual appeal courts selected candidates for the role of disciplinary spokesperson from among the judges of appeal courts, and then the NCJ selected the disciplinary spokesperson for a four-year term in a secret ballot. The NCJ needed an absolute majority of votes and first had to hear all the nominated candidates at a meeting of the Council (Sawiński 2013). The disciplinary spokesperson operated within the NCJ. As a result of the amendment, the Minister of Justice appoints the disciplinary Ombudsman and two deputies for a four-year term. The amendment to the Law on the System of Common Courts did not result in concurrent changes to the Act on the NCJ, which was a source of controversy regarding the procedure for appointing the Ombudsman and their deputies. In particular, there was a discussion about whether a resolution of the NCJ should precede the minister's appointment, as the lack of such a resolution might have caused a defective appointment leading, consequently, to allegations of abuse of the law. Representatives of the government did not see the problem, arguing that the conflict of laws directive, namely *lex posterior derogat legi priori*, applies in the case at hand. The legislative deficiency in the form of the failure to repeal Article 6 of the Act on the NCJ does not affect the correctness of the appointments. The 2023 amendment abolished the normative dualism of the procedure for appointing the disciplinary commissioner and their deputies. However, the exclusion of the judicial self-government from the selection procedure 'raises serious doubts and provides ample grounds for assuming that the personnel decisions of the Minister of Justice and the Disciplinary Commissioner may be arbitrary and lack clear and substantive criteria' (Skwarcow 2021), including in the case of a judge previously convicted of disciplinary offences. The Act establishes no procedure to dismiss a disciplinary commissioner, even if authorities appointed him improperly or if disciplinary or criminal proceedings or investigations are pending against the commissioner. This solution protects the judiciary from unjustified, arbitrary influence by the executive (political) power, which could undermine judicial independence. However, this measure becomes ineffective in situations of open support for the ruling party and the introduction of changes that violate the constitutional framework. Another significant factor is the Minister of Justice's ability to appoint the disciplinary prosecutor to handle a specific judge's case, excluding another prosecutor from action. This ability raises questions about the executive power's influence on the justice system, as it could create a 'chilling effect' among judges. Work is currently underway on an amendment to the Law on the System of Common Courts, which includes a procedure for appointing a disciplinary prosecutor for common court judges and their two deputies. The minister will appoint the prosecutor from the candidates that the general assemblies of appellate court judges nominate, thereby strengthening judicial self-governance. Until lawmakers reverse the NCJ reform, the procedure for selecting a disciplinary spokesperson should exclude the Council's participation.

The image of the politicized National Council of the Judiciary in international and domestic jurisprudence

The changes to the judiciary initiated in 2017, affecting the NCJ and subsequently implemented through amending laws, have become the subject of lively public debate in Poland and Europe, as well as numerous proceedings before tribunals and courts. This is evidenced in the judgments of the Court of Justice of the European Union (hereafter CJEU; see the judgment of 24 March 2019 in C 619/18, *European Commission* v. *Poland*, 15 July 2021 in Case C-791/19, *European Commission* v. *Poland*). Several courts, including the SAC, initiated proceedings before the CJEU by submitting requests for preliminary rulings. The SAC considered appeals from candidates for judicial appointments to the SC after the reconstituted NCJ refused to recommend these candidates. Notwithstanding the SAC's binding decisions suspending the execution of the NCJ's resolutions, the body proceeded to forward nominations to the president, who handed the nominees their acts of appointment (see the judgment of 2 March 2021 in Case C-824/18). Ordinary courts, such as the District Court in Katowice, Kraków, and Poznań, also submitted requests for a preliminary ruling to the CJEU. They sought clarification as to whether common judges appointed at the request of the NCJ – dominated by the government and parliament – may qualify as legally established and independent under EU law, and whether their judgments may be considered null and void. In its judgment of 19 November 2019, in joined cases C-585/18, C-624/18, and C-625/18, the CJEU dealt with the preliminary questions of the Polish SC of 20 September 2018 and 3 October 2018, stating that

> the reconstituted Krajowa Rada Sądownictwa (KRS – National Council of the Judiciary was formed by reducing the ongoing four-year term in office of the members of that body at that time; second, whereas the 15 members of the KRS elected among members of the judiciary were previously elected by their peers, those judges are now elected by a branch of the legislature among candidates capable of being proposed inter alia by groups of 2,000 citizens or 25 judges, such a reform leading to appointments bringing the number of members of the KRS directly originating from or elected by the political authorities to 23 of the 25 members of that body; third, the potential for irregularities which could adversely affect the process for the appointment of certain members of the reconstituted KRS.

Moreover, the CJEU issued judgments in other cases, including, for example, the judgment of 6 October 2021 in Case C-487/19 W.Ż., and that of 22

March 2022 in Case C-508/19 *M.F.* v. *J.M.* based on questions referred for a preliminary ruling by the SC, in which it was indicated that the influence of the legislative and executive powers on the personal composition of the NCJ may undermine the trust that the judiciary should inspire in individuals in a democratic society and a state ruled by law. In its judgment of 4 September 2025 (Case C 225/22/ AW 'T'), the CJEU held that a national court must treat as non-existent any judgment from a higher court that lacks independence and impartiality as required by law, meaning that it does not meet the standards of independence and impartiality guaranteed by EU law. EU law, which underscores rights and freedoms, must take precedence over national law. In this way, the CJEU seeks to protect the uniform and practical application of EU law. In such circumstances, the Polish state may be obliged to compensate parties involved in court proceedings in which adjudicating panels were improperly constituted by the authorities.

The ECtHR dealt with the impact of the 2017 amending act and the composition of the NCJ, including its participation in judicial appointment procedures, in a number of cases. These include the judgments in *Reczkowicz* v. *Poland* (application no. 43447/19, 8 November 2021), *Dolińska-Ficek and Ozimek* v. *Poland* (application nos. 49868/19 and 57511/19, 3 February 2022), *Advance Pharma sp. z o.o.* v. *Poland* (application no. 1469/20, 15 March 2022), *Grzęda* v. *Poland* (application no. 43572/18, 16 June 2022), *Żurek* v. *Poland* (application no. 39650/18, 6 October 2022), *Juszczyszyn* v. *Poland* (application no. 35599/20, 6 July 2023), *Tuleya* v. *Poland* (application nos. 21181/19 and 51751/20), as well as the ECtHR's decision of 23 January 2025 in the case of *Sarata and Others* v. *Poland* (application nos. 2415/21, 48530/21, 13972/22, 15417/22, 20791/22, 26079/22, and 40026/22), all concerning violations of Article 6(1) of the Convention for the Protection of Human Rights and Fundamental Freedoms. The pilot judgment of the ECtHR of 23 November 2023, in the case of *Wałęsa* v. *Poland* (application no. 50849/21) is of significant importance, as it confirmed that the appointment of judges based on recommendations of the NCJ established by the amending act of 8 December 2017 was flawed and incompatible with Article 6(1) of the Convention for the Protection of Human Rights and Fundamental Freedoms. This ruling confirmed that panels of judges, including new judges, did not meet the criterion of a 'court established by law', and that judgments issued by such panels entail a violation of the right to a fair trial referred to in the aforementioned provision. Notably, in December 2023, the public prosecutor's office received a notification concerning members of the neo-NCJ who voted in favour of the resolution of 23 November 2023, calling for the non-execution of the ECtHR's judgment in *Wałęsa* v. *Poland*.

In its judgments of 25 March 2019 (K 12/18), 20 April 2020 (U 2/20), and 2 June 2020 (P 13/19), the CT ruled that the amended procedure for selecting members of the NCJ appointed from among judges is consistent with the Polish Constitution, thus supporting the new procedure for appointing judges with the participation of the NCJ in its new composition. However, the composition of the CT and the appointment of its president also bear political hallmarks. Importantly, the current legal system lacks a body (tribunal) that could impartially determine the incompatibility of the 2017 Act on the NCJ with the Constitution.

The SC has emphasized that the Sejm majority politically elects most members of the NCJ, with the result that the Council does not function as a constitutional organ, as the Constitution itself determines its composition and the procedure for the election of its members (see, in particular, Article 187(1)). This was articulated in the judgment of 5 December 2019 (III PO 7/18), the resolution of the full bench of 23 January 2020 (BSA I-4110–1/20), and the resolution of the bench of seven judges of the SC of 2 June 2022 (I KZP 2/22). The case law of the SAC expresses this position in similar terms (see the judgments of 6 May 2021, II GOK 2/18, II GOK 3/18; 21 September 2021, II GOK 10/18, II GOK 13/18; 11 October 2021, II GOK 15/18, II GOK 16/18, II GOK 17/18, II GOK 18/18, II GOK 19/18, II GOK 20/18; 26 January 2022, II GSK 1812/21; 25 May 2023, III FSK 13/23; 20 February 2025, II FSK 1841/23), emphasizing that the NCJ has ceased to fulfil its role as a body safeguarding the independence of courts and judges.

The NCJ's lack of independence has resulted in a flawed judicial appointment procedure. This flaw violates the standard of judicial independence and impartiality. Notably, between 22 March 2018 and 17 June 2025,[2] 70 SC judges, 2,620 common court judges, 141 administrative court judges, and five military court judges were appointed. Consequently, the number of complaints concerning the independence of the judiciary in Poland has been rapidly and systematically increasing, particularly those alleging violations of the right to an independent and impartial court established by law. Filing a complaint with the ECtHR after a new judge has heard the case opens the possibility of seeking compensation of €10,000, payable by the Polish state (or, more precisely, by the taxpayer). By April 2025, this amount exceeded 3.5 million złoty. At the time of writing, approximately 800 cases were pending, while policymakers were considering legislation enabling the State Treasury to bring recourse claims against the SC judges appointed after 2018 for judgments that lead to complaints before the ECtHR.

The impact of the quasi-reform of the National Council of the Judiciary on the judiciary in Poland

In August 2023, Iustitia conducted a survey,[3] which showed that 41% of respondents considered the NCJ's activities, including its promotion of judges, to be illegal and contrary to the letter of the law, 40% had no opinion on the matter, and 18% of respondents deemed the NCJ's actions lawful. Furthermore, 49% of Poles gave the NCJ a negative rating in terms of political neutrality, 47% believed that the Council did not meet the standards associated with the rules of a democratic state governed by the rule of law, and 44% of respondents gave the NCJ a poor rating in regard to its safeguarding of judicial independence[4] (for more details see Markiewicz and Maj 2024). The presence of politically elected judges on the NCJ diminish its ability to safeguard judicial independence and impartiality, thereby affecting the perceived authority of Poland's judiciary. The same survey showed that only 17% of respondents gave a positive assessment of the Polish common judiciary, 10% believed that the rule of the Law and Justice Party had improved the state of the common judiciary, and 35% thought that the courts were more dependent on the government than they had been previously, while 4% believed that they had never been dependent on it.

Controversies surrounding judicial reforms and the NCJ's political affiliations, the inefficiency of the judicial system, and the protracted duration of court proceedings have contributed to a decline in public confidence in the courts and drawn increasing criticism from European and international institutions and organizations, as well as from domestic non-governmental organizations, the academic community, and judges' associations. Some actors actively express their opposition, while others call for rapid reforms in line with the current Constitution, the standards of a democratic state governed by the rule of law, and fundamental European principles. Other actors draft normative solutions aimed at remedying the effects of the introduced changes. The lack of recognition of the NCJ by certain members of the judicial community has led some judges who have reached retirement age to refrain from submitting declarations of their intention to continue in office, resulting in their automatic retirement. However, a flagrant violation of procedural law vitiates the judgments issued by the courts for the parties to the proceedings, constituting an absolute ground for appeal (see the SC's judgment of 25 June 2025, III KK 295/25). The protracted nature of court proceedings, which is part of the crisis in the judiciary resulting from a shortage of judges, exacerbates the situation in which potential candidates for judicial office, many of whom have previously worked in other legal professions, refrain from applying due to allegations of the NCJ's politicization. Their decision stems from their unwillingness to have their candidacy assessed through the prism of political preferences rather than on merit and professional suitability, and to have their appointment questioned in the future.

The defectiveness of the procedure for nominating candidates for judicial office by the NCJ is structural in nature (Grajewski 2020). Undoubtedly, the procedure for appointing judges to the judiciary is devoid of a representative system, which affects the influence of the legislative and executive powers on the appointment of judges, which in itself is inconsistent with Article 6(1) of the Convention for the Protection of Human Rights and Fundamental Freedoms of 4 November 1950 (*Journal of Laws* 1993, no. 61, item 284) and, as such, constitutes a fundamental irregularity, affecting the entire judicial process and the legitimacy of courts composed of executive judges as a result of its conduct. In turn, this situation violates an individual's constitutional right to a court (Article 45 of the Constitution), which meets the attributes of being competent, independent, and impartial. The executive and legislative branches can directly or indirectly interfere in the appointment of judges who are favourable to them, and the Disciplinary Chamber of the SC is required to discourage opposition to the introduced changes. For these reasons, the issue of changes to the Act on the NCJ has become a subject of interest for European institutions. This is reflected in the resolutions of the European Parliament, including that of 17 September 2020 on the proposal for a Council decision on the determination of a clear risk of a serious breach by the Republic of Poland of the rule of law (COM(2017)0835–2017/0360R (NLE) and that of 9 June 2022 on the rule of law and the possible approval of the Polish National Recovery Plan (2022/2703(RSP)). Furthermore, it has become a subject of attention and concern for other European bodies, including the Committee of Ministers of the Council of Europe, which, in its decision of 7 June 2023, CM/Del/Dec(2023)1468/H46–18, called on Poland to swiftly develop measures to restore the independence of the NCJ by adopting provisions guaranteeing the Polish judiciary the right to elect NCJ members from among its judges; regulating the status of all judges appointed in the flawed procedure involving the NCJ in its composition formed by the 2017 Amending Act and judgments issued with the participation of these judges; and ensuring effective judicial review of resolutions of the NCJ proposing candidates for appointment to judicial offices by the president, including candidates to the SC. The recommendations issued by the Group of States against Corruption (GRECO), adopted at its 80th Plenary Session (Strasbourg, 18–22 June 2018), called for amendments to the rules on the election of judges to the NCJ, ensuring that at least half of the Council's members are elected by the judiciary itself. Similar concerns were expressed by the Organization for Security and Co-operation in Europe (OSCE) in its Urgent Interim Opinion on the Bill Amending the Act on the National Council of the Judiciary (2024).

As a result of the 'reforms', which are incompatible with EU standards, the neo-NCJ was effectively suspended in September 2018. On 28 October 2021, the European Network of Councils for the Judiciary formally expelled the NCJ, which seriously undermined trust in Polish courts and the judgments they issue and generated problems with their recognition abroad. These actions were intended to draw attention to the need to restore standards guaranteeing the independence of the judiciary. The flawed procedure for appointing judges, involving the NCJ, established by the amending act of 2017, fundamentally impacts the independence of judges thus appointed and the authority of the Polish judiciary. Among other factors, the number of cases that the ECtHR brings against Poland influences the negative assessment of the Polish judiciary. These cases stem from violations of the right to an independent and impartial tribunal established by law through the presence of judges whom the President of the Republic of Poland appointed at the request of the neo-NCJ on adjudicating panels. According to the ECtHR (2025), consideration of such cases was to be deferred until 23 November 2026, to give the Polish government time to implement the necessary statutory changes following the pilot judgment in *Wałęsa* v. *Poland*. Simultaneously, attorneys and legal advisors have increasingly requested the exclusion of a judge due to their involvement in appointing the new NCJ, and they also raised this defect in appeals. They argued that all proceedings conducted by such judges would be invalid in civil cases or subject to absolute grounds for appeal in criminal cases.

The threats to the independence and authority of the judiciary arising from the 'reforms' provoked public outrage and sparked mass social protests and other expressions of dissent from civil society. Among these was a joint protest by 27 organizations against the amendments to the acts on the NCJ, the judiciary, and the SC. The protesting organizations included Free Courts, Democracy Action, Amnesty International Poland, the Open Dialog Foundation, the Panoptykon Foundation, Greenpeace Poland, the Helsinki Foundation for Human Rights, Inspiris, the Committee for the Defence of Democracy, Citizens of the Republic of Poland, the Polish Society for Anti-Discrimination Law, Iustitia, and the Themis Association. Actions opposing the politicization of the NCJ also included a boycott of the 2022 elections to the NCJ organized by judges' associations. To identify judges appointed by the neo-NCJ, the Committee for the Defence of Democracy developed an information technology toolkit. This was intended to serve as a basis for requesting a ruling that a judge did not meet the requirements of independence and impartiality, for seeking recusal, or for filing complaints against decisions, appeals, or complaints issued by such judges with the ECtHR. However, Resolution (7) of the SC – Civil Chamber – establishing a legal principle on 10 October 2024 (III CZP 44/23) clarified that a request or motion to exclude a judge from hearing a case solely on the basis of circumstances related to their appointment has no legal effect.

The process of reversing de-democratic processes in Poland was significantly influenced by public demonstrations in defence of judicial independence. Citizens actively participated in marches organized to defend the courts, often rallying under the slogans *Konstytucja* (Constitution) and *Wolne Sądy* (Free Courts). The most spectacular event was the March of a Thousand Robes in January 2020, which was attended by judges from Poland and across Europe, and, critically, citizens who marched alongside them. Social activists organized pickets outside courthouses, collected signatures for appeals and petitions, and compiled 'Books of Solidarity' with judges, gathering messages of support for the judiciary. This display of civic solidarity stemmed from the conviction that defending judicial independence is inseparable from the defence of the rule of law and citizens' rights. This belief arises from the understanding that courts represent the primary institution protecting citizens from potential abuses of power by the government. Although these actions did not have direct legislative force, they played a key role in maintaining the issue of violations of judicial independence in public debate; maintaining the morale of the judicial community; and exerting international pressure on Poland to return to the rule of law.

Furthermore, the academic community did not remain indifferent to changes in the judiciary, particularly the 2017 reforms, with law faculties adopting relevant resolutions. These faculties included the University of Warsaw, the University of Silesia, the University of Gdańsk, and the Jagiellonian University, with its Resolution of the Council of the Faculty of Law and Administration. These bodies emphasized that subjecting the NCJ to direct political influence did not constitute judicial reform; rather, it undermined the judiciary's most fundamental principles, namely independence and impartiality.

The judicial community also showed initiative during the crisis resulting from the amendment to the Act on the NCJ and its far-reaching legal consequences. Judges, perceiving the NCJ as having ceased to act as the guardian of judicial authority, initiated remedial measures. Their efforts are reflected, *inter alia*, in the draft law regulating the effects of resolutions issued by the NCJ between 2018 and 2024, introducing provisions to ensure stability of judgments (as a rule) of judges appointed with the participation of a compromised NCJ. The possibility of challenging them will adhere to precisely defined conditions. As a result, the draft seeks to reconcile the stability of court rulings with the protection of the rights of parties to court proceedings (Patyra 2024), contributing to the rebuilding of democratic state mechanisms based on the rule of law.

Notably, the diminishing authority of the courts has led to a weakening of citizens' trust in the state, an increased sense of injustice, and a decline in the culture of lawfulness among citizens, potentially undermining the stability of the legal system and the democratic rule of law.

Conclusion

De-democratization is a process that results in the gradual weakening of democratic institutions within a state. One of its key aspects is the restriction of judicial autonomy. Weakening the judiciary and politicizing judges removes an obstacle that could block anti-democratic or unconstitutional actions by the executive and legislative branches. Consequently, a façade system emerges, in which courts formally exist but serve as a tool to legitimize political decisions rather than to control them. The de-democratization of the judiciary in Poland, as exemplified by the NCJ, involved taking political control over this constitutional body and transforming it de facto into an instrument of political power in the process of its nomination and promotion. This transformed the NCJ de facto into a political instrument used by the governing power in the process of judicial nominations and promotions. As a result, this contributed to the questioning of the status and independence of judges and a crisis of the rule of law.

The influence of the legislature and the executive on the judiciary in a democratic state governed by the rule of law is necessary. Nonetheless, it should be based on systemic actions, in which the principle of judicial independence and impartiality play a central role. A breach of this synergy results in severe systemic problems related to the violation of cardinal constitutional principles, from the rule of law to the independence of the judiciary. Meanwhile, the model of politicization and appropriation of the judiciary, which the Law and Justice Party created and implemented in 2018–19, represents the pursuit of single-minded power (*absolutum dominium*), which contradicts the principle of separation of powers expressed in Article 10 of the Constitution of the Republic of Poland. Judicial reforms, including those affecting the NCJ, are part of the broader context of Poland's rule of law crisis, which remains unresolved, and whose essence lies in the actions of the sovereign representatives, who hold a simple parliamentary majority. These actions are a denial of the constitutional order. For these reasons, commentators began to call the changes introduced in the judiciary in 2017 and afterwards a 'hostile takeover of the constitutional order', carried out using unconstitutional and anti-constitutional methods, as seen in the reconstitution of the NCJ's membership (see Wyrzykowski 2018). As a further consequence, the political takeover of this constitutional body, which plays a significant role in appointing judges of all types and in every instance, gradually undermined the legitimacy of courts composed of such appointed judges and devalued the judicial system in Poland. The ruling party stubbornly maintained that judicial reforms were consistent with the public interest, the will of the sovereign (i.e. the nation), and European standards. It remained largely unmoved by the need for swift corrective action on the part of the Polish state arising from the judgments of the ECtHR, the CJEU, the SC, the SAC, expert analysts, EU and European institutions, demands from the judiciary, and demonstrations by those whose rights had been violated or were at risk.

The Polish government adopted the act amending the provisions on the National Court of the Judiciary on 12 July 2024 (document no. 219/X of the Sejm). Acting in a preventive capacity, the President of the Republic of Poland referred the act to the CT for review of its compliance with the Constitution (KP 2/24). At the time of writing, the case remained pending.

Notes

1 https://www.do2024.iustitia.pl/informacje/2160-odpowiedz-na-kompedium-bialej-ksiegi-w-sprawie-reform-polskiego-wymiaru-sprawiedliwosci-przedstawione-przez-rzad-rzeczypospolitej-polskiej-dla-komisji-europejskiej (accessed 2 August 2025).

2 https://www.prezydent.pl/kancelaria/archiwum/andrzej-duda/kancelaria/statystyki/statystyki-nominacji-sedziowskich-i-asesorskich (accessed 12 August 2025).

3 http://iustitia.pl/wp-content/uploads/2023/08/290823_Toplines_Justitia_cze23_1_2.pdf (accessed 31 March 2026).

4 https://biqdata.wyborcza.pl/biqdata/7,159116,30116981,miazdzace-oceny-systemu-wymiaru-sprawiedliwosci-za-rzadow-pis.html (accessed 17 August 2025).

References

Banaszak, Bogusław. 2001. *Prawo konstytucyjne*. Warsaw: C.H. Beck.

Bojarski, Łukasz. 2017. 'Udział obywateli w zarządzaniu sądownictwem: Społeczeństwo obywatelskie czy polityczny suweren?' *Krajowa Rada Sądownictwa. Kwartalnik* 2(35): 202–211.

Bojarski, Łukasz. 2023. 'Sądy i sędziowie w poszukiwaniu gospodarza. Uwagi na tle projektu ustawy o KRS przedstawionego przez SSP Iustitia w grudniu 2023 r'. *Iustitia* 4: 202–211.

Borkowski, Grzegorz and Rafał Michalczewski. 2017. 'Skład i sposób wyboru sędziów do rad sądownictwa w krajach członkowskich Unii Europejskiej'. *Krajowa Rada Sądownictwa* 2: 30–47.

Chmielarz, Krzysztof. 2024. *Administracja sądowa. Ministerialny model zarządzania i administrowania sądami powszechnymi*. Warsaw: C.H. Beck.

Dąbrowski, Stanisław. 2009. 'Granice dopuszczalnej ingerencji władzy wykonawczej i ustawodawczej we władzę sądowniczą'. In Tomasz Wardyński and Magdalena Niziołek (eds), *Niezależność sądownictwa i innych zawodów prawniczych jako fundamenty państwa prawa: Wyzwania współczesności*. Warsaw: LexisNexis, p. 110–120.

Ereciński, Tadeusz. 1994. 'Rola rady sądownictwa w państwie demokratycznym'. *Przegląd Sądowy* 5: 3–18.

Ereciński, Tadeusz, Jacek Gudowski, and Józef Iwulski. 2002. *Komentarz do prawa o ustroju sądów i ustawy o Krajowej Radzie Sądownictwa*. Warsaw: Wolters Kluwer.

European Court of Human Rights (ECtHR). 2025. 'Further extension of adjournment of Polish rule-of-law cases'. file:///C:/Users/user/Downloads/Further%20extension%20of%20adjournment%20of%20Polish%20rule-of-law%20cases.pdf.

Garlicki, Leszek. 2003. *Polskie prawo konstytucyjne. Zarys wykładu*. Warsaw: Wolters Kluwer.

Garlicki, Leszek. 2005. 'Komentarz do art. 186'. In Leszek Garlicki (ed.), *Konstytucja Rzeczypospolitej Polskiej: Komentarz*, vol. 4. Warsaw: Wydawnictwo Sejmowe, pp. 1–8.

Grajewski, Krzysztof. 2018. 'Założenia i rzeczywistość władzy sądowniczej: Uwagi w dwudziestą rocznicę wejścia w życie Konstytucji III Rzeczypospolitej'. *Przegląd Konstytucyjny* 1: 37–64.

Grajewski, Krzysztof. 2020. 'Dysfunctionality of the National Council of the Judiciary in the Polish Constitutional System after Statutory Changes: Resolution of the Combined Chambers of the Supreme Court: Civil, Criminal, Labour Law and Social Security of 23 January 2020, BSA I-4110–1/20'. *Gdańskie Studia Prawnicze* 4 (48): 161–169.

Gudowski, Jacek. 1994. 'Urząd sędziego w prawie o ustroju sądów powszechnych'. *Przegląd Sądowy* 11–12: 16–34.

Kancelaria Prezesa Rady Ministrów (Chancellery of the Council of Ministers). 2018. *Biała Księga w sprawie reform polskiego wymiaru sprawiedliwości*. Warsaw: Kancelaria Prezesa Rady Ministrów. https://share.google/iiNoArcFhTehHLRmI.

Kostyk, Bogdan. 2015. 'Niekonstytucyjność trybu wyboru części członków Krajowej Rady Sądownictwa'. *Iustitia* 2: 88–91.

Lautenbach, Geranne. 2013. *The Concept of the Rule of Law and the European Court of Human Rights*. Oxford: Oxford University Press.

Lex Super Omnia Association. 2017. *Opinion of the Lex Super Omnia Association on the Draft Act of 26 September 2017 Amending the Act on the National Council of the Judiciary and Certain Other Acts.* Warsaw: Lex Super Omnia Association. https://lexso.org.pl/2017/11/opinia-stowarzyszenia-lex-super-omnia-o-projekcie-ustawy-z-dnia-26-wrzesnia-2017-r-o-zmianie-ustawy-o-krajowej-radzie-sadownictwa-oraz-niektorych-innych-ustaw/.

Markiewicz, Krystian and Konrad Maj. 2024. 'Co ludzie myślą o sędziach i sądownictwie? Wyniki badań prowadzonych na próbie ogólnopolskiej oraz analiza danych zebranych w ramach projektu Rządy Prawa Wspólna Sprawa'. In *Sędziowie w odbiorze społecznym w czasach kryzysu praworządności w Polsce.* Warsaw: Wolters Kluwer, pp. 162–178.

Mikuli, Piotr. 2014. 'Konstytucyjność trybu wyboru sędziów sądów powszechnych do KRS'. *Krajowa Rada Sądownictwa* 4: 9–12.

Monteskiusz, Karol Ludwik. 1957. *O duchu praw*, vol. 1. Warsaw: Vis-á-Vis/Etiuda.

Olszanowski, Jan. 2025. *Nadzór administracyjny nad sądami i sędziami.* Warsaw: C.H. Beck.

OSCE Office for Democratic Institutions and Human Rights (ODIHR). 2024. *Final Opinion on the Law Amending the Law on the National Council of the Judiciary of Poland*, Opinion No. JUD-POL/504/2024 [AlC/NR]. Warsaw: ODIHR. https://legislationline.org/sites/default/files/2025-02/2025-01-03%20FINAL%20ODIHR%20Final%20Opinion%20on%20the%20Act%20Amending%20the%20NCJ%20Act_Poland_POLISH.pdf#:~:text=Pilna%20przej%C5%9Bciowa%20opinia%20w%20sprawie%20projektu%20ustawy,kwietnia%2020.

Patyra, Sławomir. 2024. 'Opinia w sprawie projektu ustawy o uregulowaniu skutków uchwał Krajowej Rady Sądownictwa podjętych w latach 2018–2023'. *Iustitia* 1–2: 78–82.

Radziewicz, Piotr. 2018. *O skutkach prawnych orzeczeń polskiego Trybunału Konstytucyjnego wydanych w składzie niewłaściwie obsadzonym.* https://konstytucyjny.pl/o-skutkach-prawnych-orzeczen-polskiego-trybunalu-konstytucyjnego-wydanych-w-skladzie-niewlasciwie-obsadzonym-piotr-radziewicz/ (accessed 28 August 2025).

Rynkun-Werner, Robert. 2023. *Niezależne sądy i niezawiśli sędziowie – polityka czy fundament demokracji? Kryzys praworządności w Polsce w latach 2015–2023.* Warsaw: C.H. Beck.

Safjan, Marek. 2009. 'O relacjach trzeciej władzy z władzą ustawodawczą i wykonawczą'. *Krajowa Rada Sądownictwa* 1: 15–22.

Sarnecki, Paweł. 2002. *Prawo konstytucyjne RP.* Warsaw: C.H. Beck.

Sawiński, Jarema. 2013. 'Odpowiedzialność dysycyplinarna sędziów'. In Górski Antoni (ed.), *Prawo o ustroju sądów powszechnych, Komentarz.* Warsaw: Wolters Kluwer.

Skwarcow, Marek. 2021. 'Status prawny i odpowiedzialność dyscyplinarna Rzecznika Dyscyplinarnego Sędziów Sądów Powszechnych'. *Iustitia* 3: 134–141.

Sokolewicz, Wiesław. 1999. 'Konstytucyjna regulacja władzy sądowniczej'. In Teresa Dębowska-Romanowska and Adam Konstytucja Jankiewicz (eds), *Ustrój. System finansowy państwa. Księga pamiątkowa ku czci prof. Natalii Gajl.* Warsaw: Biuro Trybunału Konstytucyjnego, pp. 151–196.

Thomas, John. 2009. 'Rady sądownictwa w Europie'. *Krajowa Rada Sądownictwa* 1: 36–40.

Tuleja, Piotr. 2010. 'Konstytucyjny status Krajowej Rady Sądownictwa'. In Tuleja Piotr (ed.), *Krajowa Rada Sądownictwa. XX-lecie działalności.* Toruń-Warsaw: Towarzystwo Naukowe Organizacji i Kierownictwa 'Dom Organizatora', pp. 61–90.

Wasilewski, Andrzej. 1998. 'Władza sądownicza w Konstytucji RP'. *Państwo i Prawo* 7: 3–20.

Wyrzykowski, Mirosław. 2018. '"Wrogie przejęcie" porządku konstytucyjnego'. http://konstytucyjny.pl/wrogie-przejecie-porzadku-konstytucyjnego-miroslaw-wyrzykowski/ (accessed 29 August 2025).

Zawiślak, Katarzyna. 2012. 'Pozycja ustrojowa, kompetencje i skład Krajowej Rady Sądownictwa'. *Iustitia* 3: 117–125.

5 Judicial Reform and Institutional Change in Poland

Legal and Governance Perspectives, 2015–23

Bogusław Balza

Introduction

The period between 2015 and 2023 marked one of the most dynamic phases of judicial transformation in Poland since 1989, prompting intense debate over the proper boundaries of legislative intervention in the justice system. The reforms under review were officially justified by objectives such as enhancing efficiency, increasing accountability, and strengthening public trust in the judiciary. These stated aims are examined analytically, with attention to both their legal formulation and their practical implications for institutional autonomy. Particular consideration is given to the interaction between domestic reforms and supranational oversight, including rulings and guidance issued by the Court of Justice of the European Union (CJEU) and other European bodies.

The analysis of judicial reform and institutional change in Poland requires reference to broader theoretical perspectives concerning the rule of law, constitutionalism, and the separation of powers within democratic systems. In legal scholarship, the rule of law is understood as both a normative and institutional principle aimed at ensuring that all public authority operates within the boundaries of the law and that judicial institutions retain independence and impartiality (Raz 1979; Krygier 2019). This principle constitutes a cornerstone of liberal constitutionalism and serves as a safeguard against the concentration of power within any single branch of government.

From a comparative constitutional perspective, judicial reforms often emerge at the intersection of two legitimate objectives: on the one hand, the need to enhance efficiency, transparency, and accountability within the judiciary; on the other, the imperative to preserve judicial independence as a fundamental element of democratic governance. The balance between these goals is inherently delicate, and reforms – whether in Poland or elsewhere – tend to generate debate regarding the appropriate limits of legislative and executive intervention in the judicial sphere (Sadurski 2019).

The concept of constitutional resilience provides another relevant analytical lens. It refers to the capacity of legal and political institutions to absorb shocks, adapt to change, and recover from periods of political or normative

DOI: 10.4324/9781042002030-6

stress without losing their democratic or constitutional character (Boin and Lodge 2016). This perspective facilitates an examination of the way in which domestic and supranational mechanisms, such as the interaction between national courts and the CJEU, contribute to maintaining systemic balance. Rather than assuming linear processes of de-democratization or irreversible institutional decline, this framework highlights the dynamic nature of constitutional development, where reform and resistance coexist as part of a continuous process of institutional adaptation.

By situating the Polish experience in a comparative and institutional perspective, the chapter contributes to ongoing scholarly debates regarding the relationship between legal restructuring, political authority, and judicial independence. It aims to illuminate the mechanisms through which reforms can influence the balance of power within democratic systems and to highlight the role of legal and institutional safeguards in maintaining the integrity of the judiciary. The study employs a doctrinal and comparative legal methodology, drawing on statutory texts, constitutional provisions, and reports by international organizations. This approach allows for a comprehensive evaluation of the reforms' legal foundations and their broader implications for the rule of law and democratic governance in Poland.

Legal reforms and institutional challenges in the Polish judiciary

From 2015 onwards, Poland underwent an extensive wave of legislative initiatives aimed at restructuring the judiciary and redefining the role of judicial institutions. Particularly significant were the changes to the Krajowa Rada Sądownictwa (National Council of the Judiciary – NCJ) and the Sąd Najwyższy (Supreme Court – SC) in 2017. Under the amended legislation, the method of selecting the 15 judicial members of the NCJ was altered: instead of being chosen by their peers, they were elected by the Sejm (Assembly, or lower chamber of parliament) from among candidates proposed by the Presidium of the Sejm or a group of at least 50 members of parliament.

Supporters of this reform emphasized that Article 187(4) of the Konstytucja Rzeczypospolitej Polskiej z dnia 2 kwietnia 1997 r. (Constitution of the Republic of Poland of 2 April 1997) explicitly grants the legislature authority to regulate by statute the organization, powers, mode of operation, and election procedure of the NCJ. The Constitution does not specify the detailed method of electing judicial members, leaving the ordinary legislator with discretion to determine the procedure, even if it involves institutional changes. From this perspective, entrusting the Sejm with the power to elect judicial members was framed as a legitimate exercise of national sovereignty and a mechanism to enhance democratic oversight of judicial appointments (Łabno 2017). Proponents also argued that the previous system gave disproportionate weight to judicial representatives relative to political and societal appointees, and that reforms were intended to balance these interests more evenly.

Other scholars highlighted the rationale that increasing the legislative branch's role could create a more proportional representation of the judiciary within the NCJ, while aligning the body's composition with broader societal interests (Zawiślak 2012). A comparative analysis shows that European states adopt diverse models: Austria, Germany, and the Czech Republic do not have councils equivalent to the NCJ; in Sweden, an advisory board appointed by the government participates in nominations; in France, the president and parliament play central roles in the Conseil Supérieur de la Magistrature (High Council of the Judiciary); and in Spain, the Consejo General del Poder Judicial (General Council of the Judiciary) is entirely elected by parliament. In this light, supporters contended that the Polish reforms were consistent with broader European practices, reflecting institutional diversity rather than an exceptional intervention.

Critics of the reform raised concerns about the risk of increased political influence. They argued that, by shifting the election of judicial members entirely to parliament, the reforms could reduce judicial self-governance and weaken the independence of the judiciary (Chmaj 2017). These concerns were echoed by professional organizations and international institutions, which emphasized the importance of maintaining institutional safeguards against potential political interference.

Reforms also affected the SC, where new chambers, including the Disciplinary Chamber, were established and grounds for extraordinary appeals were expanded. According to supporters, these measures were necessary to improve legal certainty, correct judicial errors, and strengthen accountability mechanisms. Critics, however, expressed concern that the structure of the new chambers and disciplinary procedures could create avenues for political influence over judges (Wróbel 2019).

Changes to the prosecution service, including the merger of the offices of the Minister of Justice and the Public Prosecutor General, were justified by the government as a means of improving efficiency, streamlining prosecutorial decision-making, and strengthening responsibility. Supporters argued that these measures would facilitate better coordination of prosecutorial functions and accelerate judicial processes. Critics cautioned that concentrating these powers could reduce institutional safeguards and increase the potential for political considerations to affect prosecutorial discretion.

Between 2015 and 2023, 25 legislative acts concerning the judiciary were enacted, covering the Trybunał Konstytucyjny (Constitutional Tribunal – CT), the SC, common and military courts, and the NCJ. These reforms reshaped judicial accountability, disciplinary procedures, and appointment mechanisms. They were accompanied by debates about the balance between independence, accountability, and responsiveness to societal demands. Proponents consistently framed the reforms as fulfilling electoral promises, enhancing transparency, and improving the efficiency of the judiciary.

These reforms triggered widespread criticism from legal scholars, professional organizations, civil society, and international bodies. Statements by the

European Network of Councils for the Judiciary and resolutions by associations of judges in Northern and Eastern Europe highlighted concerns about political influence in judicial matters. The European Commission (EC) initiated infringement procedures in April 2020, citing violations of EU law and the principles of judicial independence and impartiality. A 2023 ruling by the CJEU confirmed that certain aspects of the legislation were not fully aligned with EU obligations and emphasized the need to safeguard judicial independence.

The measures undertaken by the government led by the Prawo i Sprawiedliwość (Law and Justice Party) were intended to recalibrate the balance of power among state institutions by expanding the influence of democratically elected authorities over judicial appointments and internal governance. From this perspective, the reforms sought to strengthen the role of the executive and legislative branches in shaping the composition and direction of the judiciary, thereby reducing the autonomy traditionally afforded to judicial bodies.

The practical implications for democratic governance were significant. By increasing political control over key judicial institutions, the reforms affected constitutional safeguards designed to shield courts from majoritarian pressures. This, in turn, weakened mechanisms essential for maintaining the separation of powers, ensuring effective checks and balances, and protecting the rule of law.

The role of the Minister of Justice and the Public Prosecutor General: structural changes

The Act of 28 January 2016 – the Law on the Prosecution Service – introduced comprehensive changes to the structure, organization, and functioning of the prosecution service in Poland. The most consequential element of the reform was the merger of the offices of the Minister of Justice and the Public Prosecutor General. These functions had been separated since 2010, when legislators sought to shield prosecutorial decision-making from political influence (Kułak 2016). Under the pre-2010 model, the Public Prosecutor General operated independently of the executive, could not engage in political activity, and was appointed by the president from among candidates submitted separately by the NCJ and the Krajowa Rada Prokuratury (National Council of Prosecutors – NCP). These institutional safeguards were intended to guarantee prosecutorial independence, even in cases concerning high-ranking officials or matters of political sensitivity (Mazowiecka 2015).

The separation of the offices in 2010 had been motivated by the principle of insulating prosecutorial activity from political authority. Under the 2010 framework, the Public Prosecutor General was appointed by the President of the Republic from among two candidates: one nominated by the NCJ and the other by the NCP attached to the Public Prosecutor General's Office. The statutory framework guaranteed prosecutorial independence by prohibiting prosecutors from engaging in political activity and by limiting interference in their professional activities to direct superiors within the organizational hierarchy. The aim of the reform was to approximate the prosecution service to the model of autonomous institutions such as the judiciary, ensuring impartiality while maintaining the necessary managerial supervision (Gersdorf 2016).

According to the government's justification, however, the 2010 reform had significantly weakened the state's ability to ensure internal security and public order, which are constitutional obligations under Article 146 of the Polish Constitution. The explanatory memorandum to the 2016 Act emphasized that limiting the powers of the Public Prosecutor General restricted the government's capacity to fulfil its duties in safeguarding the state and its citizens. Supporters of the reform argued that restoring the merger of the offices of the Minister of Justice and the Public Prosecutor General would enhance efficiency, strengthen management, and enable more effective responses to organizational and administrative challenges within the prosecution system (Warciński 2016).

Article 1 of the 2016 Act explicitly stipulated that the roles of Public Prosecutor General and Minister of Justice are to be held by the same individual (art. 1 § 2). The statutory requirements for holding this position were Polish citizenship and a legal education.

The new legislation expanded the powers of the Public Prosecutor General. He or she was granted the authority to appoint and dismiss the heads of regional, district, and local prosecution offices at their discretion, without fixed terms or mandatory competitive selection procedures. This marked a departure from the previous model, in which leadership positions were filled through transparent processes designed to limit political influence. The reform also established the Internal Affairs Division within the National Prosecution Office, tasked with investigating alleged crimes committed by judges, prosecutors, and legal trainees. While presented as a measure to strengthen accountability, commentators highlighted that this arrangement raised questions about prosecutorial and judicial independence (Staszak 2016).

In terms of organizational structure, appellate prosecution offices were abolished and replaced with regional prosecution offices. The stated purpose of this measure was to simplify the institutional framework and improve the flow of information across supervisory levels. At the same time, the National Prosecution Office was placed directly under the Public Prosecutor General's control, with broad competences in managing sensitive or high-profile cases (Sakowicz 2016).

The Public Prosecutor General's disciplinary powers were also expanded. He or she could appoint disciplinary officers and chairs of disciplinary courts, and in certain circumstances suspend prosecutors from duty for periods of up to six months. He or she was empowered to oversee disciplinary proceedings, request explanations from prosecutors, and intervene in cases of alleged negligence or deficiencies. Moreover, under the amended provisions, the Public Prosecutor General was granted the authority to relocate prosecutors to other units for periods of up to six months, and in special cases up to 12 months within a year, even without their consent. Legal experts warned that such instruments could be used to exert pressure on prosecutors, as delegation to distant jurisdictions or lower-level units could serve as an informal form of punishment (Kułak 2016).

With respect to the conduct of proceedings, Articles 7–9 of the law formally affirmed the principle of prosecutorial independence, but introduced mechanisms of hierarchical subordination. Supervisors were authorized to issue instructions to subordinate prosecutors, who could request a change or seek recusal from executing a specific order, although the final decision remained at the discretion of the supervisor. This framework allowed for managerial oversight, while limiting the scope of prosecutorial autonomy. The Public Prosecutor General was empowered to alter or revoke decisions of subordinate prosecutors, issue binding guidelines, and transfer cases to the National Prosecution Office regardless of jurisdiction. He or she could also provide information about ongoing proceedings to the media, even without the consent of the case prosecutor, a competence that raised questions about the politicization of sensitive cases.

Proponents of the reform stressed that these mechanisms created the conditions for more effective coordination of prosecutorial activity, faster responses to administrative needs, and improved overall efficiency of the prosecution service (Mizera 2016). In their view, the hierarchical structure reflected the inherently centralized character of the institution and enabled the state to fulfil its constitutional obligations in the field of law enforcement. They further argued that merging the roles of Minister of Justice and Public Prosecutor General strengthened accountability by consolidating responsibility for prosecutorial policy in a single office.

Critics, however, emphasized that the combination of personnel, organizational, and disciplinary powers in the hands of a political minister risked undermining the principle of impartiality. They noted that prosecutors, who are prohibited from engaging in political activity, became subject to instructions from a political appointee who is simultaneously a member of the government. From this perspective, the reform eroded the constitutional aim of insulating certain state institutions from partisan influence, as reflected in Article 103 of the Polish Constitution on the incompatibility of offices (Seremet 2016). Concerns were also raised regarding the lack of clear legal criteria guiding supervisory interventions, which granted significant discretion to superiors in shaping prosecutorial decisions (Kułak 2016).

The reform also became the subject of international scrutiny. The Venice Commission observed that the 2016 law weakened institutional safeguards of prosecutorial independence, leaving the office vulnerable to government intervention in individual cases (Barrett et al. 2017). Scholarly debate further questioned the government's reliance on public security arguments to justify the merger of offices. As noted earlier, ensuring internal security and public order is not among the statutory tasks of the prosecution service, but rather falls within the competences of other executive bodies such as the Ministry of the Interior, the Ministry of Defence, or the Internal Security Agency. Assigning such functions to the prosecution was therefore criticized as misleading and inconsistent with established legal doctrine (Herzog 2009).

In the broader legal discourse, the 2016 Act was assessed as a departure from the prior model of prosecution, which had incorporated safeguards designed to balance efficiency with autonomy. On the one hand, the amendment standardized the chain of command, introduced mechanisms for managerial oversight, and allowed for rapid organizational adjustments (Kuchciński 2016). On the other hand, it concentrated control in the hands of the Public Prosecutor General acting as the Minister of Justice, thereby blurring the line between prosecutorial independence and political authority. While supporters highlighted improvements in coordination and responsiveness, critics underscored risks of politicization, reduced guarantees of independence, and potential violations of constitutional principles.

As a result, the 2016 reform has remained a central point of contention in Polish legal scholarship and political debate. It is analysed both as an attempt to modernize and streamline the prosecution service and as a step that compromised institutional safeguards essential for the impartial administration of justice. The balance between administrative efficiency and prosecutorial independence thus continues to shape the ongoing evaluation of the Act's systemic consequences for the rule of law in Poland.

These ongoing evaluations highlight the fact that the structural changes were not merely administrative, but had profound implications for democratic governance and the protection of constitutional principles. These structural changes had clear implications for democracy and the rule of law. By concentrating executive and political authority over the prosecution, the reforms reduced institutional checks on government power, increased the risk of politicized decision-making, and undermined the autonomy of a key judicial institution. Consequently, the capacity of the prosecution to act impartially and independently was weakened, posing a challenge to constitutional safeguards and democratic governance.

Revisions to judicial appointment processes and their implications

The reform of the Polish NCJ has become one of the central points of legal discussion concerning the independence of the judiciary and the relationship between the branches of government. As a constitutional body, the NCJ occupies a key role within the justice system: it is entrusted with safeguarding judicial independence, overseeing the appointment of judges at all levels, and functioning as a guarantor of judicial impartiality (Ejchart-Dubois et al. 2019). Its decisions and composition therefore exert significant influence over the overall functioning of the judiciary. The reform of December 2017, together with subsequent legislative amendments, has triggered divergent assessments among constitutional scholars, practitioners, and international institutions. On the one hand, proponents of the reform emphasized the constitutional legitimacy of the legislature to determine the institutional structure, procedures, and methods of selecting NCJ members. On the other hand, critics pointed to concerns regarding the erosion of safeguards of independence, the premature termination of judicial mandates, and the increased role of political organs in judicial appointments (Rakowska-Trela 2017).

The legal foundations of the NCJ are set out in Articles 186 and 187 of the Constitution of the Republic of Poland. Article 186(1) assigns the Council the task of safeguarding the independence of courts and judges, while Article 187 delineates its composition. The Council consists of representatives of all three branches of power, with 15 members drawn from among judges of the SC, the common courts, the administrative courts, and the military courts. The Constitution provides that these 15 members are elected 'from among judges' but does not specify by whom or according to what procedure. This textual lacuna has been a focal point of doctrinal debate. Article 187(3) establishes that elected members of the NCJ serve four-year terms, while Article 187(4) delegates to statute the regulation of the Council's structure, functioning, and selection of members. Thus, the constitutional design reflects a deliberate mixture of rigidity and flexibility: while the institution and its general purpose are entrenched, significant discretion is left to the ordinary legislator in shaping its detailed operation. This interplay between constitutional provisions and statutory discretion forms the basis for diverging interpretations of the 2017 reform.

The Act of 8 December 2017 on the amendment of the Act on the NCJ introduced several significant changes. Most notably, it modified the procedure for selecting the 15 judicial members of the Council. Instead of being chosen from among the judiciary, these members were henceforth to be elected by the Sejm from among candidates submitted by the Presidium of the Sejm or by at least 50 deputies. Additionally, transitional provisions terminated the ongoing four-year mandates of judicial members elected under the previous rules, requiring the appointment of new members within 30 days of the Act's entry into force (Ejchart-Dubois et al. 2019). These changes fundamentally altered the balance between judicial and political influence over the composition of the NCJ. They also raised questions concerning the protection of judicial independence, the scope of legislative discretion under the Constitution, and the proper understanding of the principle of separation of powers (Piotrowski 2017).

Supporters of the reform underscore that the Constitution grants the legislature explicit authority to regulate the structure, functioning, and procedures of the NCJ (Article 187(4)). According to this interpretation, the Constitution deliberately refrains from prescribing detailed mechanisms for selecting judicial members. Consequently, the ordinary legislator enjoys broad discretion to adopt different models, including one that assigns the power of selection to the Sejm. Some scholars argue that even fundamental changes to the method of appointment fall within constitutional competence, provided that the Council continues to consist of 15 judicial members and performs its constitutional tasks (Stelina 2017). Another justification advanced by reform proponents concerns the disproportionality within the pre-2017 Council. Before the reform, judges constituted approximately two-thirds of the body, with relatively limited representation from political and societal actors (Zalasiński 2017). Critics of this earlier arrangement contended that it fostered a corporatist system in which the judiciary effectively controlled its own appointments, potentially weakening accountability and responsiveness. By entrusting parliament with the power to elect judicial members, the reform was intended to introduce a more balanced system that acknowledges the democratic legitimacy of legislative bodies (Mikuli 2014).

Proponents also emphasize that there is no single European model of judicial councils. In fact, several democratic states, including Austria, Germany, and the Czech Republic, do not maintain specialized bodies like the NCJ at all. In those systems, judicial appointments are carried out by ministries of justice or other executive organs, without undermining their democratic credentials (Dobrowolski 2017). Where councils do exist, their composition and appointment methods vary considerably. For instance, in France, the president plays a central role in the High Council of the Judiciary, while in Spain, all members of the General Council of the Judiciary are elected by parliament (Waltoś 2002; Stefańska 2003). From this comparative perspective, the Polish reforms are consistent with a broader spectrum of legitimate models. Finally, reform advocates contend that election by parliament does not automatically politicize the NCJ. Members elected under the new system remain judges by profession, bound by standards of impartiality and subject to legal guarantees of irremovability. The decisive factor is whether structural mechanisms exist that tie Council members to political actors. Given that the statutory regime maintains the personal independence of judges, there is no reason to presume that parliamentary election alone transforms the Council into a political body (Stelina 2017).

Opponents of the reform argue that the premature termination of judicial mandates contravenes Article 187(3) of the Constitution, which guarantees four-year terms. Patyra (2017) emphasizes that the principle of fixed tenure serves as a safeguard of institutional stability and independence. Curtailing these terms by ordinary statute undermines both constitutional guarantees and the principle of separation of powers. While the CT has recognized limited circumstances in which terms may be shortened for overriding public interest, critics argue that no such justification was adequately demonstrated. Another major line of critique concerns the principle of judicial independence. Critics argue that by transferring the power to elect judicial members from judges themselves to parliament, the reform effectively deprives the judiciary of meaningful influence over the body that nominates judges. This, they contend, undermines both the perception and reality of judicial independence. As Patyra notes, decisive participation of judges in the NCJ is essential for ensuring that judicial appointments remain merit-based and insulated from political pressures (Patyra 2017).

Opponents also raise concerns about the legislative technique employed. The concept of 'common terms of office' introduced in the reform is regarded as vague and unfamiliar in Polish legal tradition. Questions arise about how to calculate terms for judges elected mid-cycle or replacing predecessors who leave office early. Such ambiguities, critics argue, weaken legal certainty and may produce inconsistent practices. Moreover, the establishment of the NCJ in 1989 symbolized a conscious move away from the politicization of the judiciary characteristic of the socialist era. By reintroducing decisive parliamentary control over judicial appointments, the 2017 reform is perceived by some scholars as a step backward, potentially re-politicizing a body that was designed as a guardian of independence. From this perspective, the reform undermines the axiological foundation of the Council as a supra-corporate institution entrusted primarily with safeguarding judicial independence.

The debate surrounding the reform cannot be separated from international and European standards. Article 6 of the European Convention on Human Rights guarantees the right to a fair trial before an independent and impartial tribunal established by law. The European Court of Human Rights (ECtHR) has consistently underscored that judicial independence requires structural and functional safeguards against political interference, including in the process of judicial appointment. While the Convention does not prohibit the executive or parliamentary appointment of judges, it condemns practices that expose judges to political dependencies. In its case law, the ECtHR has emphasized factors such as the manner of appointment, duration of office, protection against external pressure, and public perception of independence. In decisions such as *Campbell and Fell* v. *United Kingdom* and *Findlay* v. *United Kingdom*, the Court highlighted the need for sufficient guarantees against political influence. More recently, in *Urban* v. *Poland* (2010), the Court found Polish rules on judicial assessors incompatible with the Convention due to excessive dependence on the executive.

The EC, as guardian of the treaties, is responsible for ensuring that member states comply with their obligations under the Treaty on European Union (TEU) and the Treaty on the Functioning of the European Union. It has also expressed concerns regarding the Polish reform, arguing that it weakens judicial independence by reducing the judiciary's role in appointing Council members. These concerns have formed part of broader rule-of-law proceedings under Article 7 of the TEU. At the same time, it is important to recognize that European systems of judicial governance are highly diverse. Some countries rely primarily on executive appointment, while others entrust appointment powers to parliamentary bodies or mixed councils. No uniform model can be distilled as a binding 'European standard'. Nonetheless, comparative analysis suggests that a recurring feature is meaningful judicial participation in bodies responsible for appointments, particularly regarding initial entry into the judiciary. The French model, with strong presidential involvement, demonstrates that judicial independence can coexist with executive influence, provided that sufficient safeguards exist. Conversely, the Spanish model illustrates the risks of parliamentary dominance, as concerns have periodically arisen about politicization of the General Council of the Judiciary. The Swedish and Dutch systems show yet another variation, combining ministerial authority with advisory councils. Against this background, the Polish model, both before and after the 2017 reform, fits within the spectrum of European solutions, although the balance between judicial and political participation has shifted.

A central issue raised by both perspectives concerns the principle of separation of powers. This principle, enshrined in the Preamble and in Article 10 of the Constitution, requires that no branch of power dominate the others. Supporters of the reform argue that enabling parliament to elect judicial members strengthens democratic accountability and prevents excessive self-governance by the judiciary. Critics counter that judicial independence is a necessary counterbalance to political majorities and that diluting judicial influence over appointments risks undermining this equilibrium. The debate therefore reflects competing interpretations of separation of powers: one emphasizing balance and accountability through political participation, the other emphasizing autonomy and insulation from politics. Both interpretations claim grounding in constitutional principles, illustrating the inherent tension between independence and democratic legitimacy.

The concern about politicization deserves particular attention. It is undisputed that entrusting appointment powers to a political body introduces an element of political influence. The key question, however, is whether this influence reaches a level that threatens judicial independence. Supporters contend that because only judges can be elected to the Council, and because they retain personal guarantees of independence, political influence remains limited. Critics respond that the very process of election by parliamentary majority creates dependence, as judges may feel pressured to align with prevailing political forces. Moreover, public perception of politicization may itself undermine confidence in judicial impartiality, even if actual independence is preserved.

The termination of ongoing judicial mandates remains one of the most contested aspects of the reform. While some scholars view the shortening of terms as unconstitutional interference with fixed tenure, others argue that it was a necessary and unavoidable consequence of changing the system (Patyra 2017). Stelina, for example, maintains that as the old and new systems are structurally incompatible, gradual transition was not feasible. In such circumstances, termination of mandates may be justified as a proportionate measure in the service of legislative reform (Stelina 2017). This disagreement illustrates the broader difficulty of reconciling principles of continuity and stability with the need for institutional redesign.

Regardless of these debates, the cumulative effect of the reforms – particularly the transfer of decisive control over judicial appointments to the legislature – has clear implications for the functioning of constitutional democracy. These changes have significant negative implications for democracy and the rule of law. By transferring decisive control over judicial appointments to the legislature, the reforms increased the risk of politicization, weakened institutional checks on political power, and undermined the independence of the judiciary. Consequently, the capacity of the judicial system to act as an impartial arbiter and to safeguard constitutional principles has been materially reduced.

Maintaining judicial standards: disciplinary measures and European oversight

The legislative reforms introduced in Poland after 2015 affected not only the structure of the judiciary and mechanisms of judicial appointment, but also the system of disciplinary responsibility applicable to judges. A series of statutory amendments established new frameworks intended, according to government justifications, to enhance transparency, ensure accountability, and align the judiciary with broader expectations of efficiency and public trust. Critics, however, argued that these measures introduced instruments of pressure capable of discouraging independent judicial activity and reshaping the balance between the judiciary and the executive.

One of the first measures concerned the regime for judicial asset declarations. Since 2001, judges had been under an obligation to submit such declarations, but their content was previously confidential and could be accessed only under limited statutory conditions. The amendment of 30 November 2016 reversed this principle by establishing publicity as the rule. The personal details and property information of judges became publicly available, with only limited safeguards protecting sensitive data that could identify a judge's place of residence (Bielak-Jomaa 2016). While judges could request that a declaration be classified as restricted, the Minister of Justice retained the authority to revoke such classification, with no possibility of appeal. Supporters of the change argued that transparency was a prerequisite for strengthening public trust in the judiciary and ensuring that judges remained accountable in line with standards applicable to other public officials. Opponents expressed concern that the power of the executive to determine the confidentiality of declarations introduced potential for selective disclosure, exposing judges to reputational risk or pressure in ways that could affect their independence (Bojarski 2017).

Broader changes were made in the area of disciplinary proceedings. Amendments to the Law on the Organization of Common Courts transferred key powers over the disciplinary process to the Minister of Justice. The minister was granted the authority to appoint disciplinary officers, their deputies, and judges sitting on disciplinary courts, thereby reducing the role of judicial self-government bodies in these processes (Ejchart-Dubois et al. 2019). The rationale presented for this reform was the need to strengthen accountability and ensure consistent standards of professional conduct. Critics, however, stressed that such powers enabled the executive to influence both the initiation and conduct of proceedings, creating a framework in which judges involved in sensitive or controversial rulings could face an investigations.

A new institution, the Disciplinary Chamber of the SC, became a central element of the revised system. Its members were appointed through procedures involving the restructured NCJ. The Chamber was entrusted with hearing disciplinary cases, including appeals, and with deciding on matters as significant as the removal of judges from office. Government representatives described the Chamber as an important mechanism for ensuring judicial accountability at the highest level. Detractors, however, raised doubts about its independence, pointing to the role of political authorities in its establishment and the professional profiles of its members.

Supporters of the reforms maintained that the disciplinary system applied equally to all judges and served to enforce standards of professional responsibility. Critics considered these cases examples of how disciplinary instruments could be directed against judges engaged in defending constitutional principles or applying European standards of judicial independence (Gersdorf 2018).

Reforms also extended to the composition of the judiciary through modifications of retirement rules. The SC Act of 8 December 2017 lowered the retirement age for judges from 70 to 65. This change affected a significant number of sitting judges, including the First President of the SC, whose six-year term was guaranteed by Article 183(3) of the Constitution (Ejchart-Dubois et al. 2019). Government representatives explained that the change was part of an effort to rejuvenate the judiciary and harmonize retirement ages across public offices (Matusiewicz 2017). Opponents argued that it operated as a mechanism for prematurely removing experienced judges and replacing them with new appointees, thereby altering the balance within the court. The CJEU, acting in response to proceedings initiated by the EC, issued interim measures requiring Poland to reinstate the affected judges. The Polish authorities complied, although the process highlighted tensions between domestic reforms and European oversight (Gutkowski 2017).

At the level of common courts, statutory amendments expanded the powers of the Minister of Justice to dismiss and appoint court presidents. The minister was not obliged to provide reasons for such decisions. Proponents viewed this as an opportunity to improve efficiency and modernize court management. Critics emphasized the risk of politicization, noting that dismissals could be used to exert pressure on judicial administration (Czaja 2019). In parallel, competitions for judicial appointments were suspended for over two years, resulting in numerous vacancies and contributing to delays in the resolution of cases. Reports by non-governmental organizations noted that the efficiency of the judiciary declined during this period, although interpretations of the causes differed.

The Act on the Structure of Common Courts from 2019, which entered into force in February 2020, broadened the catalogue of disciplinary offences to include conduct such as questioning the legality of judicial appointments, casting doubt on the authority of judicial bodies such as the NCJ or the Disciplinary Chamber, and engaging in activities deemed political in nature. Judicial self-government bodies were prohibited from adopting resolutions that might be interpreted as political. Supporters of the statute argued that it was necessary to preserve the neutrality of the judiciary and prevent judges from overstepping their professional role. Critics contended that the vague wording of the provisions allowed for wide discretion in initiating disciplinary proceedings, which could discourage judges from engaging in public debate or applying European legal standards (Grajewski 2022).

Reactions from European institutions formed an important part of the broader context. The CJEU issued a series of rulings addressing elements of the Polish reforms, including the lowering of the retirement age, the powers of the Minister of Justice over judicial mandates, and the independence of the NCJ and the Disciplinary Chamber. In several instances, the Court concluded that the reforms were incompatible with EU law, particularly with the principles of judicial independence and effective judicial protection. The Polish government at times questioned the scope of the CJEU's authority or delayed implementation of its judgments, leading to further legal and political disputes. The Polish CT, in a 2021 ruling, declared certain provisions of the EU treaties incompatible with the Polish Constitution, further intensifying the conflict.

The Polish experience illustrates how legislative reforms in the field of judicial organization can generate complex legal debates concerning the balance between independence and accountability. Supporters of the changes emphasized the need for transparency, efficiency, and democratic oversight of the judiciary. Critics focused on the risks of politicization, the weakening of safeguards of independence, and the 'chilling effect' on judicial activity. At the European level, the case contributed to a wider discussion on the scope of supranational oversight in protecting rule-of-law standards within member states. The interaction of domestic reforms and international responses demonstrates the dynamic nature of judicial independence as a constitutional principle, shaped not only by national choices but also by obligations arising from membership of the EU and the European Convention on Human Rights.

Conclusion

The reforms affecting the Polish judiciary between 2015 and 2023 illustrate the intricate interplay between domestic legislative authority, constitutional norms, and European oversight. By reshaping the composition of the NCJ, restructuring the SC and the prosecution service, and expanding disciplinary mechanisms, these reforms significantly altered institutional design and the balance of power within the judicial system.

While proponents emphasized gains in efficiency, accountability, and transparency, critics highlighted risks of politicization, premature termination of judicial mandates, and expansive disciplinary powers. These concerns were reinforced by the scrutiny of European institutions, particularly the CJEU, which underscored tensions with EU law and the fundamental principles of judicial independence and impartiality.

The Polish case demonstrates how legal reforms can simultaneously pursue institutional modernization and create avenues for political influence. It further underscores the importance of judicial participation in appointments, robust procedural safeguards, and structural clarity in protecting judicial autonomy. The interaction between domestic reforms and supranational oversight reveals the ongoing challenges of balancing efficiency, accountability, and independence in contemporary judicial governance.

Moreover, the Polish experience illustrates that these challenges are not merely theoretical. In practice, the reforms have contributed to observable patterns of de-democratization. Judicial appointments, disciplinary measures, and institutional restructuring have increasingly been used to consolidate political control rather than to strengthen governance. Cases involving politically aligned judges, selective disciplinary proceedings, and rulings by the CT demonstrate that these measures were part of a broader strategy to instrumentalize the law and judiciary for political ends. This has weakened institutional checks on government power, undermined impartial adjudication, and reduced the judiciary's capacity to safeguard constitutional principles, confirming that the process of de-democratization in Poland was tangible and ongoing.

Ultimately, the Polish experience offers a broader lesson for comparative constitutional and legal studies. The case highlights the delicate equilibrium between national sovereignty and supranational obligations in safeguarding institutional integrity and sustaining democratic resilience.

References

Barrett, Richard, Claire Malaurie-Bazy, Richard Clayton, Philip Dimitrov, and Christoph Grabenwarter. 2017. *Opinion on the Draft Act Amending the Act on the National Council of the Judiciary, on the Draft Act Amending the Act on the Supreme Court, Proposed by the President of Poland, and on the Act on the Organisation of Ordinary Courts.* Strasbourg: Council of Europe.

Bielak-Jomaa, Edyta. 2016. *Opinion of the Inspector General for the Protection of Personal Data on the Parliamentary Bill: Introductory Provisions to the Law on the Prosecutor's Office.* Warsaw: Inspector General for the Protection of Personal Data.

Boin, Arjen, and Martin Lodge. 2016. 'Designing Resilient Institutions for Transboundary Crisis Management: A Time for Public Administration.'. *Public Administration* 94(2): 289–298.

Bojarski, Łukasz. 2017. *Legal Opinion of the Legal Experts Team at the Stefan Batory Foundation on the Assessment of the Conformity with the Constitution of the Act of*

20 July 2017 on the Supreme Court (Sejm Paper no. 1727). Warsaw: Batory Foundation.

Chmaj, Marek. 2017. *Legal Opinion on the Assessment of the Constitutionality of the Government Bill Amending the Act on the National Council of the Judiciary and Certain Other Acts (Paper no. 1423)*. Warsaw: Sejm of the Republic of Poland.

Czaja, Jacek. 2019. *Jak przywrócić państwo prawa? Sądownictwo powszechne*. Warsaw: Batory Foundation.

Dobrowolski, Marek. 2017. *Legal Opinion Concerning the Government Bill Amending the Act on the National Council of the Judiciary and Certain Other Acts*. Warsaw: Sejm of the Republic of Poland.

Ejchart-Dubois, Maria, Sylwia Gregorczyk-Abram, Paulina Kieszkowska-Knapik, and Michał Wawrykiewicz. 2019. *Działania podjęte przez instytucje Unii Europejskiej i niezrealizowane rekomendacje Komisji Europejskiej*. Warsaw: Batory Foundation.

Gersdorf, Małgorzata. 2016. *Comments on the Parliamentary Bill: Law on the Prosecutor's Office*. Warsaw: Supreme Court of Poland.

Gersdorf, Małgorzata. 2018. *Opinion on the Parliamentary Bill Amending the Act on the Supreme Court (Sejm Paper no. 2390)*. Warsaw: Supreme Court of Poland.

Grajewski, Krzysztof. 2022. *Opinion of the Presidential Bill Amending the Act on the Supreme Court and Certain Other Acts (Paper no. 2011/9th Term)*. Gdańsk: University of Gdańsk.

Gutkowski, Maciej. 2017. *Opinion of the Supreme Bar Council on the Parliamentary Bill on the Supreme Court of 12 July 2017*. Poznán: Supreme Bar Council.

Herzog, Aleksander. 2009. 'Niezależność prokuratury – mit czy nadzieja?' *Prokuratura i Prawo* 9(1): 111–128.

Krygier, Martin. 2019. 'What's the Point of the Rule of Law?' *Buffalo Law Review* 67 (3): 743–769.

Kuchciński, Marek. 2016. *Law on the Prosecutor's Office (Paper No. 162) and Introductory Provisions to the Law on the Prosecutor's Office (Paper No. 163)*. Warsaw: Sejm of the Republic of Poland.

Kułak, Krzysztof. 2016. 'Kwestia niezależności prokuratora w nowej ustawie: Prawo o prokuraturze'. *Studia Iuridica Lublinensia* 25(4): 105–127. doi:10.17951/sil.2016.25.4.105.

Łabno, Anna. 2017. *Opinia na temat zgodności z Konstytucją RP rządowego projektu ustawy o zmianie ustawy o Krajowej Radzie Sądownictwa oraz niektórych ustaw, który wpłynął do laski marszałkowej 14 marca 2017 r.* Warsaw: Biuro Analiz Sejmowych.

Matusiewicz, Andrzej. 2017. *Paper No. 1727 Pursuant to Article 118(1) of the Constitution of the Republic of Poland of 2 April 1997 and Pursuant to Article 32(2) of the Rules of Procedure of the Sejm, the Undersigned Deputies Hereby Submit a Draft Act on the Supreme Court*. Warsaw: Sejm of the Republic of Poland.

Mazowiecka, Lida. 2015. *Prokuratura w Polsce (1918–2014)*. Warsaw: Wolters Kluwer.

Mikuli, Piotr. 2014. 'Konstytucyjność wyboru sędziów sądów powszechnych'. *Krajowa Rada Sądownictwa* 4(9): 9–12.

Mizera, Katarzyna. 2016. *Druk Nr 1181 o Zmianie Ustawy: Prawo o Ustroju Sądów Powszechnych*. Warsaw: Sejm of the Republic of Poland. https://orka.sejm.gov.pl/Druki8ka.nsf/0/0182F4A900B13FC4C125809D004C3CA1/%24File/1181.pdf.

Patyra, Sławomir. 2017. *Legal Expertise on the Compliance of the Government Bill Amending the Act on the National Council of the Judiciary and Certain Other Acts with the Constitution of the Republic of Poland and with International Legal Regulations*. Warsaw: Sejm Research Centre.

Piotrowski, Ryszard. 2017. *Legal Opinion on the Government Bill Amending the Act on the National Council of the Judiciary and Certain Other Acts (Sejm Paper No. 1423)*. Warsaw: Sejm of the Republic of Poland.

Rakowska-Trela, Anna. 2017. *Assessment of the Compliance of the Government Bill Amending the Act on the National Council of the Judiciary and Certain Other Acts with the Constitution of the Republic of Poland (Paper No. 1423)*. Warsaw: Batory Foundation.

Raz, Joseph. 1979. *The Authority of Law: Essays on Law and Morality*. New York: Oxford University Press.

Sadurski, Wojciech. 2019. *Poland's Constitutional Breakdown*. New York: Oxford University Press.

Sakowicz, Andrzej. 2016. *Legal Opinion on the Parliamentary Bill – Law on the Prosecutor's Office (Papers 162 and 162A) and the Parliamentary Bill – Introductory Provisions to the Law on the Prosecutor's Office (Paper No. 163)*. Warsaw: Sejm of the Republic of Poland.

Seremet, Andrzej. 2016. *Opinion of the Prosecutor General on Papers No. 162 and 163. PG VII G 025/399/15*. Warsaw: Public Prosecutor General's Office.

Staszak, Marek. 2016. *Resolution No. 1/2016 of the National Council of Prosecutors of 11 January 2016*. Warsaw: National Council of Prosecutors.

Stefańska, Julita. 2003. 'Prokuratura w Portugalii'. *Prokuratura i Prawo* 3(12): 87–104.

Stelina, Jakub. 2017. *Legal Opinion on Selected Aspects of the Amendment to the Act on the National Council of the Judiciary (Sejm Paper No. 1423)*. Gdańsk: Sejm of the Republic of Poland.

Waltoś, Stanisław. 2002. 'Prokuratura: Jej miejsce wśród organów władzy, struktura i funkcje'. *Państwo i Prawo* 2(4): 5–18.

Warciński, Michał. 2016. *Opinion on the Compliance with European Union Law of the Parliamentary Bill: Law on the Prosecutor's Office, in the Version Including the Self-Amendment of 4 January 2016*. Warsaw: Sejm Research Centre.

Wróbel, Włodzimierz. 2019. 'Izba Dyscyplinarna jako sąd wyjątkowy w rozumieniu art. 175 ust. 2 Konstytucji RP'. *Palestra* 1(2): 17–35. https://palestra.pl/pl/czasopismo/wydanie/1-2-2019/artykul/izba-dyscyplinarna-jako-sad-wyjatkowy-w-rozumieniu-art.-175-ust.-2-konstytucji-rp.

Zalasiński, Tomasz. 2017. *Legal Opinion on the Assessment of the Compliance of the Government Bill Amending the Act on the National Council of the Judiciary and Certain Other Acts with the Constitution of the Republic of Poland and the Principles of Legislative Drafting (Sejm Paper No. 1423)*. Warsaw: Sejm of the Republic of Poland.

Zawiślak, Katarzyna. 2012. 'Pozycja ustrojowa, kompetencje i skład Krajowej Rady Sądownictwa', *Iustitia*, 3. https://www.kwartalnikiustitia.pl/pozycja-ustrojowa-kompetencje-i-sklad-krajowej-rady-sadownictwa,3702.

6 From Economic Liberalism to State-Led Capitalism

The Expanding Role of the State in Enterprise Governance

Agnieszka Faron

Introduction

The history of Poland's statehood, spanning more than a millennium, is replete with vicissitudes, including periods of both triumph and tragedy. Contemporary generations of Poles have been particularly influenced by two defining epochs: World War II and the socialist era, both of which, it is argued, offered an illusion of independence. The collapse of the communist system signified the demise of a centrally planned economy and the end of state control over society, thus marking a pivotal moment for the comprehensive reform of the Polish economy. It is evident that Poland's accession to the European Union (EU) has acted as a significant catalyst for economic growth and transformation. The 20th anniversary of Poland's accession was commemorated in 2024, and most Poles expressed appreciation for membership of the EU institutions, primarily for the sense of freedom it affords. This issue is especially pertinent in the context of recent international developments, such as the Russian Federation's aggression against Ukraine, which has further strengthened the sense of community and belonging to democratic European communities. At the same time, however, numerous EU countries and beyond have witnessed a noticeable rise in the strength of nationalist movements and a concomitant increase in support for populist parties. From the standpoint of economic liberalism, these two phenomena pose a significant threat, and were particularly evident during the 2015–23 period of government in Poland. This constitutes the focal point of this chapter, with the objective being an analysis of the impact of centralization and interventionism on the structure of the business environment in Poland. The present study will describe the actions and specific reforms undertaken by the Polish government during the specified period. Furthermore, an attempt will be made to assess the effects of these actions and reforms.

DOI: 10.4324/9781042002030-7

Populism as a path to illiberal state capitalism in Poland during the period 2015–23

The transformation that took place at the turn of the 1980s and 1990s remains the subject of considerable debate among economists, political actors, and ordinary citizens. Poland's economic progress over the past 30 years provides irrefutable evidence that the reforms undertaken were necessary. It is important to acknowledge that certain social groups were disadvantaged by these reforms, and that the privatization process itself also resulted in structural problems and an increase in the share of foreign capital in the economy. At the same time, the liquidation of Państwowe Gospodarstwa Rolne (State Agricultural Farms) further exacerbated social exclusion and the resulting discontent. In numerous regions of Poland, large segments of the population did not benefit from the economic changes, and divisions and inequalities between the rich elite and the poor majority began to emerge. Following the implementation of reforms and Poland's accession to the EU, the country experienced dynamic economic growth, although clear disparities remained between the more developed 'Poland A' and the less developed 'Poland B', a divide exacerbated by populist narratives. The Platforma Obywatelska (Civic Platform) governments emphasized the image of Poland as a 'green island', symbolizing the exceptional resilience of the economy during the 2008/09 global financial crisis, which contrasted with the feelings of a section of society affected by the economic slowdown and growing frustration. This dynamic gave rise to a pervasive lack of trust in the ruling party, the Civic Platform, precipitating a shift towards paternalistic authorities promising to protect citizens and a robust state apparatus. The consequences of these actions have provided an opportunity for populist parties to emerge, promoting the ideology of justice, equality, and the abolition of the old establishment, and purporting to represent the will of the people.

In contemporary times, populism is gaining ground across the globe, even in countries previously considered resistant to it, such as Germany and Sweden (Guriev and Papaioannou 2022). Populism can be defined as a governing logic that recentres the state within the economy, prioritizing economic nationalism and expanding state ownership. At the same time, it maintains an openness to global capital, utilizing international financial flows to underpin growth and regime stability (Ganga 2024). When right-wing populists call for a return to national greatness, they draw on its connection to one of their core strategies – the creation and deepening of social divisions. The concept of national greatness is predicated on the portrayal of 'outsiders', whether internal or external, as inferior, thereby reinforcing a pronounced distinction between 'good' and 'bad' people. This kind of nostalgia is a key component in the sustenance of the central populist narrative, which portrays elites as treacherous, detached, or foreign entities who seek to undermine the purity and unity of the populace. International organizations, human rights institutions, and transnational courts are frequently portrayed as instruments of these elites (Kotwas and Kubik 2022). This radical narrative was characteristic of Polish governments during the period under study and provided compelling justification for all actions aimed at de-democratization. While socio-political issues (described elsewhere in this volume) were evident and noticeable in a short period of time, the economic consequences are likely to be felt for many years to come.

The triumph of the Prawo i Sprawiedliwość (Law and Justice Party) represented an overt repudiation of the tenets of economic liberalism that had prevailed in Poland since 1989. A fundamental aspect of the Law and Justice Party's political strategy has been the legitimization of actions aimed at establishing an illiberal economic order. The party's official discourse focuses on the principles of social justice and economic sovereignty, which justify increased state intervention, selective redistribution, and control over strategic sectors of the economy. While the party's initial focus on social justice and an anti-elite rhetoric was evident, its economic policies began to adopt an illiberal stance, emphasizing state control, redistribution, and loyalty over competition. As Ricz (2021) postulate, a new model of capitalism was emerging, which she terms the 'illiberal model of state capitalism', and there is a preponderance of evidence indicating that this issue has been encountered in Poland.

Riedel and Anusik (2024) observe that, while certain parties contend that democracy is intrinsically liberal and that illiberal characteristics compromise its core, the notion of illiberal democracy has attained a degree of acceptance within both the political and the academic discourse, thereby challenging the simplistic view that systems are either democratic or not. The emergence of this illiberal market economy can be attributed to the state's response to the institutional void left by the neoliberal transition. The Polish government's utilization of state assets to advance partisan interests has resulted in an expanding public sector, diminished democratic oversight, and a resurgence of renationalization and price controls in pivotal industries. Despite the implication of increasing state interventionism, illiberal state capitalism remains fundamentally capitalist, characterized by private ownership, profit orientation, and market competition. From a political perspective, however, these entities frequently adopt illiberal and autocratic tendencies, often disregarding constitutional limitations on authority. Opposition actors often encounter structural disadvantages, further exacerbating the existing political climate (Piątek 2023). This duality – characterized by a capitalist economic structure coupled with illiberal governance – aptly encapsulates the economic and institutional trajectory observed in Poland from 2015 onwards. The most salient feature of the regime of illiberal state capitalism is its overarching aim: the consolidation and maintenance of political power. To achieve these objectives, a range of state interventions in the economy are employed for purely political purposes. Despite the marked rise in state interventionism within illiberal state capitalism economies, these systems remain capitalist in nature. As Ricz (2021) points out, illiberal state capitalism currently utilizes more creative and sophisticated forms of state intervention. These may be based on internal financial resources, such as EU funds or loans from alternative sources, or they may include strictly domestic measures, such as the renationalization of strategic enterprises or the use of monetary policy instruments. Economic populism may manifest as the subsidization of basic goods and services, often accompanied by costly prestige projects or ambitions to play a greater role on the global or regional stage. The existing literature on state capitalism has mainly focused on the growing importance of state ownership and policies to strengthen national champions. These issues will be addressed in the following sections of this chapter.

As Balcerowicz (2025) argues, capitalism is a necessary condition for democracy, but on its own does not guarantee it. Similarly, democracy is not a necessary condition for capitalism. Furthermore, capital is observed to flow to non-democratic states when they guarantee legal stability, market-conforming rules, and regulatory predictability.

Government reforms and their impact on the business environment

In 2016, the leader of the Law and Justice Party, Jarosław Kaczyński, attributed the slowdown in Poland's gross domestic product growth to the influence of entrepreneurs and local governments associated with the previous administration. He claimed that these entrepreneurs (whom he perceived as aligned with the opposition) were reluctant to engage in various profitable economic ventures, preferring instead to await the return of more favourable market conditions, implying that they hoped for a change in government. This view was met with immediate criticism from prominent business associations, including the Polska Rada Biznesu (Polish Business Council), the Krajowa Izba Gospodarcza (Polish Chamber of Commerce), the Konfederacja Lewiatan (Polish Confederation Lewiatan), and Pracodawcy RP (Employers of Poland). In an official joint statement, these organizations emphasized that Polish entrepreneurs are guided by rational decision-making and the sustainable development of companies and the economy, and that their investment choices are not politically motivated. Key factors shaping investment decisions are economic factors such as profitability, risk, growth prospects, and legal stability, which are influenced by government policy. Therefore, reluctance to invest is not driven by opposition to the government (Rzeczpospolita 2016). Despite this unequivocal stance, the authorities did not address the allegations substantively. Instead, they framed their statements in a narrative that delegitimized businesses as liberal and supportive of the opposition.

In December 2015, the Deputy Prime Minister and Minister of Development, Mateusz Morawiecki, lamented that Poland's economic development was overly reliant on foreign financing, and that the country required domestic savings to strengthen investment (Country Watch n.d.). It is evident that Poland's investment in research and development is insufficient, consequently maintaining a technological base that is suboptimal. Processes of globalization have resulted in Poland becoming a provider of low-cost labour for transnational corporations (Kraciuk 2016). It is not surprising that one of the principal policy documents which was aligned with the ideology of the ruling party was the Strategia na Rzecz Odpowiedzialnego Rozwoju (Strategy for Responsible Development – SRD), which was adopted in 2017. This plan delineated a comprehensive strategy, extending to 2020, with a forward-looking perspective to 2030. The plan alludes to the concept of equilibrium traps, including those associated with excessive foreign capital involvement in the economy. Consequently, the strategy espouses the expansion of Polish capital as a means of achieving economic success. It is also noteworthy that attention is paid to effective and coordinated state institutions that are responsible for the management of public policies. Thus, it is anticipated that there will be a shift from the present level of support for all sectors/industries to the provision of customized packages for specific strategic sectors that have the potential to become the drivers of the Polish economy in the future. One of the central instruments of the SRD is the Polski Fundusz Rozwoju (Polish Development Fund – PDF), designed to be instrumental in the development of a new, robust Polish economy by functioning as a mechanism for the coordination of investment and development. According to the plan, PDF-led investment will be directed towards the sustainable socio-economic development of the country, thereby complementing the private sector's involvement in addressing the needs of Polish enterprises and supporting priority segments of the economy. The implementation of government programmes pivotal to Poland's development is to be facilitated by these tools (Ministry of Development – Poland 2017).

It is important to note that the PDF was not established when the Law and Justice Party was in government (2015–23); rather, it evolved from the Polskie Inwestycje Rozwojowe (Polish Investments for Development – PID), which was established in 2013. The purpose of the PID was to ensure financing for selected long-term and profitable infrastructure investments in an economically justified manner without increasing public debt, while also mobilizing private capital over the long term. Under the new government, the PID was transformed into the PDF, incorporating it as a tool for centralization, which was supposed to deliver tangible results. This initiative aimed to streamline the operations of numerous disparate institutions and agencies, with the PDF functioning as the overarching entity, unifying, among others, the Agencja Rozwoju Przemysłu (Industrial Development Agency – IDA), Bank Gospodarstwa Krajowego (BGK – Polish Development Bank), and the Polska Agencja Rozwoju Przedsiębiorczości (PARP – Polish Agency for Enterprise Development). One of the primary functions of the fund was to implement government programmes. The 'Polish Deal', the 'National Recovery Plan', and the anti-crisis shields that were implemented during the COVID-19 pandemic, are pertinent examples of this. In principle, such an institution was regarded as being of significance, if only from the perspective of enhancing the efficacy of infrastructure management, local government, venture capital, and Pracownicze Plany Kapitałowe (Employee Capital Plan) funds. However, allegations have been made that its primary intention was to serve the policy of de-democratization. Foremost among its functions was its role as a 'second state budget', which was responsible for the management of tens of billions of złotys. Despite the public nature of these funds, they were expended outside the budgetary procedure and parliamentary oversight, thereby compromising the principle of the government's financial accountability to the parliament and the transparency of parliamentary control. A 2016 inspection by the Najwyższa Izba Kontroli (Supreme Audit Office) revealed several key findings, including the absence of a single entity designated to coordinate the whole process, and the division of supervisory responsibilities between the Treasury and the Ministry of Finance (Najwyższa Izba Kontroli 2016), which led to a diffusion of responsibility and flaws in the management of the group. Consequently, a substantial proportion of public expenditure decisions were delegated to small management groups with political affiliations to the executive branch. This phenomenon invariably gave rise to concerns regarding nepotism and the influence of political loyalty on decision-making processes. To obtain financing, companies had to meet government requirements, which, in practice, limited access to funds to entities considered loyal to the authorities. This policy excluded those who did not share the government's objectives, resulting in the selective allocation of funds. Moreover, there was a clear lack of transparency, which may be ascribed to the prevailing commercial secrecy. This, in turn, rendered it arduous for independent entities to corroborate the reliability of public expenditures. The PDF was in possession of considerable financial resources, thus enabling it to undertake high-risk investments with potentially low returns, projects which would not have been feasible for the private sector. Consequently, the state not only provided support to the economy, but also actively influenced its development, thereby displacing private investors and distorting market competition mechanisms. This finding lends further support to the notion of the creation of 'national champions', a concept that will be examined in the section that follows.

The Fund possesses a range of legal instruments that empower it to provide effective support to entrepreneurs. As of 2025, the PDF formed part of a broader system of development institutions, comprising BGK, the PARP, the Korporacja Ubezpieczeń Kredytów Exportowych (Export Credit Insurance Corporation), the Polska Agencja Inwestycji i Handlu (Polish Investment and Trade Agency), and the IDA (Woroniecki 2024). These six institutions constitute the core of the Polish system of development institutions and collectively form the Polish Development Fund Group, with the PDF coordinating their activities. Its president is the chairman of the PDF Group Council, which comprises the presidents of all the member institutions.

Despite the declarations made by the post-2023 coalition government and the measures that have been taken to date, it is regrettable that the issue has not yet been effectively isolated and made independent of the influence of the executive branch. It is anticipated that this process will require a significant investment of time. Notwithstanding the efforts to the contrary, the Fund remains a tool of economic policy, and some of its resources are outside traditional budgetary control. It is noteworthy that this is not inherently a negative development, provided its the objectives are transparent and do not serve particular political interests.

Recent institutional changes have resulted in the adoption of a more centralized state governance model and the renationalization of assets. This shift has led to an augmentation of the government's role as both owner and coordination hub, thereby diminishing the private sector's influence. This shift has involved a range of measures including nationalization and quasi-nationalization, regulatory interventions that weaken market mechanisms (including the capital market), the curtailment of minority shareholder influence, and the establishment of hybrid, opaque ownership structures.

From 2015–23, further reforms were implemented, most notably the Family 500+ programme, a central component of the Law and Justice Party's electoral platform (see Chapter 8 in this volume). Two other significant changes should also be mentioned, namely the lowering of the retirement age and the extension of compulsory schooling. The reforms were chiefly of a social nature, and the opposition regarded them as populist measures. Nevertheless, it is clear that they served to consolidate the clientelist model of state-citizen relations. From an economic perspective, however, these measures were costly. It is evident that, above all, there was an association in the long term with labour shortages and, without doubt, an increase in state budget expenditures. The primary consequences of such measures included a reduction in contribution revenues and an increase in benefit expenditures. Addressing this discrepancy is within the allocated budget inevitably adversely affected other sectors of the economy. This phenomenon also had deleterious effect on demographics, specifically on the demographic burden ratio. This, in conjunction with the skills gap that has been left in the wake of the departure of skilled workers from the market, has had a deleterious effect on the prospects for economic growth. Additional social costs included a decline in the economic activity of women (who had to spend more time caring for their children), a delay in the younger generation entering the labour market, and the costs of implementing the reforms in full.

The 'Polish Deal' is another reform that was introduced during the period under study. Its stated objective was to rebuild the Polish economy in the aftermath of the COVID-19 pandemic. As reported in the media,

> the 'Polish Deal' was intended to be a formula for a 'golden decade' for Poland. At present, the phenomenon is associated with disorder, reduced remuneration for several groups, and challenges for accountants.

> Political actors from the Zjednoczona Prawica (United Right) alliance are openly expressing the necessity to learn from past experiences.
> (Madejski 2022)

The programme encompassed the implementation of 10 key projects structured around five pillars: As stated on the website of the Polish government (Serwis Rzeczpospolitej Polskiej n.d.), these included the following pledges: 'more for health', 'your own four walls', 'increased pensions', 'lower taxes', and '500,000 new jobs'. The proposed measures included an increase in the tax-free allowance to 30,000 złoty, a reallocation of the tax burden towards higher-income earners, the introduction of tax relief for families, the financing of large infrastructure projects (including road, energy, and digital projects), an increase in the Narodowy Fundusz Zdrowia (National Health Fund) to 7% of gross domestic product, and additional support for local governments. At the same time, local governments experienced a reduction in their financial autonomy as a consequence of changes to revenues from personal income tax and corporate income tax, which had an impact on their budgets (a situation that was addressed by a system of targeted subsidies granted by the Prime Minister and BGK and the suspension of EU funds (a development that ensued from a dispute with the European Commission over the rule of law). Such actions served to limit the autonomy of local governments, while the centralized distribution of funds created the risk of discretionary allocation according to political criteria and the establishment of a divide between those who were seen to be in favour of the government (i.e. supporters of the ruling party) and those who were seen to be against it (i.e. opposition supporters, particularly residents of large cities). The avalanche-like nature of the changes and the numerous last-minute amendments resulted in legal chaos. The regulations were unclear, contradictory, and subject to change even after they came into force (as reflected in successive iterations such as Polish Deal 2.0, 3.0, etc.). The introduction of the tax reform in January 2022 was characterized by insufficient systemic preparation and a lack of independent public and expert consultations, and consequently engendered a pervasive lack of trust in state institutions and a concomitant deterioration of their image among entrepreneurs and foreign investors.

In sum, as demonstrated by Brzezinski and Sałoch-Drożdż (2024), the period 2016–19 was marked by the attainment of commendable outcomes in economic growth, public debt management, and revenue collection, thanks to the actions of a populist government. Notably, this policy did not lead to a rise in inflation or excessive public expenditure, while substantially reducing overall absolute poverty and nearly eradicating child poverty. Nevertheless, the authors emphasize that although 'sophisticated' populists can implement effective short-term macroeconomic policies, their long-term sustainability remains uncertain. It is conceivable that, in the longer term, this may result in a decline in economic growth and prosperity due to the erosion of democratic institutions in Poland.

Centralization and renationalization in the business sector: developing national champions

Spółki skarbu państwa (state-owned enterprises – SOEs) have historically engaged in the acquisition and consolidation of commercial entities, a practice euphemistically referred to as the 'promotion of national champions'. The government's 're-Polonization' policy is intended to increase the level of domestic ownership, particularly in the finance, energy, defence, and media sectors (Jasiecki 2017). The reindustrialization process was officially initiated by the Civic Platform-led government under Prime Minister Donald Tusk, which unveiled the 'Polish Investments' programme in 2012. This initiative was strategically designed to revitalize the economy through substantial investment in the transport infrastructure and energy sectors. The programme was facilitated through a public-private partnership, with credit assistance from BGK (Górka et al. 2017). The global financial crisis of 2007–09 and the COVID-19 pandemic both significantly contributed to the strengthening of two distinctive trends: a growing wave of state interventionism and an increasing role for SOEs in the economy, coupled with a regression of democracy and growing populism (Piątek 2023). Immediately after its electoral victory in 2015, the United Right government declared its intention to phase out privatization, a decision that was formalized with the abolition of the Ministry of the State Treasury on 1 January 2017. This action entailed the transfer of coordination responsibilities over ownership processes to the office of the Prime Minister, accompanied by the dispersal of supervisory functions among the relevant ministers. In 2019, the Ministry of State Assets was established to replace the Ministry of the State Treasury, thus signifying a progression in the centralization of oversight of state assets.

The prevailing official narrative asserts the necessity for a more state-centric economic policy, aimed at rectifying market deficiencies and fortifying domestic growth. The argument is made that the state can mobilize resources to mitigate global crises and curtail the influence of foreign investors. This standpoint accentuates perceived missteps in antecedent privatization programmes, particularly the transfer of pivotal sectors to foreign capital (Kozarzewski 2016).

The way in which SOEs function within market economies has long been a subject of debate among economists. It is evident that SOEs possess the capacity to function as market regulators, thereby eradicating detrimental elements. In this context, the following aspects are of particular relevance: first, the promotion of competitive practices; second, the guarantee of state control over key sectors; and third, the assurance of the provision of public services in areas where private sector participation is limited. Consequently, the retention of strategic industries under state control can serve to safeguard national interests during periods of crisis (Wałęga 2024).

The term 're-Polonization' refers to the range of practices that governing populists employed to re-establish national ownership of assets held by specific, predominantly foreign-owned, companies in designated sectors of the economy (Benczes and Orzechowska-Wacławska 2024). In Poland, a notable prevalence of acquisitions and consolidations was observed in the banking, energy, and media sectors, particularly in the context of re-Polonization and the establishment of prominent Polish enterprises. The term 'national champion' is employed to describe a large company that has received various forms of state support with the objective of enhancing its competitiveness in the global market. Such companies are generally presumed to be a source of national pride. According to Stanikunas and Burinskas (2011), national champions are large companies that are dominant in their field and favoured by the government of the country in which they are based in the belief that it will be in that country's interests if such companies are successful in foreign markets. It is widely anticipated that national champions will engender benefits that are congruent with the state's economic interests, thereby serving to fortify the strength of the economy and the state itself. This encompasses the execution of high-risk, security-relevant strategic projects, the upgrading of technological capacity, and the serving of the role of 'fiscal agent' (the payment of domestic taxes and the avoidance of aggressive tax planning). Moreover, the roles of these actors encompass the creation of employment opportunities and the provision of support for less developed regions. (Lewandowski 2014). Not all enterprises are deemed national champions solely by virtue of receiving state support, as historically they were often used to secure the provision of various public services (Kociubiński 2023). As Błaszczyk (2025) argues, populists characteristically engage in the nationalization of industrial enterprises, subsequently transforming them into state-owned champions. This phenomenon exerts a substantial negative influence on their productivity, as evidenced by the imposition of lax budgetary constraints and diminished incentives for cost reduction and innovation. In the instances where such corporations begin to exercise dominance over the national economy, there is a concomitant weakening of the entrepreneurial spirit and innovation. Furthermore, it is evident that incoming authorities often appoint their own personnel to key positions within SOEs. In the case of large corporations, such appointments can result in frequent changes in strategy and difficulties in effective management. This issue thus prompts further investigation into the manner and extent to which this may impact the market position and developmental prospects of large companies (Toborek-Mazur 2022).

The initial manifestation of re-Polonization during the period 2021–23 was the establishment of a multi-energy concern under the Polish leader, PKN Orlen (now known as Orlen SA). A significant milestone in PKN Orlen's efforts to establish a robust multi-energy conglomerate was the formalization of a cooperation agreement between Grupa Lotos, PKN Orlen, Polskie Górnictwo Naftowe i Gazownictwo (PGNiG – Polish Oil and Gas Company), and the State Treasury, endorsed on 12 May 2021 at the headquarters of the Ministry of State Assets. The four-party agreement stipulated a merger formula designed to ensure the new company's financial stability, while also considering the interests of shareholders from all participating companies, including minority shareholders (Grupa Lotos n.d.). In 2022, the long-awaited agreements were finally signed, resulting in the consolidation of Lotos (fuels, refineries) and PGNiG (natural gas, gas storage, extraction) with PKN Orlen. A substantial and cohesive multi-energy group of this nature has the potential to bolster the energy autonomy of Poland and the broader Central and Eastern European region, particularly in the context of market disruptions associated with the ongoing conflict stemming from the Russian Federation's military invasion of Ukraine in early 2022. However, the operation of such a complex system necessitates a coordinated and professional management approach, rather than one driven by short-term political agendas. (Toborek-Mazur 2022). The rationale for establishing a national champion in Poland's energy market is grounded in the context of the authoritarian regime in Russia and the imperative of ensuring energy security. However, two issues require further consideration. The establishment of a market giant of this nature requires a long-term development strategy. Concurrently, there is a grave risk of managerial turnover contingent on the prevailing political party. The most controversial case was the acquisition of 100% of the shares in Polska Press, a large regional press previously owned by the German Verlagsgruppe Passau media group. The controversy was primarily concerned with the fact that this action afforded the government a significant degree of control over a substantial proportion of the regional news media. The subsequent stage in the endeavour to exert influence over media content distribution channels – a matter of considerable significance in terms of media pluralism – was the acquisition of 65% of the shares in Ruch SA (a national press distribution network). These developments, which took place in 2020–21, clearly illustrated the re-Polonization of the media and the weakening of its independence. In the aftermath of the takeover, a significant realignment of editor-in-chief positions ensued, a development that could only be interpreted as a deliberate strategy to enhance political allegiance rather than professional competence. This realignment served to reinforce the government's narrative through the medium of the media.

With regard to the banking sector, it is noteworthy that during the Civic Platform-Polskie Stronnictwo Ludowe (Polish Peasant Party) coalition government in 2010, PKO Bank Polski made an attempt to purchase Bank Zachodni WBK, suggesting that previous governments also recognized the potential advantages of such actions. In addition, J.K. Bielecki, the former Chief Executive Officer of Bank Pekao SA and then Chief Economic Adviser to the liberal Prime Minister, Donald Tusk, commented following the joint acquisition of the Bank Pekao SA by the major Polish insurance company Polski Zakład Ubezpieczeń (PZU) and the PDF:

> Pekao is a highly reputable financial institution … The acquisition of Bank Pekao SA by any party is a judicious decision. Prior to my

> departure, I undertook the task of installing a bison sculpture in front of the banki's headquarters … This bison [Pekao's corporate logo] was removed by the headquarters in Milan, but I am glad that it will now be restored.
>
> (Naczyk 2022)

This objective was accomplished in 2017, when the state-owned insurer PZU and the PDF acquired 32.8% of the shares from Italy's UniCredit (the PDF's share was 12.8%). It is evident that the transaction resulted in a significant shift in the composition of the bank's shareholding structure, thereby conferring a dominant position to Polish capital. The re-Polonization of the banking sector also encompassed Alior Bank, which since 2015 has been under the control of PZU, following the insurer's acquisition of over 25% of its shares and its designation as its largest shareholder. Alior Bank played a pivotal role in subsequent acquisition processes, particularly in the context of the takeover of Ruch SA. The bank (which was acquired in 2015 by PZU) took over 100% of the shares of this Polish distributor and subsequently, on the basis of an agreement with PKN Orlen, resold them. The bank, which operated commercially, was included in a large-scale project to consolidate the assets of SOEs. Consequently, the re-Polonization of Alior Bank not only entailed a transfer of ownership, but also functioned as a political and economic instrument, thereby strengthening the dependence of a segment of the financial sector on the interests of those in positions of authority.

In sum, re-Polonization can be defined as a political process aimed at increasing the role of the state in key sectors, leading to the centralization of economic power. As Prime Minister Morawiecki articulated, 're-Polonization signifies a discernible shift in the prevailing system'. This shift entails the state's expansion into new areas of public life, leading to a form of nationalization of the public sphere (Forsal 2017). It is important to note that the impact of centralization measures was not restricted to the business sector. To illustrate, during Morawiecki's tenure, a programme was initiated that led in 2018 to the establishment of the Państwowe Gospodarstwo Wodne Wody Polskie (State Water Holding 'Polish Waters'). This institution was entrusted with the oversight of the management of all water resources in the country. It is noteworthy that no other European country has a water management system that is as centralized as that of Poland (Górka et al. 2017). A parallel may be drawn between the energy sector and the situation under study. While the concept of infrastructure development appears to be a rational one, given that diversification of supply sources has been shown to result in reduced prices, the government led by the Law and Justice Party introduced regulations that served to limit competition in the market, namely the Act on Reserves, which significantly reduced the profitability of gas imports to Poland by private companies. This development served to reinforce the position of the state-controlled PGNiG, while posing a threat to an escalation in the cost of raw materials within the domestic market (Forsal 2017).

Business and investment consequences

Since 2015, the state authorities have adopted a markedly sceptical stance towards large segments of Poland's business elite and leading business interest associations. The authorities perceive these actors as legacies of a neoliberal and corruption-tainted transition, and as continuities with the post-communist nomenklatura, and are viewed as insufficiently aligned with national interests. This reconfiguration of the relationship between the state and business has resulted in a shift towards more distant interaction patterns, diminished levels of trust, and an increase in conflictual modes of interest intermediation (Jasiecki 2017).

In line with the government's official stance, the measures outlined in this chapter were intended to bolster the Polish economy, with the overarching objective being to enhance its competitiveness. The elements of the SRD that were implemented produced significant social benefits in the short term; however, in the long term, they presented challenges for public finances. Following the general election that brought the Civic Coalition to power, the newly established Ministry of Finance issued a document that offered an overview of the prevailing state of public finances in the wake of the Law and Justice Party's tenure. The White Paper asserts that 'the state's policy in 2016–23 resulted in a substantial diminution of transparency in public finances and engendered a further complication of procedures through the establishment of unjustified links between entities, thereby impeding economic planning and management' (Ministry of Finance – Poland 2024). The authors of the White Paper draw attention to a number of irregularities, including (1) the transfer of nearly 66 billion złoty to public finance entities in the form of treasury securities rather than subsidies, which meant that these transfers were not recorded as state budget expenditures; (2) the excessive use of expenditures not expiring before the end of the fiscal year, which represented a departure from the constitutional principle of a single-year budget and allowed for the creative implementation of significantly higher expenditures than those resulting from the limit of the stabilising expenditure rule; (3) the transfer of part of the profits made by the Narodowy Bank Polski (NBP – National Bank of Poland) to the COVID-19 Counteraction Fund, which allowed negative revenues to be recorded in the state budget; (4) restrictions on transparency in reporting on state expenditures; and (5) the circumvention of fiscal rules through the financing public tasks via entities not designated for this purpose. In recent years, Poland has been among the five EU countries with the largest public finance imbalances. An increasingly significant role in the debt is played by the extra-budgetary funds of BGK and the PDF, which incur debt guaranteed by the State Treasury, despite the lack of their own funds to service it. Ultimately, the burden of the debt is shouldered by the budget. Furthermore, the introduction of 22 new taxes (levies, fees, and other charges) resulted in numerous alterations to the tax system and an escalation in the scope of collection, consequently leading to a deterioration in Poland's position in the 2023 tax competitiveness ranking across all categories, with the exception of personal income taxation (Ministry of Finance – Poland 2024). In addition, Polish populists have implemented further taxation on financial and retail corporations. A bank levy was imposed in February 2016, and subsequently a new retail sales tax was introduced (effective from 1 January 2021). During the electoral campaign, the Law and Justice Party announced its intention to introduce new taxes which were to be applied to banks and supermarkets. It was anticipated that the project would generate approximately 7 billion złoty. However, it was subsequently revealed that the retail sales tax had become the subject of a dispute with the European Commission (EC). The EC accused the government of favouring small stores at the expense of large international chains, thus providing illegal state aid; the tax was ultimately levied from 2021. Conversely, the levy imposed on banking institutions yielded revenues that fell short of initial projections. However, it is important to note that their introduction demonstrated a certain unpredictability in Polish law and sent a clear signal to investors that other sectors could also be subject to taxation in the future. Moreover, as is the case with other forms of taxation, it is inevitable that the additional financial burden will ultimately be transferred to consumers.

As discussed elsewhere in this volume, there is ample evidence to support the assertion that the crisis in the Polish judiciary has had a significant impact on the confidence of foreign investors and partners in Poland. It is also noteworthy that, notwithstanding the emphatic rulings of the Sąd Najwyższy (Supreme Court) regarding Poland's rule-of-law crisis, the national authorities have thus far responded with incremental legislative amendments. These adjustments recalibrated the scope and design of the judicial reforms, while preserving their autocratic objectives, thus enabling the government to continue them despite the Court's interventions (Bornemann 2023). Furthermore, the government's non-compliance with the legal rulings and the penalties imposed on Poland by the Court of Justice of the EU in the Turów mine and the Disciplinary Chamber cases resulted in losses of approximately 2.9 billion złoty in 2022–23. Consequently, strained relations with the EU, coupled with the absence of financial resources from the Krajowy Plan Odbudowy (National Recovery Plan) have contributed to a decline in the perception of Poland among international credit rating agencies. As highlighted in the White Paper, economic growth in 2021–23 was lower than anticipated (Ministry of Finance – Poland 2024).

It is difficult to dispute the assertion that several of the government's initiatives displayed a pronounced populist character. A salient example occurred in the run-up to the parliamentary election in 2023, when the government increased the one-off benefit to 2,650 złoty, thereby raising the minimum pension amount to 1,588.44 złoty. To finance these payments in 2023, the Solidarity Fund took out a loan of 5 billion złoty from the Demographic Reserve Fund; repayment was scheduled to commence in 2026 and to continue until 2037 (Ministry of Finance – Poland 2024). In addition, the government provided pensioners with extra payments beyond the standard 12-monthly pensions, disbursing what are commonly referred to as the 13th and 14th pensions prior to elections to the European Parliament; it also allocated complimentary laptops to fourth-grade students and teachers, with the latter also receiving specific monetary bonuses. On Teachers' Day (14 October), a payment of 900 złoty was made. These initiatives occurred precisely one year prior to the election date. This decision was preceded by a similar move from the NBP, which had earlier lowered its interest rates. Consequently, the SOE PKN Orlen reduced the prices of gasoline and diesel fuel 15 times in the month preceding the election, to 5.99 złoty per litre. As a result of the subsequent depletion of fuel supplies at petrol stations, the company declared that the pumps were out of order (Anioł 2024). The Law and Justic Party's use of advertising as a mechanism to finance favourable media outlets and undermine independent journalism is also a cause for concern, as it places financial pressure on the media. While independent media outlets (primarily TVN) have so far demonstrated resilience due to their foreign ownership, the current economic climate may prompt many of these investors to withdraw. This could have a devastating impact on media pluralism. In addition, millions of złotys in public subsidies were allocated to the purchase of new headquarters. Houses in Warsaw's Mokotów and Ursynów districts, premises in a historic tenement building, a plot of land with two ponds, its own forest and a 'beekeeper's cottage' are just some of the properties that Minister of Education Przemysław Czarnek financed with public money (TVN24 2023). Another example of mismanagement was the establishment in 2017 of the Narodowy Insytut Wolności (National Freedom Institute – NFI), whose task was to support non-governmental organizations in Poland. Although the NFI was allocated funding, allegations quickly arose that grants were being distributed at the institute's discretion. Indeed, most of the grants went to Catholic, right-wing, conservative, and even extreme nationalist organizations, many of which have openly supported the Law and Justice Party for years, and some are directly linked to the current government. Many of these organizations were established in 2018 and 2019, at the time when the NIF began distributing funds (Onet 2020).

Conclusion

Several factors are currently undermining the promotion of democracy. These include the limited influence of international actors in the face of domestic conditions within individual countries, as well as efforts by the People's Republic of China and Russia to challenge the global order based on democratic values, demonstrating that economic growth is possible without democracy. Nevertheless, the decline in credibility and trust in traditional promoters of democracy (particularly the United States) and the conflicting goals and interests between the originators and recipients of pro-democratic actions are of key importance (Waśko-Owsiejczuk 2023). Moreover, the prevailing global economic and political circumstances, in conjunction with China's escalating influence, serve to dispel the notion that democracy is a prerequisite for economic advancement (Waśko-Owsiejczuk 2023). The rise of populist parties additionally threatens the effectiveness of European integration through the phenomenon of the 'captured state'. A defining feature of these networks is that informal political and economic networks have the capacity to influence, and indeed control, formally democratic public institutions and the free market. The primary aim of these networks is to secure economic gains for the private benefit of their members (Nonchev 2019; Abby 2014).

The aim of this chapter is not to assess the changes or reforms being introduced, as their full effects will only become evident in the long term. Both the COVID-19 pandemic and the outbreak of war in Ukraine compelled the government to take swift action to mitigate the potential socio-economic damage, which justifies some of the measures described in this chapter aimed at increasing state interventionism. As noted by Szarzec and Nowara (2017), in Poland, SOEs, especially strategic ones, tend to achieve better economic outcomes compared to the Polish average for such enterprises. The reasons for this phenomenon can be attributed to the characteristic features of the network sectors in which SOEs operate, the impact of economies of scale, or the dominant position of SOEs on domestic markets. Therefore, caution should be exercised when assessing short-term economic decisions made between 2015 and 2023, many of which were still being implemented at the time of writing. For example, the government elected in 2023 chose not to discontinue the Family 800+ programme, even though it became clear after a relatively short period of time that it had no significant impact on population growth. Similarly, the PDF continues to operate despite harsh criticism.

However, it should be noted that many of the measures implemented during this period were perceived as detrimental to democratic institutions. It is necessary to determine whether the main goal of those in power was to consolidate control over society, which could have jeopardized the pursuit of economic progress. Populist measures that were supposedly intended to support Polish citizens and the Polish economy may simultaneously have sought to subordinate citizens to the authorities. Totleben et al. (2019) suggest that, according to data from the Polish National Court Register, there is a clear correlation between changes in SOE management boards and political elections in Poland. Political parties often assume control of SOEs, viewing them as a form of reward for electoral success. These changes can lead to the departure of experienced managers, the disruption of projects, sudden modifications to strategies and investment plans, and the appointment of less qualified individuals with political connections, which ultimately reduces the financial performance and competitiveness of companies and increases uncertainty both within their structures and among their business partners. It is therefore difficult to interpret many of the actions described in this chapter as anything other than populist measures aimed at establishing a clientelist system.

References

Abby, Innes. 2014. 'The Political Economy of State Capture in Central Europe'. *Journal of Common Market Studies* 52(1): 88–104. doi:10.1111/jcms.12079.

Anioł, Włodzimierz. 2024. 'Wellbeing for Own PeopleL Specificity of Populist Social Policy'. Public Policy Studies 11(3): 7–36. doi:10.33119/KSzPP/2024.3.1.

Balcerowicz, Leszek. 2025. 'Stability of Law and Potential Profit Attract Capital: The Political System Is of Lesser Importance'. *Profits and Principles: When Global Finance Meets Democratic Values.* Sopot: Centrum Myśli Strategicznych. https://www.efcongress.com/wp-content/uploads/2025/05/Profits-and-Principles-e-book.pdf.

Benczes, István and Joanna Orzechowska-Wacławska. 2024. 'Governing the Economy under Populist Rule: The Cases of Hungary and Poland'. *Problem of Post-Communism* 71(4): 341–355. doi.org/10.1080/10758216.2023.2301085.

Błaszczyk, Barbara. 2025. 'Populism in World Literature: Its Essence, Sources and Some Effects in the Sphere of Economy'. *Ekonomista: Online First*: 1–26. https://ekonomista.pte.pl/Online-first. doi:10.52335/ekon/200858.

Bornemann, Jonas. 2023. 'Of Autocratic Incrementalism and Inadvertent Inspirations: The Interaction between the European Court of Justice and National Lawmakers in the Rule of Law Crisis in Poland'. *European Law Open* 2: 302–321. doi.org/10.1017/elo.2023.34.

Brzezinski, Michał and Katarzyna Sałach-Dróżdż. 2024. 'The Short-Term Macroeconomic Impact of Populism: A Case Study of Poland'. *Economics & Politics* 36: 832–867. doi.org/10.1111/ecpo.12273.

Country Watch. n.d. 'Poland Country Review'. www.countrywatch.com.

European Centre for Press and Media Freedom. 2023 'Media Freedom at a Crossroads: Journalism in Poland Faces Uncertain Future Ahead of Election'. https://www.ecpmf.eu/wpcontent/uploads/2023/10/MFRR-Report-Media-Freedom-at-a-Crossroads.pdf.

Eurostat. 2025. 'Employment and Activity by Sex and Age: Annual Data'. www.ec.europa.eu; doi.org/10.2908/LFSI_EMP_A.

Forsal. 2017. 'Polska Gospodarka jest centralnie sterowana. To sposób na wyjście z pułapki średniego rozwoju?', 30 October.https://forsal.pl/artykuly/1081836,polska-gospodarka-jest-centralnie-sterowana-to-sposob-na-wyjscie-z-pulapki-sredniego-rozwoju.html.

Fundacja Batorego. 2023. 'Ocena odporności państwa na nadużycia władzy. Raport'. ('Assessment of the State's Resilience to Abuse of Power'). www.batory.org.pl.

Ganga, Paula D. 2024. 'Bringing the State Back In: Populism and Economic Nationalism in Europe'. *Social Science Quarterly* 105: 2003–2016. doi.org/10.1111/ssqu.13461.

Górka, Kazimierz, Brygida Grzeganek-Więcek, and Romuald Szopa. 2017. 'Premises and Directions for Reindustrialization of the Economy'. *Research Papers of Wroclaw University of Economics* 491: 181–191. doi.org/10.15611/pn.2017.491.17.

Grupa Lotos. n.d. 'Historia połaczenia z ORLENEM'. https://www.lotos.pl/3454/poznaj_lotos/o_nas/historia_polaczenia_z_orlenem.

Guriev, Sergei and Elias Papaioannou. 2022. 'The Political Economy of Populism'. *Journal of Economic Literature* 60(3): 753–832. doi.org/10.1257/jel.20201595.

Jasiecki, Krzysztof. 2017. 'The Nature of Capitalism in Poland. Controversy over the Economy since the End of 2015: The Prospects of Business Elite and Employer Associations'. *Corvinus Journal of Sociology and Social Policy* 8(3): 171–193. doi:10.14267/cjssp.2017.3s.08.

Kociubiński, Jakub. 2023. 'Using the Free Market Against Itself? The Strategy of Promoting National Champions by Authoritarian Regimes: Motivations and Limitations'. *Studia nad Faszyzmem i Zbrodniami Hitlerowskimi (Studies of Fascism and Nazi Crimes)* 45(2). doi.org/10.19195/2300–7249.45.2.3.

Kotwas, Marta and Jan Kubik. 2022. 'Beyond "Making Poland Great Again". Nostalgia in Polish Populist and Non-Populist Discourses. *Sociological Forum* 37(S1). doi:10.1111/socf.12842.

Kozarzewski, Piotr. 2016. 'Changes in the Ownership Policy of the Polish State'. *Economic Studies* 91: 555–578.

Kozarzewski, Piotr and Maciej Bałtowski. 2022. 'State Capitalism in Poland'. *Annales Universitatis Mariae Curie-Skłodowska, Sectio H – Oeconomia* 56(1). doi:10.17951/h.2022.56.1.61–77.

Kraciuk, Jakub. 2016. 'Economic Development of Poland against the Background of other EU Member States'. *Folia Pomeranae Universitatis Technologiae Stetinensis, Oeconomica*, 331(85)4: 69–78. doi:10.21005/oe.2016.85.4.07.

Lewandowski, Remigiusz. 2014. 'Building Economic Potential Based on National Champions Strategy: A Case Study of PWPW'. *Zeszyty Naukowe Uniwersytetu Szczecińskiego 803, Finanse, Rynki Finansowe, Ubezpieczenia* 66: 767–783.

Madejski, Mateusz. 2022. 'Kto stoi za Polskim Ładem? Te nazwiska padają najczęściej'. *Business Insider*, 11 January. https://businessinsider.com.pl/gospodarka/kto-stworzyl-polski-lad-te-nazwiska-padaja-najczesciej/hm81e5m.

Ministry of Development (Poland). 2017. 'Strategy for Responsible Development'. Warsaw: Ministry of Development. https://www.gov.pl/web/fundusze-regiony/informacje-o-strategii-na-rzecz-odpowiedzialnego-rozwoju.

Ministry of Finance (Poland). 2024. 'Stan Polskich Finansów Publicznych 2016–2023. Biała Księga'. Warsaw: Ministry of Finance. https://www.gov.pl/web/finanse/stan-polskich-finansow-publicznych-2016-2023-biala-ksiega2.

Naczyk, Marek. 2022. 'Taking Back Control: Comprador Bankers and Managerial Developmentalism in Poland'. *Review of International Political Economy* 29(5): 1650–1674. doi:10.1080/09692290.2021.1924831.

Najwyższa Izba Kontroli. 2016. 'NIK o realizacji programu "Inwestycje Polskie"', 2 May. https://www.nik.gov.pl/najnowsze-informacje-o-wynikach-kontroli/nik-o-realizacji-programu-inwestycje-polskie.html.

Nonchev, Andrei. 2019. 'State Capture of the Post-Socialist State: Challenges to European Integration'. *Nauchni Trudove* 3: 203–213.

Onet. 2020. 'Miliony dla swoich. Tak PIS wspiera swoje organizacje, cz.1, 15 September. https://wiadomosci.onet.pl/tylko-w-onecie/pis-i-organizacje-pozarzadowe-partia-rzadzaca-przelewa-miliony-zl-dla-swoich/51d421f.

Piątek, Dawid. 2023. 'The Illiberal Model of State Capitalism in Poland'. *Ekonomia i Prawo (Economics and Law)* 22(1): 157–175. doi:10.12775/EiP.2023.009.

Rzeczpospolita. 2016. 'BCC, Krajowa Izba Gospodarcza, Konfederacja Lewiatan, Polska Rada Biznesu, Pracodawcy RP – biznes stanowczo odpowiada Jarosławowi Kaczyńskiemu', 17 November. https://www.rp.pl/biznes/art10822801-bcc-krajowa

-izba-gospodarcza-konfederacja-lewiatan-polska-rada-biznesu-pracodawcy-rp-biznes-stanowczo-odpowiada-jaroslawowi-kaczynskiemu.

Ricz, Judit. 2021. 'The Anatomy of the Newly Emerging Illiberal Model of State Capitalism: A Developmental Dead End?' *International Journal of Public Administration* 44(14): 1253–1263. doi:10.1080/01900692.2021.1874984.

Riedel, Rafał and Jakub Anusik. 2024. 'Capitalist Backsliding? From Neoliberalism to "Illiberal Market Economy" in Poland and Hungary'. *The Open Journal of Sociopolitical Studies* 17(2): 352–568. doi:10.1285/i20356609v17i2p452.

Serwis Rzeczpospolitej Polskiej. n.d. 'Polski Ład – o programie'. https://www.gov.pl/web/polski-lad/o-programie.

Stanikunas, Romantas Antanas and Arunas Burinskas. 2011. 'National Champions: The Controversial Industry Policy'. *Transformations in Business & Economics* 10(1) (22): 98–112.

Szarzec, Katarzyna and Wanda Nowara. 2017. 'The Economic Performance of State-Owned Enterprises in Central and Eastern Europe'. *Post-Communist Economies* 29 (3): 375–391. doi:10.1080/14631377.2017.1316546.

Toborek-Mazur, Joanna. 2022. 'Mergers and Acquisitions on the Example of the PKN Orlen in 2022'. *Academic Quarterly Publication* 26(4): 12–17.

Totleben, Bartosz, Katarzyna Szarzec, and Andreas Kardziejonek. 2019. 'Rent-Seeking by Politicians in State-Owned Enterprises'. *Ekonomia i Prawo* (*Economics and Law*) 18(4): 515–529. doi:10.12775/EiP.2019.034.

TVN24. 2023. 'Willa plus. Publiczne pieniądze dla organizacji bliskich PIS. Lista', 31 January. https://tvn24.pl/willa-plus.

Wałęga, Katarzyna. 2024. 'External Conditions for the Functioning of State-Owned Enterprises (SOEs) in Poland on the Example of Grupa Azoty'. *Kwartalnik Nauk o Przedsiębiorstwie* 3: 103–122. doi.org/10.33119/KNoP.2024.73.3.7.

Waśko-Owsiejczuk, Ewelina. 2023. 'A Critical Perspective on Democracy Promotion'. *Polityka i Społeczeństwo* 1(21): 280–296. doi:10.15584/polispol.2023.1.18.

Woroniecki, Paweł. 2024. 'Polish Development Fund Support Mechanisms for Entrepreneurs: A Legal Perspective)'. *Przedsiębiorczość – Edukacja* (*Entrepreneurship – Education*) 20(1): 29–40. doi.org/10.24917/20833296.201.2.

7 The Reconfiguration of Ownership

State Participation and Structural Change in Poland's Banking Sector from 2015

Bogusław Balza

Introduction

The banking sector plays a central role in the functioning of contemporary economies, not only by safeguarding financial stability but also by facilitating the efficient allocation of credit and supporting investment (Douglas 2008). In countries undergoing systemic transformation, such as Poland, the structure and orientation of the banking system acquire an additional dimension of importance, as they directly influence the trajectory of economic modernization and integration into global markets. Since the early 1990s, the Polish banking sector has been shaped by rapid liberalization and the growing presence of foreign capital. While this process has facilitated the transfer of know-how, strengthened regulatory standards, and improved efficiency, it has also given rise to concerns regarding the dependence of the domestic economy on external decision-making centres.

In response to these concerns, political debates in Poland have increasingly emphasized the notion of 're-Polonization' of the banking system. Advocates of this approach have argued that greater domestic ownership of banks would translate into enhanced national sovereignty, a more development-oriented credit policy, and improved resilience against external shocks. Alongside these structural transformations, the sector has also been influenced by targeted state interventions, particularly in the area of household finance, where mortgage-related policies have reflected both economic and political considerations.

The aim of this chapter is to examine the implications of these changes for the functioning of the banking sector and for the broader Polish economy. Particular attention is devoted to three interrelated issues: the ownership and concentration structure of the banking sector; the allocation of credit and its relationship with investment dynamics; and the impact of politically motivated interventions on financial stability. By situating the Polish case in a comparative international context, the analysis seeks to assess whether recent transformations have enhanced or constrained the capacity of the banking sector to fulfil its fundamental economic functions.

DOI: 10.4324/9781042002030-8

Shifts in ownership: from privatization to increased state participation

The ownership structure of the Polish banking sector has undergone profound changes since the late 1980s. As in other Central and Eastern European countries, Poland's banking system transitioned from the state-dominated model characteristic of socialist economies to a mixed system shaped by privatization, foreign direct investment, and, more recently, renewed state intervention (Pyka and Pyka 2017). These shifts illustrate the broader tensions between liberalization and sovereignty, as well as between the integration of foreign capital and the political imperative of re-Polonization.

At the outset of systemic transformation, Poland inherited the post-communist 'monobank' model. Until the mid-1980s, the system consisted of only a handful of state-owned institutions: Narodowy Bank Polski (NBP – National Bank of Poland), Bank Gospodarki Żywnościowej (BGŻ – Polish Development Bank), Bank Handlowy w Warszawie, and Bank Pekao SA. Cooperative banks existed, but played only a marginal role. Within this structure, the central bank performed both regulatory and commercial functions, and competition in banking was virtually absent (Gostomski and Lepczyński 2019). The first steps towards modernization came in 1986, even before political and economic reforms were launched in 1989. The pivotal year was 1989, when two landmark laws – the Banking Law of 31 January 1989 and the Act on the National Bank of Poland of 31 January 1989 – introduced a two-tier banking system. The NBP was designated as the central bank, and commercial banks began to operate independently. The reform allowed domestic and foreign investors to establish joint-stock banks, thereby opening the market to competition.

The 1989 Banking Law, together with a liberal licensing policy pursued by the NBP, encouraged the rapid entry of new players. The requirements were modest, and included limited initial capital, a one-year business plan, and qualified management staff. To attract foreign capital, additional incentives were provided, such as three-year tax holidays, the possibility of holding capital in foreign currency to hedge against inflation, and full repatriation of profits (Szelągowska 2004). The results were immediate. In 1990 alone, 49 licenses for new banks were issued, followed by 17 in 1991. By 2003, a total of 104 licenses had been granted (Domański et al. 2008). The first bank dominated by foreign capital, Bank of America in Poland, began operations in 1990, soon followed by Raiffeisen Bank International (Raiffeisen Bank Polska), Citibank Poland, and others. By the end of the decade, foreign institutions had established a strong presence: in 1999, 16 banks with 100% foreign ownership and 23 with majority foreign ownership operated in Poland, controlling more than 69.5% of total banking assets (Balcerowicz 2001). Foreign banks were particularly attractive to corporate clients, especially subsidiaries of multinational companies. However, the newly established Polish banks lacked both experience and technological sophistication, whereas foreign institutions provided advanced financial services, often replicating their global standards.

The most decisive changes in the ownership structure of Polish banks occurred through the privatization of state-owned banks. Under the Act of 13 July 1990 on the Privatization of State Enterprises, along with amendments to the Banking Law in 1992, Poland began to permit the sale of public banks. Given the scarcity of domestic capital, privatization relied heavily on foreign investors. The rationale was threefold: recapitalization, managerial efficiency, and the transfer of know-how and technology (Uiboupin 2004). In the mid-1990s, a wave of privatizations took place. Notably, in 1999, the Irish group AIB took control of Bank Zachodni, while UniCredito Italiano acquired Bank Pekao SA following its merger with three regional banks. By 2001, privatization of the 'big nine' had largely been completed. Only Powszechna Kasa Oszczędności Bank Polski, BGŻ, and the state development bank Bank Gospodarstwa Krajowego remained under direct state control (Kwaśniak 2002). Critics of this model argued that subsidiaries of foreign banks acted primarily in the interests of their parent companies, potentially neglecting their domestic priorities. Concerns were voiced that profits would be transferred abroad and that Polish savings could be siphoned off. However, empirical evidence indicated the opposite: in many cases, parent banks injected capital into their Polish subsidiaries to support credit expansion, especially during the 2000s (Osiński and Wyczański 2006).

The global financial crisis of 2007–09 altered the dynamics of ownership. Some foreign parent banks faced solvency challenges and were forced to restructure, repay public assistance, and divest assets. This created openings for changes in bank ownership in Poland. For instance, in 2011, the Irish group AIB sold its majority stake in Bank Zachodni WBK to Spain's Santander, while the Greek group EFG Eurobank sold Polbank to Austria's Raiffeisen Bank International (Kotowicz 2012). A landmark event occurred in 2017, when UniCredit, struggling with its own balance sheet problems, sold its majority stake in Bank Pekao SA. The buyers were Powszechny Zakład Ubezpieczeń (PZU), Poland's largest insurance company, and the Polski Fundusz Rozwoju (PRF – Polish Development Fund), both under significant state influence. This transaction marked a turning point: for the first time, a major bank previously controlled by a foreign group was repurchased by domestic, state-backed institutions (Kotowicz 2018).

By 2015, foreign investors controlled 59% of banking sector assets, down from their peak in earlier years (Kotowicz 2017). The reduction reflected both the withdrawal of some international players and deliberate policies by the right-wing government led by the Prawo i Sprawiedliwość (Law and Justice Party). The Law and Justice Party framed re-Polonization as a matter of economic sovereignty and financial security, arguing that excessive foreign ownership was undermining national interests.

An examination of the period 2000–25 shows that the share of domestic capital increased steadily from 30.5% in 2000 to 57.2% in 2025, while foreign capital decreased from 69.5% to 42.8%. In the early 2000s, foreign ownership dominated, with over two-thirds of banking assets held by international investors. Between 2015 and 2017, domestic participation surged significantly, with domestic capital surpassing 50% in 2017 (54.5%) for the first time in the post-privatization era. From 2017 onwards, domestic ownership remained above 50%, reflecting a consolidation of state and domestic investor influence, peaking at 58.1% in 2024 before decreasing slightly to 57.2% in 2025. These data illustrate the pronounced trend of re-Polonization in the Polish banking sector over the last quarter of a century.

Thus, the process of ownership reconfiguration in Poland's banking sector can be divided into three broad phases. The first, from 1989 to the early 2000s, was characterized by liberalization and privatization dominated by foreign strategic investors. The second, spanning the 2000s and early 2010s, witnessed consolidation under foreign groups, with occasional domestic participation. The third, from 2015 onwards, was marked by re-Polonization and increased state participation, symbolized by the Bank Pekao SA transaction (Siemiątkowski 2011).

This trajectory illustrates a cyclical logic: from state ownership under socialism, through privatization and foreign dominance during the transition period, to renewed state involvement under right-wing governance. Each stage was shaped not only by economic considerations but also by political narratives concerning sovereignty, stability, and the control of strategic sectors.

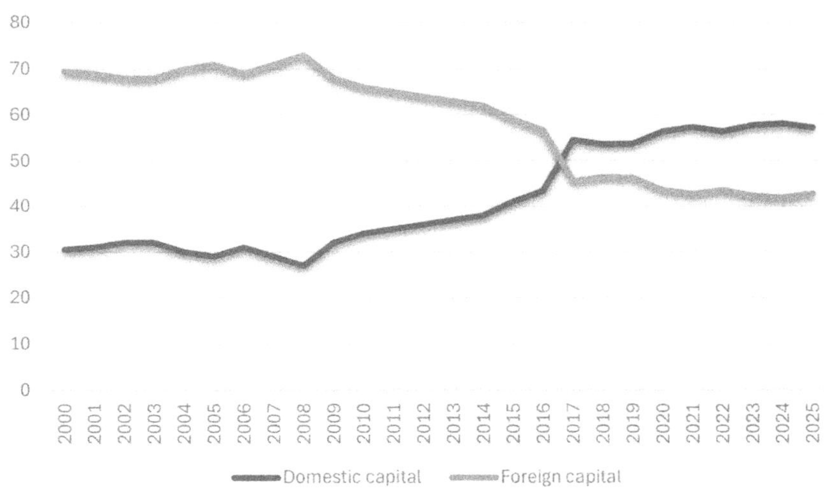

Figure 7.1 Ownership structure of the banking sector (share of total assets)
Source: author's compilation based on data from the Urząd Komisji Nadzoru Finansowego (Polish Financial Supervision Authority) and the Narodowy Bank Polski (National Bank of Poland) for the period 2015–23. See the list of references at the end of the chapter for further details.

While the narrative emphasizes sovereignty and control, these interventions also provided politically aligned actors with well-remunerated positions within key institutions, creating incentives to operate beyond rational economic considerations. In this sense, state involvement served not only economic or strategic objectives but also reinforced mechanisms of political patronage, illustrating an early intersection between economic policy and the broader process of de-democratization.

Economic sovereignty and the narrative of re-Polonization

The narrative of re-Polonization in Poland's banking sector, prominently advanced under the Law and Justice government, has been strongly tied to the broader objective of economic sovereignty. Central pillars of this strategy include reducing dependence on foreign capital, holding profits within the country, and ensuring that large domestic banks are equipped to finance investment and support economic development (Mleczko 2016). The process of re-Polonization has not occurred in isolation; rather, it has coincided with a broader trend of banking sector consolidation, aimed at strengthening financial institutions that are crucial to Poland's economic and strategic security.

A key indicator used to measure market concentration in banking is the CR-5 ratio, which calculates the share of total banking sector assets controlled by the five largest banks in a country. In general, a CR-5 below 40% indicates a fragmented market with high competition, where no single bank dominates, whereas a CR-5 above 70% reflects a highly concentrated market dominated by a small number of large institutions. High concentration in banking carries special significance because it directly affects systemic stability, risk-taking behaviour, and the capacity of banks to finance large-scale investment projects. In Poland, the CR-5 ratio has historically been lower than in many European Union (EU) countries, indicating a relatively fragmented sector. In recent years, however, following a series of mergers and acquisitions, such as the takeover of Bank Pekao SA by PZU and the PRF, the absorption of Idea Bank by Bank Pekao SA, and Bank BPH's acquisition by Alior Bank, the CR-5 ratio in Poland increased from 42% in 2010 to 59% in 2025, reflecting a steady trend of consolidation. This reflects a deliberate policy of consolidation and re-Polonization, aimed at establishing a smaller number of robust banks with strong market positions.

Economic theory and empirical studies offer compelling arguments for the benefits of a more concentrated banking sector. Increased concentration enhances the financial stability of banks, as larger institutions with greater market power tend to adopt more cautious credit policies. Empirical evidence indicates that banks with greater market power monitor borrowers more carefully, extend lower-risk loans, and maintain safer loan portfolios, a phenomenon referred to as the 'franchise value' hypothesis (Yağlı 2020). In other words, banks with strong brand value and market dominance are

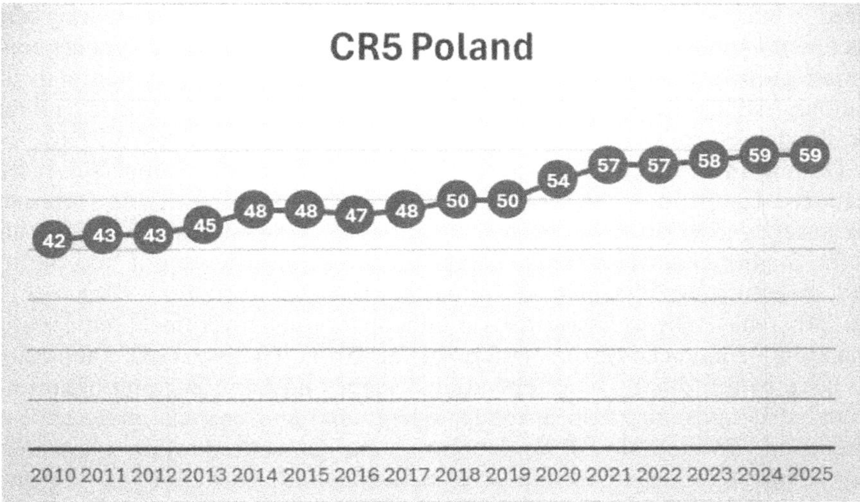

Figure 7.2 Poland's CR-5 ratio (2010–25)
Source: author's compilation based on data from the Urząd Komisji Nadzoru Finansowego (Polish Financial Supervision Authority) and the Narodowy Bank Polski (National Bank of Poland) for the period 2015–23. See the list of references at the end of the chapter for further details.

motivated to preserve their long-term profitability and stability by avoiding high-risk lending.

Furthermore, banks with a concentrated market position are better positioned to develop long-term relationships with borrowers, which enhances information quality and reduces credit risk. Studies demonstrate that higher banking concentration improves loan quality and monitoring, even if it restricts overall credit volume (Jayaratne and Strahan 1996; Braggion et al. 2017). This mechanism is particularly relevant for large banks capable of financing strategic investments, which aligns with Poland's objective of using domestic banks to support national economic priorities.

From a macroeconomic perspective, larger banks with consolidated market power possess greater capital buffers, enabling them to absorb shocks and contribute to the stability of the financial system. Tran et al. (2022) found that banking sectors with higher concentration levels are generally more stable, particularly when supported by strong equity positions. Similarly, İbrahim Yağlı (2020) notes that increased market power reduces credit risk, as dominant banks engage in more careful credit assessment and maintain safer loan portfolios.

In the context of post-communist economies such as Poland, consolidation also addresses structural weaknesses caused by excessive fragmentation. Historically, the Polish banking sector included many small and medium-sized banks with limited capacity to fund large investments, making the sector more vulnerable to insolvency and reducing its ability to support economic growth. Rising market concentration has strengthened domestic institutions, reduced their reliance on foreign capital, enabled them to retain profits domestically, and reinforced financial sovereignty (Mleczko 2016).

Despite these advantages, market concentration carries important risks. Reduced competition may lead to higher lending rates, which in turn can encourage riskier borrower behaviour and increase systemic risk (Boyd et al. 2009; Stiglitz and Weiss 1981). Large banks may also develop a 'too big to fail' mentality, while systemically important financial institutions (Acharya et al. 2017) may take excessive risks in anticipation of government support in the event of financial distress (Afonso et al. 2014). The increased complexity of large banks, due to wider operational scope and more intricate organizational structures, may also introduce operational and financial management challenges (Wu et al. 2019). Moreover, market concentration may limit the competitive incentives that drive efficiency and innovation. In a highly concentrated market, banks may be less pressured to improve customer service, adopt technological innovations, or optimize operational efficiency (Berger et al. 2017). Harasim (2010) emphasizes that bank soundness is particularly important for customer confidence in deposit-taking institutions, illustrating the delicate balance between market power and public trust.

Empirical findings regarding the relationship between market concentration and financial crises are mixed. Bretschger et al. (2012) analysed 160 countries between 1970 and 2009 and found that higher profitability (measured by return on assets) contributes to stability, while higher interest margins increase the likelihood of crises. This suggests that concentration alone does not guarantee stability; indeed, the quality of bank management and regulation is critical. Nevertheless, studies focusing on developing economies (Tran et al., 2022) support the notion that higher concentration can improve stability, especially when banks maintain adequate equity capital.

While market concentration supports stability, competition has its own benefits. Greater competition in banking lowers interest rates, expands credit access, and reduces financing obstacles, enhancing overall economic welfare (Van Leuvensteijn et al. 2013; Chortareas et al. 2012; Rice and Strahan 2010; Claessens and Laeven 2005; Beck et al. 2004). However, competition may reduce the incentive for banks to screen borrowers carefully, potentially decreasing credit quality (Vives 2016; Biswas and Koufopoulos 2020). In fragmented markets, borrower-specific information becomes dispersed, and rejected applicants may simply apply to other banks, further increasing the likelihood of suboptimal lending (Chiesa 1998; Marquez 2002). Concentration mitigates these risks by allowing banks to internalize the benefits of long-term monitoring and lending relationships (Petersen and Rajan 1995; Cetorelli and Peretto 2012).

The literature thus highlights a trade-off: while competition improves efficiency and social welfare, market concentration enhances credit quality and systemic stability. In the case of Poland, moderate consolidation through re-Polonization appears to strike a pragmatic balance between these competing objectives. By supporting larger, financially robust domestic banks, policymakers have sought to simultaneously increase economic sovereignty, improve financial stability, and ensure that banks have sufficient resources to finance domestic investment.

The re-Polonization strategy has therefore been twofold: to reduce foreign ownership and to consolidate the banking sector. Limiting foreign capital prevents the outflow of profits abroad, strengthens domestic control over financial resources, and aligns the banking sector with national economic priorities (Mleczko 2016). Increasing market concentration ensures that these domestic banks have the capital and stability required to support investment, even in times of economic stress.

Overall, the policy of re-Polonization and consolidation represents a deliberate effort to align financial stability, credit allocation, and economic sovereignty. By concentrating ownership in a smaller number of large, domestic institutions, Poland has increased the resilience of its banking system while maintaining an appropriate level of competition to support efficiency, innovation, and consumer welfare. This approach reflects the broader strategic narrative of re-Polonization: ensuring that the banking sector serves both economic and national security objectives in a complex, globalized financial environment.

However, when these measures are considered alongside other state actions, including off-budget expenditures, NBP interventions, and policies that fostered higher inflation than economically justified, it becomes clear that re-Polonization also served a hidden purpose. By consolidating control over the financial system, the state effectively insulated itself from accountability to citizens, pursuing a form of economic autonomy that parallels the broader process of de-democratization. This strategy masked political objectives under the guise of economic sovereignty, allowing policymakers to prioritize regime interests over economically rational outcomes.

Impact of banking sector changes on credit allocation and investment

The re-Polonization of Poland's banking sector, initiated by the ruling right-wing government, was promoted as a strategy to strengthen national economic sovereignty and support domestic enterprises. The primary argument put forward was that increasing domestic ownership of banks would result in a higher volume of credit directed to the private sector, thereby stimulating investment and contributing to economic growth. However, empirical evidence suggests that these objectives have not been achieved.

From 2015 to 2024, the total value of loans extended by banks to the private sector, expressed as a percentage of Poland's gross domestic product (GDP), declined sharply from 53.3% to 33.6%. This indicates a substantial reduction in the role of banks in financing the Polish economy. By contrast, more developed economies, such as the United States, maintain a credit-to-GDP ratio of 197%, while the euro area averages 77.7%, demonstrating a significantly higher degree of financial intermediation and support for investment (see Table 7.1).

The decline in lending suggests that the re-Polonization and consolidation policy had objectives beyond supporting domestic investment. By restricting credit flows to the private sector, the state could maintain influence over financial resources, reinforcing a system in which economic outcomes were shaped more by political priorities than by market logic. This pattern illustrates how interventions ostensibly designed to enhance economic sovereignty also facilitated mechanisms associated with de-democratization, whereby the state operates with reduced accountability to citizens.

The decrease is particularly pronounced in the corporate sector, where loans to Polish enterprises fell from 18% of GDP in 2015 to 11.8% in 2023. Despite the increased domestic ownership of banks, Polish financial institutions have not significantly increased support for local firms, leaving Poland near the bottom of the EU in terms of banking sector contribution to economic growth, with only Ireland performing worse (World Bank 2025a).

Several structural factors have contributed to the observed decline in credit allocation. The re-Polonization process has led to consolidation in the banking sector, resulting in fewer players and reduced competition. While this has improved profitability for individual banks, it has simultaneously

Table 7.1 The value of loans to the private sector, expressed as a percentage of GDP

Country	*2015*	*2016*	*2017*	*2018*	*2019*	*2020*	*2021*	*2022*	*2023*	*2024*
Australia	136.3	142.6	140.6	140	136.2	142.2	138.6	134	127.4	129.6
New EU members	45.4	44.9	43.6	42.7	42	43.4	42.5	41.1	38.7	38.9
China, People's Rep.	149.6	153.1	152	154.9	162.2	179.1	173.5	181.7	189.6	194.1
Euro area	89	88	87	85.8	85	93.7	89.1	85.3	80.1	77.7
EU	89	88.2	87	85.6	84.7	92.6	88.2	84	78.7	75.9
Poor countries	18.7	19.5	19.4	19.3	19.3	20.6	20.6	21.5	–	–
Ireland	51.2	47.3	42.6	39.7	36	32.2	26.4	25.4	25.9	25
Japan	163	163.9	169.1	168.8	177.3	195.5	195.6	196.5	195.2	196.8
Korea, Rep.	132.1	134.8	136.4	141.1	151.2	164.1	170.8	174.9	176.1	–
OECD members	138.8	141	143.6	138.5	145.3	161.9	159.6	144.5	143.1	149.3
Poland	53.3	54.3	52.2	51.8	50.2	49.2	45.7	39.3	34.7	33.6
United States	183.6	186.3	194	183	194.7	218.3	220.3	187.5	192.5	197.8

Source: World Bank (2025a).

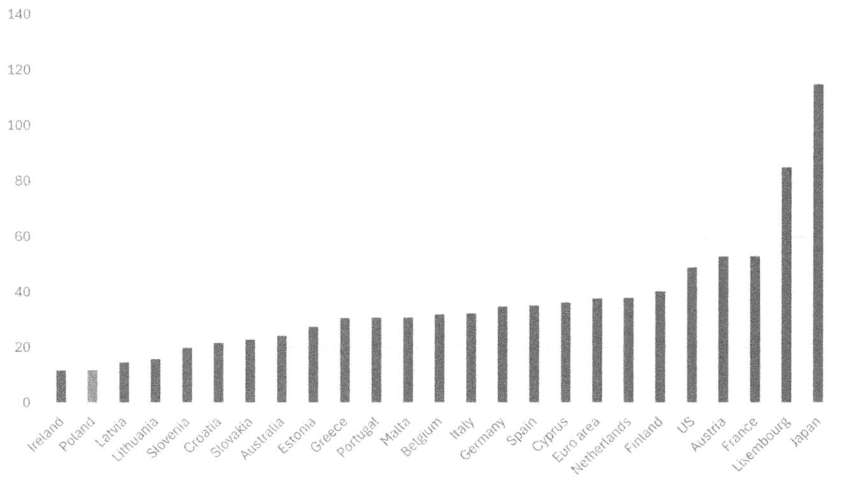

Figure 7.3 Credit-to-GDP ratio in 2023 (corporate loans in %)
Source: World Bank (2025b).

diminished incentives to extend credit to a broader range of borrowers, particularly small and medium-sized enterprises. Higher concentration allows banks to raise their profit margins because clients face fewer alternatives, yet this comes at the cost of reduced credit availability. The operational efficiency of banks improved during this period, as reflected by the cost-to-income (C/I) ratio, which fell from 75.7% in 2015 to 46.3% in 2023. This improvement indicates greater profitability; however, it was largely driven by market concentration and cost reduction rather than by an expansion of lending to the private sector.

The decline in credit allocation has important consequences for investment and economic growth. Access to bank financing is critical for enterprises seeking to undertake new projects, expand operations, or innovate. Reduced credit availability limits the ability of firms to compete domestically and internationally, potentially discouraging foreign investment, which often favours markets with well-capitalized and dynamic local enterprises. The relatively small size of Poland's banking sector relative to GDP is consistent with trends observed in other 'new' EU member states, which generally exhibit smaller financial systems than those of 'old' EU member states. While smaller banking systems are often associated with lower financial development, excessively large systems in older member states may also introduce inefficiencies, highlighting a complex balance between size, efficiency, and the capacity to support economic growth.

The observed decline in credit allocation coincides with a slowdown in Poland's GDP growth in certain years. According to World Bank data, Poland's GDP grew by 4.4% in 2015, before falling to 0.2% in 2023 and to

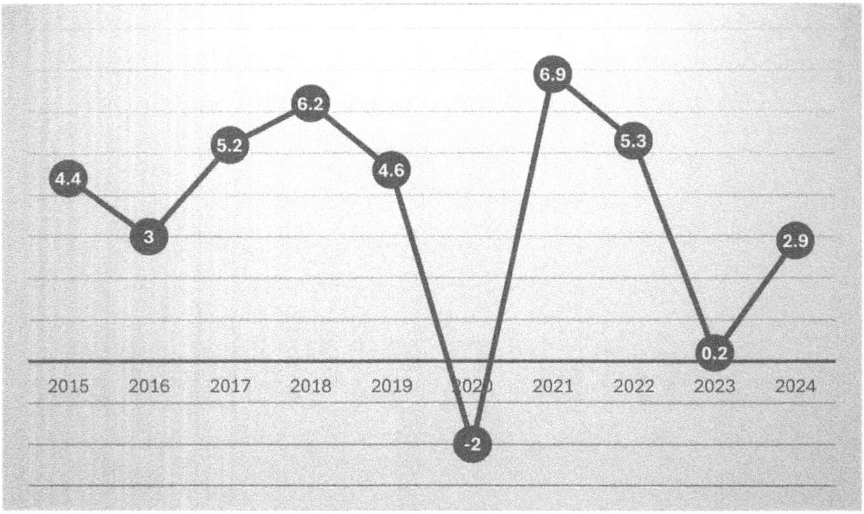

Figure 7.4 GDP growth in Poland
Source: World Bank (2025b).

2.9% in 2024. The sharp drop to 0.2% in 2023, immediately following the period of reduced credit allocation, highlights the potential negative impact of constrained bank lending on economic activity (World Bank 2025b). Lower credit levels hinder investment, business expansion, and innovation, which are essential drivers of GDP growth. The data suggest that limited access to financing from the banking sector have contributed to slower economic performance, particularly in the post-re-Polonization period.

In sum, the re-Polonization of Poland's banking sector has not fulfilled its stated objectives of increasing credit allocation to the private sector or supporting domestic investment. Although banks have become more profitable and the sector more concentrated, credit provision has declined, leaving domestic firms with limited access to financing. The political argument that re-Polonization would stimulate investment and benefit the broader economy has therefore proven largely unfounded. The observed trends underscore structural limitations within the banking sector and highlight the need for policy reconsideration to improve competition, enhance credit allocation, and strengthen the role of banks in supporting Poland's economic development.

From a de-democratization perspective, the failure to increase credit to the private sector underscores the divergence between the declared goals of re-Polonization and its hidden objectives. While formal targets were unmet, the state achieved a more fundamental aim: increasing control over financial institutions and resources, reinforcing political influence over economic outcomes. Evidence such as irrational fiscal decisions, off-budget spending, and NBP interventions points to a deliberate strategy in which the appearance of economic sovereignty served to consolidate political power.

Political considerations and financial stability: policy interventions and their effects

The introduction of mortgage payment holidays in Poland illustrates the close link between political considerations and financial stability. Adopted in the run-up to the parliamentary election in 2022, the measure was motivated less by systemic concerns and more by the desire of the ruling government to secure electoral support. The programme was therefore strongly tied to the political calendar, rather than to the long-term stability of the financial system.

The context for the intervention was rising inflation and the response of the NBP. Since October 2021, the NBP had been systematically increasing its reference rate to counteract accelerating price rises. These decisions translated into higher interbank rates and, consequently, into rapidly increasing mortgage instalments. The government identified the burden of variable rate mortgages as a pressing social issue and responded with a legislative solution. On 7 July 2022, the Act on Crowdfunding for Business Ventures and Assistance to Borrowers was passed, giving eligible mortgage holders the right to suspend four monthly instalments in 2022 and an additional four in 2023. Banks were prohibited from charging any fees or interest during this suspension period, effectively granting borrowers an interest-free loan equivalent to eight monthly mortgage payments. Importantly, the law applied universally to all borrowers with mortgages in złoty for their own housing needs, without income or wealth criteria, and irrespective of whether they experienced actual repayment difficulties.

From a borrower's perspective, the suspension of repayments was financially advantageous. The repayment schedule was extended by the number of suspended instalments, but in mathematical terms the client always benefited from the payment holiday due to the time value of money. The borrower effectively postponed repayment at no additional cost, while inflation eroded the real value of future payments. From the bank's perspective, however, this shift represented a measurable financial loss. Although the nominal value of the loan remained unchanged, the value of expected cash flows decreased. In accounting terms, this constitutes a so-called "non-substantial modification of a financial asset. Consequently, banks were required to recognize an immediate negative adjustment to their financial results, equivalent to the difference between the discounted value of cash flows under the original repayment schedule and the discounted value of cash flows under the modified schedule after the suspension. This mechanism explains why banks reported significant losses in 2022, even though the nominal repayments were not reduced.

The scale of participation in the programme was massive: nearly 1.5 million people took advantage of the payment holiday option, representing 54% of all mortgage loans in złoty and 68% of their total value (Zaliwska 2022). For the banking sector, this translated into substantial costs and capital pressures. According to estimates, the total burden amounted to between US $5.8 and US $7.7 billion, depending on the final participation rate (Marcinkowska 2022).

The impact on return on equity (ROE) was severe. In 2022, the losses represented 81.0% of equity for Pekao Bank Hipoteczny, 34.3% for mBank Hipoteczny, 28.9% for PKO Bank Hipoteczny, 21.9% for Millennium, and 10.8% for Bank ING. Although short-term liquidity and solvency were not immediately threatened, the erosion of profitability and capital adequacy significantly increased systemic risk and reduced banks' ability to finance economic development (Adamska 2025). As the President of the Polish Bank Association pointed out, the scale of capital erosion meant that over the next three years, the banking sector's capacity to finance Poland's growth would be reduced by more than US $82.5 billion (Pietraszkiewicz 2022).

It is also noteworthy that mortgage prepayments reached a record level in 2022, amounting to US $14.4 billion, compared to US $7.3 billion in the previous year, thereby effectively doubling the scale of this phenomenon (Adamska 2025). Although at first glance this surge may be linked to 'freed-up' funds from payment holidays, experts emphasize that it cannot be explained solely by this factor. The dramatic increase in prepayments was also driven by borrowers' concerns about further interest rate increases and their desire to reduce the cost of loans in a high-inflation environment. In practice, some households used the suspension of repayments while simultaneously allocating other available resources to accelerate loan repayment. This development had a dual effect: on the one hand, it lowered household credit risk and enabled borrowers to lower their indebtedness more rapidly; on the other hand, it deprived banks of a portion of their expected interest income, compounding the costs already generated by the payment holiday scheme itself. Combined with the slowdown in capital accumulation, this further weakened the banking sector's ability to finance economic development in subsequent years.

The payment holiday scheme also had macroeconomic side effects. By temporarily increasing disposable household income, it boosted consumption, thereby adding to inflationary pressures. This directly contradicted the NBP's monetary policy, which relied on higher interest rates to curb inflation. The measure thus undermined the effectiveness of anti-inflationary efforts, creating policy inconsistency between the government and the central bank.

Another controversial aspect of the programme was its universal design. The Urząd Komisja Nadzoru Finansowego (Polish Financial Supervision Authority) initially supported the idea of providing assistance but subsequently recommended restricting eligibility to borrowers in genuine financial distress, noting that only about 8% of borrowers had a debt-to-income ratio exceeding 50% – a commonly used benchmark for financial distress. Instead, the legislation extended eligibility to all mortgage holders, regardless of income or repayment capacity. This not only increased fiscal and sectoral costs but also weakened the principle of targeting social support to vulnerable groups.

In sum, mortgage payment holidays exemplify a politically motivated intervention with significant unintended consequences for financial stability. While they provided temporary relief to households, they simultaneously eroded banks' profitability, weakened their capital base, and reduced their lending capacity. By injecting liquidity into the household sector, they fuelled inflationary pressures and undercut monetary policy objectives. The universal design of the programme amplified its cost and undermined its justification as a social policy tool. Ultimately, this case demonstrates how short-term political considerations can conflict with long-term financial stability, thereby reducing the resilience of the banking sector and the broader economy.

This intervention foreshadows the broader implications of politically driven financial policy in Poland. It highlights the hidden objectives behind state actions, namely providing short-term electoral gains, consolidating political loyalty, and reinforcing control over financial institutions. As such, mortgage holidays can be seen as an illustrative example of how economic instruments were employed to advance political priorities, consistent with the patterns of de-democratization identified throughout this chapter.

Conclusion

The analysis of the Polish banking sector over the past decade highlights the complexity of the relationship between ownership structure, credit allocation, and financial stability. While the process of re-Polonization has altered the formal balance between domestic and foreign capital, it has not produced the expected improvement in access to finance for enterprises or households. On the contrary, declining credit-to-GDP ratios suggest that the sector's contribution to investment and growth has weakened. Increased concentration has enhanced banks' profitability while simultaneously reducing competitive pressures and incentives to expand lending.

The introduction of universal mortgage payment holidays illustrates how political objectives may overshadow considerations of financial stability. Although the Polish programme provided temporary relief to households, it generated significant costs for banks, undermined the effectiveness of monetary policy, and weakened the capacity of the sector to support long-term economic development. The case demonstrates that interventions motivated by short-term electoral considerations may produce unintended consequences that extend beyond the immediate horizon of policymaking.

Taken together, these findings indicate that the challenges facing the Polish banking sector are not reducible to questions of ownership or capital structure. Rather, they reflect broader tensions between political agendas and the requirements of financial intermediation in a modern economy. Strengthening the banking sector's role in supporting sustainable growth requires a regulatory and institutional environment that balances stability, competition, and developmental orientation, while insulating financial policy from short-term political pressures. The Polish experience provides valuable lessons for other emerging European economies, illustrating both the opportunities and the risks associated with politically driven transformations of the financial system.

Incorporating the lens of de-democratization, it becomes evident that Polish banking sector reforms were not solely economic initiatives. Ownership changes, consolidation, and politically motivated interventions collectively facilitated a system in which state authorities could exercise significant control independent of citizen oversight. This highlights the dual character of such reforms: while they offered certain stability benefits, they simultaneously entrenched political influence and reduced democratic accountability. Future analysis must recognize that these patterns reflect a broader trend in which economic instruments are leveraged to serve hidden political objectives, thereby offering lessons on the risks of conflating state sovereignty with unaccountable control over financial and economic resources.

References

Acharya, Viral V., Lasse H. Pedersen, Thomas Philippon, and Matthew Richardson. 2017. 'Measuring Systemic Risk'. *The Review of Financial Studies* 30(1): 2–47. doi:10.1093/rfs/hhw088.

Adamska, Izabela. 2025. 'Mortgage Holidays and the Stability of the Financial Situation of Mortgage Banks in Poland'. *Ruch Prawniczy, Ekonomiczny i Socjologiczny* 25(1): 239–264.

Afonso, Gara, João A. C. Santos, and James Traina. 2014. 'Do "Too-Big-to-Fail" Banks Take on More Risk?' *Economic Policy Review* 20(2): 41–58.

Balcerowicz, Leszek. 2001. *Raport Roczny 2001 r.* Warsaw: Narodowy Bank Polski.

Beck, Thorsten, Asli Demirguc-Kunt, and Vojislav Maksimovic. 2004. 'Bank Competition and Access to Finance: International Evidence'. *Journal of Money, Credit and Banking* 36(3): 627–648.

Berger, Allen, Leora Klapper, and Rima Turk-Ariss. 2017. 'Bank Competition and Financial Stability'. In *Handbook of Competition in Banking and Finance*. Cheltenham: Edward Elgar Publishing.

Biswas, Subrata S., and Konstantinos Koufopoulos. 2020. 'Bank Competition and Financing Efficiency under Asymmetric Information'. *Journal of Corporate Finance* 101504.

Boyd, John, Gianni De Nicolo, and Abdul Jalal. 2009. 'Bank Competition, Risk and Asset Allocations.' *International Monetary Fund* 9(143): 1–39.

Braggion, Fabio, Nandini Dwarkasing, and Lyndon Moore. 2017. 'Nothing Special About Banks: Competition and Bank Lending in Britain'. *The Review of Financial Studies* 30(10): 3502–3537.

Bretschger, Lukas, Veronika Kappel, and Thomas Werner. 2012. 'Market Concentration and the Likelihood of Financial Crises'. *Journal of Banking & Finance* 36: 3336–3345.

Cetorelli, Nicola, and Pietro F. Peretto. 2012. 'Credit Quantity and Credit Quality: Bank Competition and Capital Accumulation'. *Journal of Economic Theory* 147(3): 967–998.

Chiesa, Giancarlo. 1998. 'Information Production, Banking Industry Structure and Credit Allocation'. *Research in Economics* 52(4): 409–430.

Chortareas, Georgios E., Jesús G. Garza-García, and Claudia Girardone. 2012. 'Competition, Efficiency and Interest Rate Margins in Latin American Banking'. *International Review of Financial Analysis* 24: 93–103.

Claessens, Stijn, and Luc Laeven. 2005. 'Financial Dependence, Banking Sector Competition, and Economic Growth.' *Journal of the European Economic Association* 3(1): 179–207.

Departament Bankowości Komercyjnej i Specjalistycznej Zespół Analiz Sektora Bankowego. 2021. *Informacja na temat sytuacji sektora bankowego w 2020 r.* Warsaw: Urząd Komisji Nadzoru Finansowego.

Departament Bankowości Komercyjnej i Specjalistycznej Zespół Analiz Sektora Bankowego. 2022. *Informacja na temat sytuacji sektora bankowego w 2021 r.* Warsaw: Urząd Komisji Nadzoru Finansowego.

Departament Bankowości Komercyjnej Zespół Analiz Sektora Bankowego. 2023. *Informacja na temat sytuacji sektora bankowego w 2022 r.* Warsaw: Urząd Komisji Nadzoru Finansowego.

Departament Bankowości Komercyjnej Zespół Analiz Sektora Bankowego. 2024. *Informacja na temat sytuacji sektora bankowego w 2023 r.* Warsaw: Urząd Komisji Nadzoru Finansowego.

Departament Bankowości Komercyjnej Zespół Analiz Sektora Bankowego. 2025. *Informacja na temat sytuacji sektora bankowego w 2024 r.* Warsaw: Urząd Komisji Nadzoru Finansowego.

Domański, Piotr, Tomasz Hoffman, Andrzej Kotowicz, Włodzimierz Maciaszczyk, Ewa Miętkiewska, Marcin Mikołajczyk, Małgorzata Pawłowska-El Berrah, and Filip Świtała. 2008. *Raport o sytuacji banków w 2007 r.* Warsaw: Urząd Komisji Nadzoru Finansowego.

Douglas, John. 2008. 'The Role of a Banking System in Nation-Building'. *Maine Law Review* 8(60): 510–531.

Gostomski, Eugeniusz and Błażej Lepczyński. 2019. *Zmiany struktury własnościowej sektora bankowego w Polsce.* Warsaw: Warszawski Instytut Bankowości.

Harasim, Janina. 2010. 'Retail Banking in the New Market Conditions'. *Zeszyty Naukowe Uniwersytet Ekonomiczny w Poznaniu* 10(140): 119–131.

Jayaratne, Jith, and Philip E. Strahan. 1996. 'The Finance-Growth Nexus: Evidence from Bank Branch Deregulation'. *The Quarterly Journal of Economics* 111(3): 639–670.

Kotowicz, Andrzej. 2012. *Raport o sytuacji banków w 2011 r.* Warsaw: Urząd Komisji Nadzoru Finansowego.

Kotowicz, Andrzej. 2017. *Raport o sytuacji banków w 2016 r.* Warsaw: Urząd Komisji Nadzoru Finansowego.

Kotowicz, Andrzej. 2018. *Raport o sytuacji banków w 2017 r.* Warsaw: Urząd Komisji Nadzoru Finansowego.

Kotowicz, Andrzej. 2019. *Sytuacja sektora bankowego w 2018 r.* Warsaw: Urząd Komisji Nadzoru Finansowego.

Kotowicz, Andrzej. 2020. *Sytuacja sektora bankowego w 2019 r.* Warsaw: Urząd Komisji Nadzoru Finansowego.

Kotowicz, Andrzej. 2025. *Raport o sytuacji banków w 2025 r.* Warsaw: Urząd Komisji Nadzoru Finansowego.

Kwaśniak, Wojciech. 2002. *Sytuacja finansowa banków w 2001 r.* Warsaw: Narodowy Bank Polski.

Marcinkowska, Monika. 2022. 'Credit Holidays: Analysis of Potential Effects of the Regulation on Key Stake-Holders'. *Journal of Finance and Financial Law* 2(34): 125–159.

Marquez, Roberto. 2002. 'Competition, Adverse Selection, and Information Dispersion in the Banking Industry.' *The Review of Financial Studies* 15(3): 901–926.

Mleczko, Jakub. 2016. 'Konkurencyjność sektora bankowego a problem repolonizacji: Szanse i zagrożenia'. *Zeszyty Naukowe Wydziału Zamiejscowego w Chorzowie Wyższej Szkoły Bankowej w Poznaniu* 1(18): 73–89.

Osiński, Jacek and Paweł Wyczański. 2006. *Raport o stabilności systemu finansowego 2005.* Warsaw: Narodowy Bank Polski.

Petersen, Mitchell A., and Raghuram G. Rajan. 1995. 'The Effect of Credit Market Competition on Lending Relationships'. *The Quarterly Journal of Economics* 110(2): 407–443.

Pietraszkiewicz, Krzysztof. 2022. *Złożonych zostało ok. 850 tys. wniosków o wakacje kredytowe.* Warsaw: Bank.pl. https://bank.pl/krzysztof-pietraszkiewicz-prezes-zbp-zlozonych-zostalo-ok-850-tys-wnioskow-o-wakacje-kredytowe/.

Pyka, Irena, and Jan Pyka. 2017. 'Przesłanki i dylematy repolonizacji banków krajowych'. *Zeszyty Naukowe Politechniki Śląskiej* 17(108): 349–361.

Rice, Thomas and Philip E. Strahan. 2010. 'Does Credit Competition Affect Small-Firm Finance?' *The Journal of Finance* 65(3): 861–889.

Siemiątkowski, Piotr. 2011. 'Rola kapitału zagranicznego w transformacji polskiej gospodarki'. *Toruńskie Studia Międzynarodowe* 1(4): 63–76.

Stiglitz, Joseph and Andrew Weiss. 1981. 'Credit Rationing in Markets with Imperfect Information'. *The American Economic Review* 71(3): 393–410.

Szczepańskia, Olga. 2025. *Raport o stabilności systemu finansowego.* Warsaw: Narodowy Bank Polski.

Szelągowska, Anna. 2004. *Kapitał zagraniczny w polskich bankach.* Warsaw: Poltext.

Tran, Son, Dat Nguyen, and Liem Nguyen. 2022. 'Concentration, Capital, and Bank Stability in Emerging and Developing Countries'. *Borsa Istanbul Review* 22(6): 1251–1259. doi:10.1016/j.bir.2022.08.012.

Uiboupin, Janek. 2004. 'Implications of Foreign Bank Entry on Central and East European Banking Market'. *Kroon & Economy* 4(1): 25–31.

Van Leuvensteijn, Michiel, Claus K. Sorensen, Jacob A. Bikker, and Arjen A. Van Rixtel. 2013. 'Impact of Bank Competition on the Interest Rate Pass-Through in the Euro Area'. *Applied Economics* 45(11): 1359–1380.

World Bank. 2025a. *Domestic Credit to Private Sector (% of GDP).* https://data.worldbank.org/indicator/FS.AST.PRVT.GD.ZS.

World Bank. 2025b. *GDP Growth (Annual %).* https://data.worldbank.org/indicator/NY.GDP.MKTP.KD.ZG.

Wu, Jith, Meng Guo, Ming Chen, and Byung-Nak Jeon. 2019. 'Market Power and Risk-Taking of Banks: Some Semiparametric Evidence from Emerging Economies'. *Emerging Markets Review* 41: 100630.

Vives, Xavier. 2016. 'Competition, Regulation, and Stability in Banking: Theory and Evidence'. In *Competition and Stability in Banking: The Role of Regulation and Competition Policy.* Princeton, NJ and Oxford: Princeton University Press, pp. 106–140.

Yağlı, İbrahim. 2020. 'Bank Competition, Concentration and Credit Risk'. *Intellectual Economics* 14(2): 17–35. doi:10.13165/IE-20-14-2-02.

Zaliwska, Grażyna. 2022. 'Jakie są skutki wakacji kredytowych dla sektora bankowego w Polsce?' *Biuletyn Ryzyka* 3(22): 1–3.

8 Society's Dependence on Social Benefits as a Hidden Economic Process of De-democratization

Wojciech Maciejewski

Introduction

The relationship between economic policy, social welfare, and the quality of democracy has become an increasingly important subject of contemporary political economy. In recent decades, many democratic states have expanded social transfer systems as instruments of redistribution, poverty reduction, and electoral stabilization. While such measures are often justified by social and economic objectives, they also have the potential to reshape the balance of power between citizens and the state. Government transfers, especially unconditional and recurrent ones, may gradually evolve from temporary support mechanisms into structural tools of political influence. As dependency on social benefits increases, the autonomy of individuals and households in the economic sphere may weaken, leading to forms of economic subordination that extend beyond material welfare.

In this context, fiscal instruments such as child benefits, supplementary pension payments, and income compensation schemes can become not only economic stabilizers but also mechanisms reinforcing citizens' loyalty to governing elites. This creates a subtle yet significant link between redistribution and political control. When political legitimacy derives not from institutional trust or civic participation but from the expectation of continued financial support, the democratic process risks being distorted. The expansion of welfare policies without sufficient transparency and accountability can thus become a hidden driver of de-democratization, in which social gratitude and material dependency replace deliberative choice and programmatic evaluation.

To provide analytical clarity, the chapter proposes a theoretical framework outlining the pathways through which social transfers may interact with political incentives and institutional dynamics. Welfare expansion, by reducing poverty, stabilizing consumption, and correcting market failures, strengthens the material security of households. However, when benefits become unconditional, recurrent, and substantial relative to income, they may generate forms of economic dependency, particularly under labour market conditions that weaken incentives for labour market participation, or shift expectations towards the state as the primary guarantor of welfare. Such

DOI: 10.4324/9781042002030-9

dependency can, over time, evolve into clientelistic expectations, whereby beneficiaries increasingly associate their material well-being with specific political actors. In this context, governing elites may strategically use welfare expansion to consolidate political loyalty when institutional safeguards limiting political influence over redistribution are weak. As redistribution becomes increasingly politicized and discretionary, democratic accountability may erode, leading to a hidden form of de-democratization that emerges not through formal institutional change, but through subtle shifts in voter incentives, reduced transparency of public finances, and the growing concentration of executive control over redistributive instruments. This model does not claim determinism; rather, it identifies the conditions under which welfare policies may become politicized in ways that compromise voter autonomy and the integrity of democratic processes.

Economical ways of influencing de-democratization processes

According to the classical school of economics, the state's function is limited to a 'nightwatchman' role, delegating nearly all aspects of social and economic life to market mechanisms (Smith 1776/2007; Ricardo 1817/2001; Mill 1848/2008). In such a framework, the state has only the financial resources to perform tasks such as providing security, protecting private property, creating and enforcing laws, and supplying public goods that the free market cannot deliver. As the economy develops, classical theories prove insufficient to ensure the continued growth of production and the enrichment of societies. For example, the advent of the Great Depression of 1929–33 necessitated a reassessment of the state's role in the economy (Skidelsky 2009; Blaug 1995; Keynes 1936/2018; Ferguson 2013).

Under the principles of interventionism, governments gain financial resources to conduct investments and influence the economy. Their main goal is to counter economic crises, but this has the effect of shifting some responsibility for the economy from society to state. Governments derive political benefits from such an arrangement, gaining public support among citizens who are willing to relinquish personal responsibility for economic decisions. Over time, this contributes to a system in which economic failures and financial crises are regarded as the mistakes of decision-makers. As a result, the public comes to expect politicians to take action to improve the economic situation (Rigby and Hatch 2017). The main tools available to political actors are monetary and fiscal policies, which can influence resource allocation and tax rates, thereby shaping economic outcomes (Acemoğlu et al. 2008). The complex and multifaceted nature of these tools requires careful analysis at both the micro and the macro level, making it difficult for economic researchers to establish relationships, while providing opportunities for political actors to manipulate them by invoking external influences (Killick 2021), thereby evading responsibility for their decisions. When the economy enters an upward phase, political actors tend to attribute observed growth to the effectiveness of their governance. However, although fiscal and monetary policies undoubtedly play a crucial role in shaping national economic performance, their effects are complex, context-dependent, and should be analysed from both short- and long-term perspectives (Javed et al. 2019).

What may seem obvious in economics is not always obvious in politics, where decision-making is expected to produce immediate effects. The most pertinent example of the economic influence of political actors on societies and electoral decisions can be seen in campaigns featuring numerous promises related to economic issues such as welfare, unemployment, minimum wages, or social benefits. From a political point of view, such promises are not unusual and convey a vision of the state according to a given political option. From an economic point of view, many political promises represent costs that must be financed with public funds derived from tax revenues. In principle, political actors rarely make statements about direct public participation in financing the functioning of the state, instead framing expenditures as the responsibility of their party or its leaders.

It is difficult to attribute such actions to de-democratization processes; indeed, they can be considered normal democratic processes. It should be added, however, that election promises, especially economic ones, can somehow make voters dependent on a particular political option, especially when it concerns promises of material improvements without additional conditions on the part of the beneficiaries. There is no clear evidence indicating that the implementation of social benefits by states drives de-democratization processes. Furthermore, research on this topic remains limited. This is influenced by many factors, starting with the methodological difficulties in distinguishing when the state is pursuing its goals and when political actors are using them to win voters' votes. However, any form of dependency, including economic dependency, affects individuals' ability to make independent decisions (Verdejo-Garcia et al. 2018). This knowledge of a universal and scientific nature is used by entities and organizations to achieve their goals. In the case of governments, which are tasked with building socio-economic well-being, actions aimed at obtaining political benefits may be conflated with actions for the development of the country. Sotiropoulos (2018) points out that 'political clientelism consists of material benefits … dispensing welfare state benefits to one's own political clients'. Similarly, Cayton and Rosenfeld (2025) observe that the 'politicization of public employment … allows incumbents to dole out patronage jobs … [and] utilize state funds for political purposes'. Such actions can indirectly increase citizens' dependence on the state or political actors. Even without directly influencing voters' decisions, individuals tend to support those in power who improve their well-being through government transfers.

Selected examples of social benefits that can influence voter behaviour

Shaping voters' dependence on a particular political group can take many forms, one of which is the provision of economic benefits to the public in the form of subsidies, market pricing, or any other transfers that improve material conditions that do not result from the effects of productive labour output. Receiving such benefits from political actors fosters the belief that citizens' needs are recognized and met. Social transfers from the authorities are indeed one of the areas of activity and duties of the state to provide equal opportunities and counteract social exclusion, but they should be implemented strategically rather than in an ad hoc manner. An example of such a social programme in Poland is the Family 500+ initiative that was launched in April 2016. This was one of the most ambitious social interventions in the country, premised on the idea that cash transfers to families with children could act as a procreative stimulus, thereby alleviating the demographic crisis. Pre-implementation analyses assumed that increasing the net income of families with children would help to raise the national fertility rate. In 2015, just before the programme was introduced, the fertility rate in Poland stood at 1.289 children per woman. It is worth noting that in the years following the programme's launch this rate increased moderately, to approximately 1.357 children per woman in 2016 and to 1.453 in 2017 (Demagog 2020). Empirical studies using Bayesian Structural Time Series models suggest that, by the end of 2017, the programme had increased the birth rate by 4.5% per month, corresponding to an average of an additional 1,420 births per month (Bartnicki and Alimowski 2022). On an annual basis, however, this effect – while significant – represented a small boost relative to expectations. However, macro-level demographic data show that, despite these effects, the programme has failed to reverse the overall trend of declining birth rates. In 2023, there were only about 272,000 live births in Poland, down by 33,000 (11%) from the previous year – the lowest birth rate since World War II (Główny Urząd Statystyczny 2023; Polska Agencja Prasowa 2024). In the first half of 2025, preliminary data indicated that the number of births had fallen to about 115,500 live births, more than 10,000 fewer than a year earlier, while the number of deaths far exceeded the number of births (the number of deaths increased by about 6,000 in that year) (Główny Urząd Statystyczny 2025). The findings of cross-sectional studies suggest that the programme's impact on procreation decisions varied among demographic group. It was more effective among women aged 30–40 years, but was limited among younger women or those with higher incomes (Bokun 2024). Moreover, as a financial instrument, the programme did not eliminate the key barriers (e.g. access to housing, employment conditions, the cost of parenting, labour market flexibility) that largely shape people's decisions to have children. In sum, although the Family 500+ initiative has contributed to reducing child poverty (particularly in larger families) and generated a short-term increase in the number of births, its effectiveness in fostering a long-term demographic recovery has proved limited. Despite the many aspects that the evaluation of the Family 500+ programme can be considered valid, researchers indicate that it can lead to the phenomenon of citizens' economic dependence on social transfers. The regular and unconditional nature of the benefit reinforces expectations of the state as the main guarantor of welfare, which can weaken individual motivation for labour participation and deepen households' dependence on transfer policies in the long term (Magda et al. 2018; Sawulski 2016). This phenomenon fits into the broader context of analyses of the impact of income redistribution on the relationship between the state and society, highlighting the risk of forming clientelistic attitudes, in which political support may be conditioned by the continuation of certain benefit programmes (Inglot 2008).

Another programme illustrating the potential economic dependence of citizens on the state is the introduction of financial support for pensioners. The Law of 9 January 2019 on the Additional Annual Cash Benefit for Pensioners saw the introduction of an additional 13th pension, followed two years later by the Law of 26 May 2024 on Another Additional Annual Benefit, which introduced a 14th pension. These benefits are paid to pensioners as one-off lump sums in April and September of any given year and are separate from standard pension payments. According to a EU-SILC study, average net equivalent income in 2023 increased by 15.7% in nominal terms (1.1% in real terms), reflecting the impact of these additional benefits for pensioners (see Łysoń et al. 2024). The 13th pension is paid as a lump sum and is structured to have a progressive effect relative to the base pension, resulting in a larger percentage increase in income for retirees with lower pensions. A similar effect is fulfilled by the 14th pension which, thanks to a threshold of 2,900 złoty (in 2023), concentrates support on the lower-income deciles of the population. Evaluating the legitimacy of this programme only from the perspective of the standard of living of pensioners, it can be considered a positive one allowing to protect the elderly from poverty. Analysing the programme from the perspective of economic de-democratization processes, one can see another social group that can become dependent on a particular political option that offers unconditional additional benefits. In the short term, politicians' actions can have the intended effect of increasing pensioners' total annual income and reducing the risk of poverty (Minister do spraw Polityki Senioralnej 2024). The long-term effects of such measures and their potential effects will be discussed later in the chapter.

The potential effects of using economic tools for political purposes

Although many of the social programmes introduced during the period 2015–23 addressed social objectives (e.g. reducing child poverty, supporting families, and providing for the elderly), they are not entirely without potential long-term drawbacks, as they may, under certain conditions, foster a degree of dependence on benefits or weaken incentives for economic activity. Moreover, the injection of non-labour money into the economy can contribute to rising inflation, which may diminish the real value of the benefits provided.

Table 8.1 shows core inflation figures, which exclude price changes outside the control of state monetary policy. While social benefits alone cannot

Table 8.1 Core inflation in Poland in 2015–23

Year	*2015*	*2016*	*2017*	*2018*	*2019*	*2020*	*2021*	*2022*	*2023*
Inflation (%)	0.6	–0.2	0.4	0.7	2.0	3.9	4.1	9.1	10.1

Source: author's compilation based on data from the Narodowy Bank Polski (National Bank of Poland) for the period 2015–23. See the list of references at the end of the chapter for further details.

account for such a large increase in inflation, they nonetheless contributed to it.

Similar conclusions can be drawn from an analysis of the budget deficit in 2015–23 (see Table 8.2). Economic theory suggests that an extensive social system, characterized by large transfers and extensive support programmes, may lead to a permanent widening of the budget deficit in the long term. While social spending can act as an economic stabilizer in the short term (e. g. by boosting demand during a crisis), its steady growth necessitates increasing tax revenues or incurring ever greater debt (the so-called deficit multiplier effect; see US Department of the Treasury 1984). This carries the risk that fiscal consolidation may be necessary in the long term, which often involves reducing social spending. Consequently, in conditions of limited resources, the social system is often the target of cuts, while its expansion frequently leads to fiscal tensions (Blossey 2025). Finally, an analysis of government spending shows that rapid growth in social spending without an adequate tax base tends to be a major factor in generating deficits (Edwards 2023). In the context of Polish data drawn from the period 2015–23, during which public debt rose sharply, particularly after 2020, it can be argued that excessive expansion of the social system without maintaining long-term fiscal balance carries the risk of imposing a permanent burden on the state budget.

Social security benefits may also generate a work distortion effect, seen in citizens' decreased motivation to take up employment. Critics argue that if benefits are relatively high relative to possible labour income, they may discourage low-skilled or tenured individuals from taking employment, as the

Table 8.2 General government deficit in Poland in 2015–23

Year	*2015*	*2016*	*2017*	*2018*	*2019*	*2020*	*2021*	*2022*	*2023*
Debt (in millions of złoty)	46,666	41,614	30,404	7,987	15,883	161,544	49,008	112,833	179,935
Debt (as a % of gross domestic product)	2.6%	2.2%	1.5%	0.2%	0.7%	7.0%	1.9%	3.7%	5.3%

Source: author's compilation based on data from the Główny Urząd Statystyczny (Central Statistical Office of Poland) for the period 2015–23. See the list of references at the end of the chapter for further details.

'loss' of benefits can be substantial. In the case of the Family 500+ programme, some studies suggest that some women are quitting their jobs or reducing their working hours to avoid losing eligibility for benefits (Chądzyński and Osiecki 2017). Analyses of labour force participation data using difference-in-differences methods indicate that labour force participation among women with children had declined by mid-2017, with the effect being more noticeable among women with lower skill sets and those residing in smaller towns (Magda et al. 2018). An increase in state benefits lowers the incentive to work among some social groups, reflecting the classic income effect in the labour supply models (Oshio et al. 2018; Halvorsen et al. 2015). As a result, individuals may underestimate the potential benefits of working longer, motivated by the sense of short-term security provided by social benefits (Liebman and Luttmer 2015).

A further consequence is the potential persistence of beneficiary status over time. When a benefit becomes a permanent component of a household's income, it can be difficult to switch to economic independence, particularly in the face of educational, infrastructural (e.g. lack of childcare), or low skill set barriers. Households that have become accustomed over the years to relying on assistance may develop patterns of dependency, making it more difficult to address their economic problems outside the social support system. In the sociological literature this is sometimes referred to as the 'poverty trap' or the effects of a permanent beneficiary-state relationship (Kaźmierczak-Kałużna 2019). Another aspect is the political effect: when a benefit becomes widely expected by voters, it becomes socially difficult to reduce or remove it. Consequently, political actors may be compelled to maintain or even expand the programme, which reduces the flexibility of fiscal policy and increases the budget's reliance on social transfers. In this context, Poland's Family 500+ programme has become a political 'commitment' that is difficult to scale back (Ceglarz 2022). Analyses of the 'Polish welfare state' say that many transfer expenditures (involving cash transfers) replace, but do not improve public services, which can lead to dependence on transfers, and at the same time to the privatization of social services, whereby citizens are required to 'buy', or finance, education, care, or health care independently (Wigura et al. 2019). As some initiatives (e.g. Family 500+ programme) operate without restrictive conditionality (i.e. the beneficiary is not required to meet certain behavioural conditions, such as job seeking), this weakens incentives for economic activity and may encourage passive waiting for assistance (Jurek et al. 2019).

It remains difficult to assess and evaluate unequivocally the impact of the developments described earlier on the processes of de-democratization, given the multidimensional nature of this phenomenon. This is particularly evident in the attempt to provide an economic justification for the influence of political actors and parties on the voter intentions and behaviours. Within the field of economics, there is no clear consensus on the way in which monetary and fiscal policy should be shaped, and the number of variables that need to be taken into account does not guarantee the success of any of the options chosen. Changes in the economy are slower to emerge than politicians would like, and the public demands that political actors take action with immediately visible effects, which further hinders rational economic decisions. It should also be recognized that there are social groups that cannot survive without state assistance, and facilitating the fair distribution of income seems virtually impossible in such conditions.

This analysis has some limitations, due to the lack of conclusive empirical research to confirm that initiatives such as the Family 500+ programme, for example, have led to widespread economic dependency (i.e. long-term inactivity). It should be noted that the mere existence of benefits does not determine dependency; much depends on the economic context, the structure of the labour market, the level of public services (such as education, care, transport), as well as infrastructure and local conditions.

Conclusion

The analysis of the relationship between the use of economic instruments for political purposes and the phenomenon of citizens' economic dependence on the state faces significant theoretical and empirical limitations. This stems primarily from the dual role of the state in the economy – as a regulator ensuring macroeconomic balance and as an entity responsible for redistributive and social functions. In a democracy, the state is not only the initiator of fiscal and monetary policy, but also the guarantor of the socio-economic well-being of its citizens. For this reason, it is difficult to clearly distinguish between economically motivated actions and those that serve social or political purposes (Blaug 1995; Skidelsky 2009).

From the perspective of welfare economics, state interventionism aims to reduce income inequality, protect groups at risk of poverty and compensate for market failures. In this context, social benefits – such as Poland's Family 500+ programme or the introduction of supplementary pension payments – have a stabilizing and compensatory function, which makes it difficult to interpret them solely in terms of 'economic dependency'. On the one hand, their introduction may weaken incentives for economic activity in certain social groups (Magda et al. 2018), but on the other hand, they may reduce the risk of economic and social marginalization, which in the long term may promote social inclusion and increase human capital.

During the period 2015–23, declining transparency in public finances emerged as a significant obstacle to assessing the effects of socio-economic policy in Poland. This phenomenon was linked to the transfer of a portion of public expenditure outside the state budget, mainly to extra-budgetary funds and agencies, such as the Polski Fundusz Rozwoju (Polish Development Fund), Bank Gospodarstwa Krajowego (Polish Development Bank), and the Fundusz Przeciwdziałania COVID-19 (COVID-19 Counteraction Fund). This practice led to a concealment of the actual scale of the deficit and public debt, which made it difficult for citizens and researchers alike to assess the effectiveness and direction of fiscal policy (Supreme Audit Office 2024; Ministry of Finance 2023). As a result, political and social accountability for the way in which public funds were spent was weakened, and redistribution decisions – including those concerning social programmes – were increasingly made in conditions of limited transparency and without full parliamentary control. This problem is particularly significant in the context of the theory of economic clientelism, according to which a lack of transparency in public finances can contribute to the perpetuation of mechanisms that make social groups dependent on financial transfers (Sotiropoulos 2018; Sawulski 2016).

Furthermore, there is no clear empirical evidence to suggest that the mere fact of receiving benefits leads to widespread permanent economic inactivity or political dependence among citizens. This dependence is highly contextual and depends on many variables, such as the structure of the labour market, the quality of public institutions, welfare infrastructure, and access to education (Shimizutani and Oshio 2013). Thus, the phenomenon of economic dependency is not a simple consequence of social transfers, but the result of a complex interaction between social policy and the socio-economic structure of a country.

However, empirical data from Poland indicate that between 2015 and 2023 this interaction took place in an increasingly complex political and institutional environment. During this period, the quality of democracy declined markedly, as reflected in the V-Dem Institute's Liberal Democracy Index, which fell from approximately 0.73 in 2015 to 0.59 in 2023 (V-Dem Institute 2024). This downward trend coincided with a marked increase in social expenditure, rising from about 15.4% of gross domestic product in 2015 to nearly 20% in 2023 (Eurostat 2024; Ministry of Finance 2023). While the expansion of redistributive transfers strengthened the social safety net and reduced the risk of economic marginalization, it also coincided with a concentration of decision-making power within the executive branch and a decline in fiscal transparency.

Such parallel developments suggest that the relationship between social spending and democratic quality may be more nuanced than simple causality implies: the expansion of welfare programmes can simultaneously encourage inclusion and stability, while also creating opportunities for the political instrumentalization of economic policy. This duality highlights the importance of transparency and institutional safeguards in preventing welfare policies from becoming tools of political control. The ethical and political dimension of this discussion is also significant. A state that would abandon redistribution mechanisms in the name of 'market neutrality' would cease to function as a guarantor of social security. Citizens, expecting the public authorities to ensure a minimum standard of living, legitimize the state's social policy actions as part of the social contract, rather than as a form of clientelism (Wigura et al. 2019). From this perspective, redistributive policy can be understood less as a tool for creating dependency and more as a mechanism for maintaining social cohesion.

The analysis demonstrates that the relationship between welfare expansion and democratic quality cannot be reduced to a simple causal mechanism. Social transfers fulfil essential functions related to poverty reduction, social inclusion, and macroeconomic stability. However, in political environments marked by declining transparency, weakened institutional checks, and the increasing use of extra-budgetary financing, welfare instruments may acquire a political dimension that extends beyond their social purpose. In sum, the difficulty in clearly linking social programmes to citizens' economic dependence on the state stems from the multidimensional nature of social policy in the economy. The state, acting as a guarantor of welfare and macroeconomic stability, pursues both economic and social goals, which often overlap. However, the declining transparency of public finances and the systematic transfer of expenditure outside the budget during the period under review make it difficult to fully assess the effects of these measures and may lead to a weakening of democratic control over public finances. Only long-term comparative studies – taking into account structural changes, economic cycles, the level of social capital and the transparency of finances – can provide a more precise assessment of whether the programmes in question lead to economic dependency or instead constitute an element of responsible social policy in a modern welfare state.

References

Acemoğlu, Daron, Michael Golosov, and Aleh Tsyvinski. 2008. 'Political Economy of Mechanisms'. *Econometrica* 76(3): 619–641. doi:10.1111/j.1468-0262.2008.00849.x.

Bartnicki, Sławomir and Maciej Alimowski. 2022. 'W poszukiwaniu demograficznych efektów rządowego programu "Rodzina 500+"'. *Studia Socjologiczne* 1: 193–219. doi:10.24425/sts.2022.140601.

Blaug, Mark. 1995. *Metodologia ekonomii*. Warsaw: PWN.

Blaug, Mark. 1997. *Economic Theory in Retrospect* (5th edn). Cambridge: Cambridge University Press.

Blossey, Nils. 2025. 'Austerity and Social Spending: Estimating the Long-Run Effects of Fiscal Adjustment'. *British Journal of Political Science* 55: 1–13. doi:10.1017/s0007123425000018.

Bokun, Anna. 2024. 'Cash Transfers and Fertility: Evidence from Poland's Family 500+ Policy'. *Demographic Research* 51 (July–Dec.): 855–910. https://www.jstor.org/stable/48797805.

Cayton, Frances and Bryan Rosenfeld. 2025. 'Autocracy and Resilience'. In Valerie J. Bunce, Thomas B. Pepinsky, Rachel Beatty Riedl, and Kenneth M. Roberts (eds.), *Global Challenges to Democracy: Comparative Perspectives on Backsliding*. Cambridge: Cambridge University Press, pp. 89–117. doi:10.1017/9781009602570.006.

Ceglarz, Jakub. 2022. 'Tyle pieniędzy poszło na programy socjalne PiS. To już pół budżetu'. *Business Insider*. https://businessinsider.com.pl/gospodarka/500-plus-300-plus-13-i-14-emerytura-tyle-wydalismy-na-programy-socjalne-pis/dqyr50m?utm.

Chądzyński, Marek and Grzegorz Osiecki. 2017. *500 plus – jak poprawić, żeby nie zepsuć*. Warsaw: Warsaw Enterprise Institute. https://wei.org.pl/wp-content/uploads/2017/12/old/images/file-9454b35f48b7c167c7bf42ebafbf8005.pdf.

Demagog. 2020. *Czy wskaźnik dzietności wzrósł po wprowadzeniu 500+?*15 September. https://demagog.org.pl/wypowiedzi/czy-wskaznik-dzietnosci-wzrosl-po-wprowadzeniu-500/.

Edwards, Chris. 2023. *Deficits Caused by Broad-Based Spending Increases.* Cato Institute. https://www.cato.org/blog/deficits-caused-broad-based-spending-increases?utm.

Eurostat. 2024. *General Government Expenditure by Function (COFOG): Social Protection.* https://ec.europa.eu/eurostat/databrowser/view/gov_10a_exp/default/table?lang=en.

Główny Urząd Statystyczny (Central Statistical Office of Poland). 2016. *Komunikat dotyczący deficytu i długu sektora instytucji rządowych i samorządowych w 2015 roku.* Warsaw: Główny Urząd Statystyczny. https://stat.gov.pl/obszary-tematyczne/rachunki-narodowe/statystyka-sektora-instytucji-rzadowych-i-samorzadowych/komunikat-dotyczacy-deficytu-i-dlugu-sektora-instytucji-rzadowych-i-samorzadowych-w-2015-roku%2C1%2C22.html.

Główny Urząd Statystyczny (Central Statistical Office of Poland). 2019a. *Komunikat Prezesa Głównego Urzędu Statystycznego.* Warsaw: Główny Urząd Statystyczny. https://stat.gov.pl/sygnalne/komunikaty-i-obwieszczenia/listWartośćinwestycji poczynionych po otrzymaniu dotacjia-komunikatow-i-obwieszczen/wynik-nominalny-sektora-instytucji-rzadowych-i-samorzadowych-za-lata-2015–2018%2C292%2C5.html.

Główny Urząd Statystyczny (Central Statistical Office of Poland). 2019b. *Komunikat dotyczący deficytu i długu sektora instytucji rządowych i samorządowych w 2018 r.* Warsaw: Główny Urząd Statystyczny. https://stat.gov.pl/files/gfx/portalinformacyjny/pl/defaultaktualnosci/5483/1/29/1/komunikat_dotyczacy_deficytu_i_dlugu_sektora_instytucji_rzadowych_i_samorzadowych_w_2018.pdf.

Główny Urząd Statystyczny (Central Statistical Office of Poland). 2022. *Komunikat dotyczący deficytu i długu sektora instytucji rządowych i samorządowych w 2021 roku (za lata 2018–2021).* Warsaw: Główny Urząd Statystyczny. https://stat.gov.pl/obszary-tematyczne/rachunki-narodowe/statystyka-sektora-instytucji-rzadowych-i-samorzadowych/komunikat-dotyczacy-deficytu-i-dlugu-sektora-instytucji-rzadowych-i-samorzadowych-w-2021-roku-za-lata-20182021%2C1%2C34.html.

Główny Urząd Statystyczny (Central Statistical Office of Poland). 2023. *Komunikat dotyczący deficytu i długu sektora instytucji rządowych i samorządowych w 2022 roku.* Warsaw: Główny Urząd Statystyczny. https://stat.gov.pl/obszary-tematyczne/rachunki-narodowe/statystyka-sektora-instytucji-rzadowych-i-samorzadowych/komunikat-dotyczacy-deficytu-i-dlugu-sektora-instytucji-rzadowych-i-samorzadowych-w-2022-roku%2C1%2C37.html.

Główny Urząd Statystyczny (Central Statistical Office of Poland). 2024a. *Komunikat dotyczący deficytu i długu sektora instytucji rządowych i samorządowych w 2023 Roku.* Warsaw: Główny Urząd Statystyczny. https://stat.gov.pl/obszary-tematyczne/rachunki-narodowe/statystyka-sektora-instytucji-rzadowych-i-samorzadowych/komunikat-dotyczacy-deficytu-i-dlugu-sektora-instytucji-rzadowych-i-samorzadowych-w-2023-roku%2C1%2C39.html?pdf=1&utm.

Główny Urząd Statystyczny (Central Statistical Office of Poland). 2024b. *Sytuacja demograficzna Polski do 2023 r.* Warsaw: Główny Urząd Statystyczny. https://stat.gov.pl/obszary-tematyczne/ludnosc/ludnosc/sytuacja-demograficzna-polski-do-2023-roku,40,4.html.

Główny Urząd Statystyczny (Central Statistical Office of Poland). 2025. *Sytuacja demograficzna – dane wstępne.* Warsaw: Główny Urząd Statystyczny. https://ssgk.stat.gov.pl/Ludnosc.html.

Ferguson, Niall. 2013. *The Great Degeneration: How Institutions Decay and Economies Die.* New York: Penguin.

Halvorsen, Rune, Bjørn Hvinden, and Mi Ah Schøyen. 2015. 'The Nordic Welfare Model in the Twenty-First Century: The Bumble-Bee Still Flies!' *Social Policy and Society* 15(1): 57–73. doi:10.1017/s1474746415000135.

Inglot, Tomasz. 2008. *Welfare States in East-Central Europe, 1944–2021*. Cambridge: Cambridge University Press.

Javed, Farhan, Muhammad Sahail, Khan Alam, and Brekhna Gul. 2019. 'Asymmetric Effects of Monetary Policy Shocks on Output Growth: Evidence from Nonlinear ARDL and Hatemi-J Causality Tests'. *Global Economics Review* 4(4): 157–181. doi:10.31703/ger.2019.

Jurek, Łukasz, Cyprian Kozyra, and Magdalena Rojek-Nowosielska. 2019. 'Postrzeganie świadczeń socjalnych – perspektywa międzynarodowa'. *Studia Oeconomica Posnaniesia* 7(4): 75–88. doi:10.18559/SOEP.2019.4.5.

Kaźmierczak-Kałużna, Izabela. 2019. 'W orbicie "500+": Funkcjonowanie ubogich rodzin wielodzietnych w warunkach zmiany polityki rodzinnej w Polsce'. *Kultura i Społeczeństwo* 63(4): 125–149. doi:10.35757/KiS.2019.63.4.7.

Keynes, John Maynard. 2018. *Ogólna teoria zatrudnienia, procentu i pieniądza*. Warsaw: PWN. (Originally published 1936.)

Killick, Anna. 2021. 'Not "My Economy": A Political Ethnographic Study of Interest in the Economy'. *The British Journal of Politics and International Relations* 24(1): 171–186. doi:10.1177/13691481211007064.

Liebman, Jeffrey B. and Erzo F. Luttmer. 2015. 'Would People Behave Differently if They Better Understood Social Security? Evidence from a Field Experiment'. *American Economic Journal: Economic Policy* 7(1): 275–299. doi:10.1257/pol.20120081.

Łysoń, Piotr, Justyna Bortnowska, Aleksandra Kusy, Kinga Molasy, Robert Wieczorkowski, Dorota Cybart-Napiórkowska, Tomasz Piasecki, Magdalena Fijałkowska-Kaczorowska, Marek Kowalewski, Renata Łokietek, Martyna Topuszczak, Joanna Wawrzyniak, and Agata Kaczmarek. 2024. *Dochody i warunki życia ludności Polski – raport z badania EU-SILC 2023*. Warsaw: Główny Urząd Statystyczny. https://stat.gov.pl/files/gfx/portalinformacyjny/pl/defaultaktualnosci/5486/6/17/1/dochodyiwarunkizycialudnoscipolski.pdf.

Magda, Iga, Aneta Kiełczewska, and Nicola Brandt. 2018. 'The "Family 500+' Child Allowance and Female Labour Supply in Poland'. IBS Working Paper 01/2018. https://ibs.org.pl/app/uploads/2018/03/IBS_Working_Paper_01_2018.pdf.

Mill, John Stuart. 2008. *Principles of Political Economy with Some of their Applications to Social Philosophy*. Ed. J. Riley. Oxford: Oxford University Press. (Originally published 1848.)

Minister do spraw Polityki Senioralnej. 2024. *Informacja o sytuacji osób starszych w Polsce za 2023 r. 2024*. Warsaw: Minister do spraw Polityki Senioralnej. https://das.mpips.gov.pl/source/2024/Informacja%20o%20sytuacji%20osob%20starszyc%20w%20Polsce%20za%202023%20r.pdf.

Ministry of Finance. 2023. *Public Finance Report 2023*. Warsaw: Government of the Republic of Poland. https://www.gov.pl/web/finance/annual-reports.

Najwyższa Izba Kontroli (Supreme Audit Office). 2024. *Epidemia COVID-19 – czas chaosu i nietrafionych decyzji – wybrane zagadnienia w świetle ustaleń kontroli NIK*. Warsaw: Najwyższa Izba Kontroli. https://www.nik.gov.pl/plik/id,31301,vp,34402.pdf.

Narodowy Bank Polski (National Bank of Poland). 2016. *Sprawozdanie z wykonania założeń polityki pieniężnej na rok 2015*. Warsaw: Narodowy Bank Polski. https://nbp.pl/wp-content/uploads/2022/07/wykonanie2016.pdf.

Narodowy Bank Polski (National Bank of Poland). 2017. *Sprawozdanie z wykonania założeń polityki pieniężnej na rok 2016*. Warsaw: Narodowy Bank Polski. https://nbp.pl/wp-content/uploads/2022/07/wykonanie2016.pdf.

Narodowy Bank Polski (National Bank of Poland). 2018. *Sprawozdanie z wykonania założeń polityki pieniężnej na rok 2017*. Warsaw: Narodowy Bank Polski. https://nbp.pl/wp-content/uploads/2022/07/wykonanie2017.pdf.

Narodowy Bank Polski (National Bank of Poland). 2019. *Sprawozdanie z wykonania założeń polityki pieniężnej na rok 2018*. Warsaw: Narodowy Bank Polski. https://nbp.pl/wp-content/uploads/2022/07/wykonanie2018.pdf.

Narodowy Bank Polski (National Bank of Poland). 2020. *Sprawozdanie z wykonania założeń polityki pieniężnej na rok 2019*. Warsaw: Narodowy Bank Polski. https://nbp.pl/wp-content/uploads/2022/07/wykonanie2019.pdf.

Narodowy Bank Polski (National Bank of Poland). 2021. *Sprawozdanie z wykonania założeń polityki pieniężnej na rok 2020*. Warsaw: Narodowy Bank Polski. https://nbp.pl/wp-content/uploads/2022/07/wykonanie2020.pdf.

Narodowy Bank Polski (National Bank of Poland). 2022. *Sprawozdanie z wykonania założeń polityki pieniężnej na rok 2021*. Warsaw: Narodowy Bank Polski. https://nbp.pl/wp-content/uploads/2022/07/wykonanie2021.pdf.

Narodowy Bank Polski (National Bank of Poland). 2023. *Sprawozdanie z wykonania założeń polityki pieniężnej na rok 2022*. Warsaw: Narodowy Bank Polski. https://nbp.pl/wp-content/uploads/2023/05/Sprawozdanie-z-wykonania-zalozen-polityki-pienieznej-na-rok-2022.pdf.

Narodowy Bank Polski (National Bank of Poland). 2024. *Sprawozdanie z wykonania założeń polityki pieniężnej na rok 2023*. Warsaw: Narodowy Bank Polski. https://nbp.pl/wp-content/uploads/2024/05/Sprawozdanie-z-wykonania-ZPP-PL-2023-WWW.pdf.

Oshio, Takashi, Emiko Usui, and Satoshi Shimizutani. 2018. 'Labor Force Participation of the Elderly in Japan'. NBER Working Paper 24614. Cambridge, MA: National Bureau of Economic Research. doi:10.3386/w24614.

Polska Agencja Prasowa. 2024. 500 + nie pomogło? Liczba urodzeń w Polsce wciąż spada. https://www.pap.pl/aktualnosci/500-nie-pomoglo-liczba-urodzen-w-polsce-wciaz-spada.

Ricardo, David. 2001. *On the Principles of Political Economy and Taxation*. Kitchener, ON: Batoche Books. (Originally published 1817.)

Rigby, Elizabeth and Megan E. Hatch. 2017. 'For Richer or Poorer: The Politics of Redistribution in Bad Economic Times'. *Political Research Quarterly* 70(3): 590–603. doi:10.1177/1065912917706549.

Sawulski, Jakub. 2016. *Public Finance in Poland: Evolution, Characteristics and Perspectives*, IBS Policy Paper. Warsaw: Instytut Badań Strukturalnych.

Shimizutani, Satoshi and Takashi Oshio. 2013. 'Revisiting the Labor Supply Effect of Social Security Earnings Test: New Evidence from its Elimination and Reinstatement in Japan'. *Japan and the World Economy* 28: 99–111. doi:10.1016/j.japwor.2013.08.003.

Skidelsky, Robert. 2009. *Keynes: The Return of the Master*. New York: PublicAffairs.

Smith, Adam. 2007. *An Inquiry into the Nature and Causes of the Wealth of Nations*. Ed. Edwin Cannan. Prague: MetaLibri. (Originally published 1776.)

Sotiropoulos, Dimitri A. 2018. *The Backsliding of Democracy in Today's Greece*. London: Hellenic Observatory, European Institute, London School of Economics. https://www.lse.ac.uk/Hellenic-Observatory/Assets/Documents/Publications/Sta

ff-Publications/Sotiropoulos-Backsliding-of-Democracy-Crisis-2019-paper-Fr-Ebert-Stiftun..-.pdf (26 June 2025).

Sumarto, Mulyadi and John F. McCarthy. 2025. 'Welfare and Democratisation: How Electoral Politics Shape Indonesian Social Policy and Citizen's Social Rights'. *Contemporary Politics*: 1–21. doi:10.1080/13569775.2025.2502637.

US Treasury Department. 1984. *The Effect of Deficits on Prices of Financial Assets: Theory and Evidence.* Washington, DC: US Government Printing Office. https://home.treasury.gov/system/files/226/deficits-base.pdf.

V-Dem Institute. 2024. *Democracy Report 2024: Democracy Winning and Losing at the Ballot*. Gothenburg: University of Gothenburg. https://v-dem.net/documents/43/v-dem_dr2024_lowres.pdf.

Verdejo-Garcia, Antonio, Trevor T.-J. Chong, Julie C. Stout, Murat Yücel, and Edythe D. London. 2018. 'Stages of Dysfunctional Decision-Making in Addiction'. *Pharmacology Biochemistry and Behavior* 164: 99–105. doi:10.1016/j.pbb.2017.02.003.

Wigura, Kinga, Jakub Bodziony, and Jan Chodorowski. 2019. *Polskie państwo socjalne: Prywatyzacja zamiast opiekuńczości. Raport opracowany przez*. Warsaw: Fundację Kultura Liberalna in partnership with Orange Polska. https://kulturaliberalna.pl/wp-content/uploads/2020/01/Raport-socjalny_KL.pdf.

9 Human Rights Violations in the Process of De-democratization in Poland, 2015–23

Grzegorz Krawiec

Introduction

Between 2015 and 2023, Poland became the subject of extensive scholarly analysis and reports by international organizations documenting systematic processes of de-democratization and widespread human rights violations (Freedom House 2025; International IDEA n.d.; Mieńkowska-Norkiene et al. 2024). During this period, Poland's democratic framework underwent significant erosion, characterized by the weakening of the rule of law, the dismantling of checks and balances, and deliberate violations of the separation of powers (Freedom House 2025; V-Dem Institute 2023). The Varieties of Democracy (V-Dem) project reclassified Poland from a liberal democracy to an 'electoral democracy' in 2016, noting some of the most severe declines in judicial independence, media freedom, and civil liberties in Central and Eastern Europe (V-Dem Institute 2023; see too the introduction to this volume). This intensification of analyses reflects the international community's concerns about the deteriorating state of the rule of law and the protection of human rights in Central and Eastern Europe.

The process of de-democratization manifested across a wide range of domains, encompassing the judiciary, the media, civil society, public administration, and the protection of fundamental rights. Although not all measures undertaken by those in power achieved their intended effects, their cumulative scope reveals an extensive and systematic attempt to reshape the relationship between the state and its citizens – a dynamic that forms the core of the subsequent analysis.

Reports from International IDEA highlight Poland's regression in executive oversight, institutional autonomy, the rule of law, and the protection of fundamental rights, positioning Poland as a prominent example of democratic backsliding (International IDEA n.d.).

The analysis draws on the theoretical framework developed by Charles Tilly (2007). According to Tilly, democracy is a process – not a static state – in which state-citizen relations become increasingly broad, equal, protected, and based on mutually binding consultations (Tilly 2007, 13–14). Democratization entails a net movement towards breadth, equality, protection, and

DOI: 10.4324/9781042002030-10

mutually binding consultation between the state and citizens, while de-democratization occurs when these relations become narrower, less equal, less protected, and less binding (Tilly 2007, 14–15). As noted in Chapter 1 in this volume, this theoretical perspective has already been introduced; it is revisited here to clarify its relevance to the present analysis.

In Poland, these dimensions were undermined through legislative, judicial, and administrative measures that centralized power, politicized institutions, restricted civil liberties, and marginalized vulnerable groups. The centralization of power, which intensified from 2015 to 2023, was a decisive factor shaping de-democratization processes. The transfer of increasing decision-making powers to the central state significantly weakened decentralization mechanisms and societal oversight of legislative and administrative processes, thereby creating fertile ground for restricting fundamental rights and freedoms (Kulesza 2006).

This analysis examines how Poland's de-democratization from 2015 to 2023 entailed systematic human rights violations that reduced the breadth of citizen participation (e.g. through restrictions on assemblies and media control), undermined equality (e.g. through the marginalization of women, minorities, and migrants), weakened protection (e.g. through the politicization of the judiciary), and eroded mutually binding obligations (e.g. through the repression of civil society). By linking these violations to Tilly's framework, the chapter demonstrates how state actions systematically dismantled democratic mechanisms, consistent with international assessments of Poland's democratic regression (Freedom House 2025; V-Dem Institute 2023).

The period 2015–23 marked a systemic retreat from democratic principles in Poland, characterized by the centralization of power, the erosion of institutional independence, and targeted restrictions on civil liberties. This process aligns with Tilly's de-democratization framework, in which the state reduces the breadth of citizen participation by limiting access to governance, undermines equality by favouring certain groups, weakens protection against arbitrary state actions, and erodes mutually binding obligations by prioritizing state control over mutual accountability (Tilly 2007).

Prior failures significantly facilitated the de-democratization processes from 2015 to 2023. Although the public administration reforms of 1990 and 1998 appeared to introduce decentralization, they were never fully consolidated, thereby creating fertile conditions for a later resurgence of centralization. As early as 1991, Michał Kulesza warned that prioritizing administrative tasks over strategic functions in local governance could weaken democratic mechanisms (Kulesza 1991, 90). In 1993, he noted that the absence of further reforms would entrench a model of centralized management, fostering inefficiency and corruption (Kulesza 1993, 46). By 2006, he emphasized the need for a comprehensive analysis of administrative structures, the lack of which facilitated organizational pathologies and declining public trust in governance (Kulesza 2006, 5–6).

These trends were facilitated by structural weaknesses stemming from incomplete decentralization reforms in 1990 and 1998. As Kulesza cautioned, these reforms overly emphasized administrative tasks at the expense of strategic management, planning, and public utility functions, leaving local governments weak and vulnerable to centralizing tendencies (Kulesza 1991, 90). In 1993, Kulesza warned that without further reforms, the centralized management system – familiar to political elites – would persist, thereby fostering inefficiency, corruption, and diminished citizen trust (Kulesza 1993, 46).

The legacy of these incomplete reforms became starkly evident from 2015 onwards. Central government initiatives, often bypassing local authorities, exposed weaknesses in public consultation and participation. Tensions at the central and local level manifested in disputes over education policy, urban planning, and the allocation of funds disbursed by European Union (EU) institutions, repeating past mistakes and highlighting the limitations of top-down modernization in Polish administration.

Annual reports published by the Polish Ombudsman, officially the Rzecznik Praw Obywatelskich (Commissioner for Human Rights), document a steady increase in citizen complaints, rising from 57,000 in 2018, to 72,000 in 2020, and to a record 79,698 in 2023, reflecting growing societal distrust and systemic failures in rights protection and governance transparency (Commissioner for Human Rights 2018, 2019, 2020, 2021, 2022, 2023). International indicators corroborate this trend, with Freedom House downgrading Poland's democratic status and V-Dem noting regression in judicial independence, media freedom, and civil liberties (Freedom House 2025; V-Dem Institute 2023). Poland's failure to comply with rulings issued by the Court of Justice of the European Union (CJEU) and the European Court of Human Rights (ECtHR) led to restrictions in judicial cooperation, such as the suspension of European Arrest Warrants, further damaging Poland's international standing (Commissioner for Human Rights 2021). These changes reflect a retreat from Tilly's dimensions of protection and mutually binding obligations, as the state prioritized control over ensuring citizen rights and fostering mutual trust. The following subsections analyse specific de-democratization mechanisms, linking each to Tilly's framework to illustrate how they facilitated human rights violations.

Instrumentalization of the legal system and politicization of the judiciary as tools of human rights violations

The instrumentalization of law and the politicization of the judiciary were central to Poland's de-democratization, reducing Tilly's dimensions of protection and equality by undermining safeguards against arbitrary state actions and ensuring unequal access to justice (Tilly 2007). From 2015, legislative changes systematically targeted key judicial institutions such as the Trybunał Konstytucyjny (Constitutional Tribunal – CT), the Krajowa Rada Sądownictwa (National Council of the Judiciary – NCJ), and the Sąd

Najwyższy (Supreme Court – SC) to subordinate them to executive and legislative control.

Successive amendments to the Act on the CT paralysed its operations through the non-publication of rulings, delaying procedures, and allowing interference in its composition, as well as introducing disciplinary powers over judges, resulting in its subordination to the Sejm (Assembly, the lower house) and the executive (Commissioner for Human Rights 2016).

The Ombudsman's 2016 report details how amendments to the Act on the CT introduced procedural barriers, such as requiring a two-thirds' majority for rulings and delays in case hearings, effectively paralysing its oversight function (Commissioner for Human Rights 2016). The non-publication of CT rulings, beginning in 2016, neutralized the Tribunal's role as an independent arbiter of constitutional law, limiting citizens' ability to challenge unconstitutional legislation and reducing the breadth of their participation in governance (Tilly 2007). Legislative amendments enabled increased political control over judicial proceedings and the premature termination of judges' tenures, thereby violating the principle of judicial independence and irremovability, and leading to a rise in citizen complaints about delays and perceived bias in proceedings (Commissioner for Human Rights 2017). Judges who publicly defended their independence or criticized political interference faced social and professional repercussions. Intimidation in courtrooms, the withholding of promotions, and public denunciations became tools to enforce conformity, fostering a climate of self-censorship and professional uncertainty within the judiciary (Commissioner for Human Rights 2017, 2018, 2019).

These reforms allowed the Minister of Justice to appoint and dismiss court presidents, thereby deepening political actors' influence over judicial proceedings and undermining citizens' equality before the law. The SC faced similar attacks, with 2018 amendments mandating early retirement for judges over the age of 65, including the SC's First President, and requiring presidential approval for continued service, creating dependency on political decisions in violation of constitutional guarantees (Commissioner for Human Rights 2018). For example, the forced retirement of the SC's First President in that year sparked widespread protests, underscoring the erosion of judicial autonomy and the state's retreat from its mutual obligation to maintain independent institutions (Tilly 2007). The Ombudsman noted a rise in complaints about prolonged and biased judicial proceedings, with pre-trial detentions increasing from 4,162 in 2015 to 8,520 by 2019, often without clear justification, reflecting arbitrary judicial practices (Commissioner for Human Rights 2019). Moreover, several analyses linked the rise in pre-trial detentions to broader trends in punitive state actions, particularly those targeting anti-government activism and public protest leaders. These changes demonstrate how hastily enacted legislative reforms, without oversight, can permeate the judicial system and exacerbate societal fragmentation. For instance, the number of cases of prolonged pre-trial detentions without

adequate justification increased, particularly for political activists, undermining due process.

Significant international scrutiny emerged when the Venice Commission and the European Network of Councils for the Judiciary issued critical assessments, warning that insufficient judicial independence threatened not only internal stability but also disconnection from European legal frameworks. For instance, judges questioning the legitimacy of politically appointed colleagues faced harassment and disciplinary proceedings, further eroding trust in the judiciary. Non-compliance with CJEU and ECtHR rulings, particularly those challenging the legality of judicial appointments, entrenched this politicization, with the Ombudsman reporting systemic deficits in judicial independence from 2021 to 2023 (Commissioner for Human Rights 2021, 2022, 2023).

These actions transformed the judiciary into a tool for advancing political agendas, limiting access to impartial justice and violating the rule of law. This is consistent with Tilly's de-democratization framework, as it reduced protection against arbitrary state decisions and undermined equality in access to legal remedies (Tilly 2007; Freedom House 2025; V-Dem Institute 2023).

Analysis of legislative changes in the judiciary and their impact on equality before the law and the protection of individual rights

Legislative changes in the judiciary from 2015 to 2023 had profound consequences for equality before the law and the protection of individual rights, aligning with Tilly's framework by undermining safeguards against arbitrary state actions and creating unequal access to justice (Tilly 2007). Amendments to the Act on the CT in 2016 introduced procedural obstacles, such as requiring a two-thirds' majority for rulings and enabling the government to delay or ignore decisions, effectively neutralizing its role as a constitutional safeguard (Commissioner for Human Rights 2016). The CT effectively lost its position as an independent arbiter, leading to a surge in preliminary questions referred by Polish courts to the CJEU to verify whether a court composed of politically controlled NCJ appointees met independence standards (Commissioner for Human Rights 2019).

Legal experts noted that the introduction of 'stand-in judges' and rapid legislative changes created an environment in which legal certainty was routinely violated. Citizens facing administrative or criminal proceedings reported greater difficulties in obtaining a transparent judicial review, particularly in politically sensitive cases. Widespread delays in court hearings and legal ambiguities undermined due process and fostered a climate of fear regarding arbitrary intervention (Commissioner for Human Rights 2018, 2019).

The presence of 'stand-in judges' in the CT, challenged by the ECtHR in 2023, rendered many rulings non-binding under international standards, creating legal uncertainty and weakening the protection of individual rights

(Commissioner for Human Rights 2023). The need to verify the legality of judicial panels before hearings caused significant delays and chaos, with the Ombudsman noting that citizens faced prolonged proceedings and uncertainty regarding the validity of court decisions (Commissioner for Human Rights 2023).

This unpredictability further discouraged civic engagement and led many individuals to seek legal remedies in international forums, as confidence in domestic remedies steadily declined. These legislative changes directly impacted equality before the law. A politicized judiciary limited citizens' ability to challenge state actions, as courts increasingly served political interests rather than delivering impartial justice. The impact on individual rights was equally severe. The absence of an independent judiciary hindered effective appeals against administrative decisions, such as restrictions on public assemblies or penalties imposed during protests (Commissioner for Human Rights 2020). For example, individuals challenging state-imposed fines for participating in peaceful protests frequently encountered biased judicial processes, with courts often uncritically upholding state decisions (Commissioner for Human Rights 2021).

The legislative assault on the judiciary was compounded by broader governance failures, such as a lack of transparency in the legislative process. The Ombudsman noted that laws were often rushed through parliament without adequate consultations or impact assessments, as seen in the 2022 'Polish Deal' tax reforms, which deepened public distrust and limited civic participation (Commissioner for Human Rights 2022). These practices violated constitutional and international standards, drawing criticism from both the European Commission and the Venice Commission, which highlighted Poland's abandonment of democratic principles (Commissioner for Human Rights 2021). The cumulative effect of these legislative changes was a judiciary that functioned as an extension of the executive, undermining the rule of law and leaving citizens vulnerable to systemic human rights violations.

These changes created a judicial system where political loyalty often trumped impartiality, severely undermining the rule of law and the protection of individual rights. This aligns with Tilly's de-democratization framework, as state actions reduced protection against arbitrary decisions and undermined equality, creating a judicial system that favoured politically aligned actors, leaving citizens without effective legal remedies (Tilly 2007; Freedom House 2025; V-Dem Institute 2023).

Curtailment of civil liberties: freedom of assembly, freedom of speech, and the right to privacy

The curtailment of civil liberties, including the freedom of assembly, the freedom of speech, and the right to privacy, was a hallmark of Poland's de-democratization, reducing the breadth and equality of citizen participation in public life, consistent with Tilly's framework (Tilly 2007). The introduction in

2017 of regulations on 'cyclical assemblies' privileged pro-government demonstrations, allowing authorities to prioritize them over opposition protests. For example, events such as Kraków's Critical Mass in 2016 – an environmentally focused bicycle event – were denied authorization on vague 'public safety' grounds (Commissioner for Human Rights 2016, 2017), thereby limiting access to public spaces for dissent.

During the COVID-19 pandemic, the authorities imposed bans on public assemblies through regulations rather than constitutional states of emergency, a practice the Ombudsman deemed unconstitutional as it violated legal certainty, proportionality, and the principle of statutory exclusivity, further reducing protection against arbitrary state action (Commissioner for Human Rights 2020, 2021). These measures disproportionately targeted dissent, with police dispersing peaceful protests, particularly those defending women's and minority rights, while tolerating pro-government gatherings, thereby undermining equality in civic participation (Commissioner for Human Rights 2021).

Freedom of speech was severely undermined by political control over public media, reducing the breadth of public discourse. In 2016, the National Broadcasting Council was marginalized in favour of a politically appointed National Media Council, which disciplined journalists for critical reporting and restricted access to parliamentary proceedings, thereby limiting transparency and public debate (Commissioner for Human Rights 2016, 2017, 2018, 2019, 2021, 2022, 2023). The Ombudsman documented cases of public media employees being disciplined or dismissed for addressing politically sensitive topics, such as judicial reforms or women's rights protests, contributing to a chilling effect on expression (Commissioner for Human Rights 2017).

The practice of subordinating public radio and television to political control continued, and despite a 2016 CT ruling the National Broadcasting Council remained stripped of actual influence over the appointment of public media leadership, violating constitutional guarantees of media freedom (Commissioner for Human Rights 2023). The impact extended to digital platforms, where state-supported social media campaigns and disinformation undermined trust and disrupted civic dialogue. Patterns of online harassment and coordinated smear tactics against activists were documented and linked to declining pluralism in Polish political discourse (Commissioner for Human Rights 2018, 2019, 2020, 2021).

The independence of local media was also compromised, with media ownership consolidated by state-controlled companies, reducing informational pluralism and further limiting the breadth of citizens' access to diverse information (Commissioner for Human Rights 2022). The right to privacy was eroded by the 2016 'surveillance' law, which gave police and services broad access to telecommunications data without effective judicial oversight, a practice consistently criticized by the Ombudsman for violating privacy rights and lacking accountability, weakening protection against state interference (Commissioner for Human Rights 2016, 2017, 2018, 2019, 2020, 2021, 2022, 2023; Tilly 2007). Attempts to curtail the independence of the private broadcaster TVN, which was perceived as critical of the government, further illustrated the weakening of media pluralism. These moves provoked wide public protests, underscoring continuing societal resistance to the erosion of democratic standards.

Amendments to digital and telecommunications regulations further expanded the scope of permissible surveillance, raising serious concerns about the protection of journalistic sources and the confidentiality of private communications. Annual reports published by the Ombudsman between 2019 and 2021 highlight a discrepancy between formal privacy regulations and effective remedies, particularly in a cross-border context, where European privacy standards diverge from national practice (Commissioner for Human Rights 2019, 2020, 2021).

By 2023, amendments to penitentiary law further restricted prisoners' telephone contact with families, often violating their constitutional right to family life, and leading to a growing number of complaints about restricted communication rights (Commissioner for Human Rights 2023). These restrictions suppressed public expression, limited civic engagement, and eroded personal autonomy, consistent with Tilly's de-democratization framework, reducing the breadth of participation, equality in access to public spaces, and protection against arbitrary state actions (Tilly 2007). More broadly, such measures reflected a wider tendency to strengthen state control at the expense of individual rights and social oversight. These changes served to consolidate executive power and weaken institutional and civic mechanisms capable of holding it to account.

Examples of laws and practices restricting protest, free expression, and citizens' privacy

Specific laws and practices illustrate the restriction of civil liberties, highlighting the state's systematic efforts to suppress dissent and control public spaces, consistent with Tilly's framework, reducing breadth, equality, and protection in state-citizen interactions (Tilly 2007). Increasingly, such legal instruments were supported by overt police strategies designed to prevent the organization of protests. For instance, a coordinated police presence at anticipated protest sites, alongside the targeted monitoring of social media groups engaged in activism, became routine. New administrative procedures allowed local authorities to suspend assembly rights with short notice, sometimes on the basis of broad 'national security' or 'morality' clauses not subject to judicial review, thereby reinforcing the arbitrary nature of restrictions (Commissioner for Human Rights 2016, 2017, 2018, 2019, 2020, 2021).

For example, in 2019, local authorities in Lublin and Rzeszów sought to prohibit Pride marches, claiming that they posed risks to public order despite their peaceful nature, thereby limiting the breadth of civic participation in public spaces (Commissioner for Human Rights 2019). During the COVID-19 pandemic, regulations imposed through constitutionally questionable means were used to ban protests, with police dispersing gatherings and imposing administrative fines, particularly against those protesting against the October 2020 CT ruling, which declared abortions on the grounds of severe or fatal foetal abnormalities unconstitutional (Commissioner for Human Rights 2020, 2021). These developments also reflected a broader struggle in the cultural and moral sphere over the dominant public narrative. Efforts to restrict demonstrations concerning gender equality and reproductive rights often aligned with attempts to appeal to conservative social values and to maintain the political alliance with the Catholic Church, reinforcing a state-sanctioned hierarchy of values within the public sphere.

The landscape of free expression also shifted beyond the media sector. Critical voices within academia faced new pressures, including threats of funding cuts for university centres engaged in open political criticism or the organization of opposition events. This chilling effect extended to cultural institutions, where artistic projects linked to protest movements were subject to censorship, withdrawal of public support, or heavy bureaucratic oversight (Commissioner for Human Rights 2018, 2019). In practice, criticism of the authorities could lead to administrative harassment, which significantly limited the public space for free debate.

The Ombudsman documented cases involving arrests, excessive use of force, and the transportation of protesters to remote locations, practices that limited access to legal representation and infringed due process guarantees, thereby undermining protection against arbitrary state action (Commissioner for Human Rights 2021). Media freedom was severely compromised by the National Media Council's control over public radio and television. A 2016 CT ruling mandating apolitical media appointments was ignored, facilitating political influence over content, with public media increasingly promoting government-aligned narratives, thereby narrowing the scope of public discourse (Commissioner for Human Rights 2016, 2017, 2018, 2019, 2020, 2021, 2022, 2023).

Independent journalists faced marginalization through restricted access to parliamentary proceedings and denials of public information requests, limiting transparency and further undermining equality in access to information (Commissioner for Human Rights 2017). Surveillance practices, enabled by the 2016 'surveillance' law, allowed unchecked data collection, with the Ombudsman noting illusory judicial oversight and frequent violations of detainees' communication rights, such as restrictions on family contact, weakening protection against state interference (Commissioner for Human Rights 2016, 2017, 2018, 2019, 2020, 2021, 2022, 2023). By 2023, the misuse of coercive measures, such as the application of handcuffs in pre-trial detentions, further deepened violations of privacy and dignity (Commissioner for Human Rights 2023).

Exclusion and marginalization: women's, minority, and migrant rights in state policy

De-democratization disproportionately affected marginalized groups, including women, the LGBT community, migrants, and people with disabilities, through state policies that entrenched exclusion and discrimination, thereby undermining equality and protection under Tilly's framework (Tilly 2007). The October 2020 CT ruling, which drastically restricted abortion rights, curtailed women's reproductive autonomy and contributed to tragic cases in which delayed medical interventions resulted in deaths. These developments sparked nationwide protests that were met with police repression and administrative penalties (Commissioner for Human Rights 2020, 2021). For example, an activist was subjected to criminal proceedings for assisting a woman in obtaining an abortion, further escalating social tensions (Commissioner for Human Rights 2022).

This struggle for human and civil rights was most visibly expressed in the mobilization of women around reproductive rights, as well as in wider movements advocating equality for sexual minorities, which became emblematic of resistance to the shrinking space for civic freedoms and pluralism. The CT ruling, widely criticized as politically motivated in light of concerns over the Tribunal's compromised independence, further deepened gender inequalities and limited access to health care. The Ombudsman noted a rise in complaints about barriers to health care, particularly for women in rural areas (Commissioner for Human Rights 2022).

Anti-LGBT rhetoric escalated, with local authorities declaring 'LGBT-free zones' in 2019–20, effectively denying equal legal protection and fostering a climate of stigmatization and violence, thereby undermining equality and protection (Commissioner for Human Rights 2019, 2020, 2021, 2022, 2023; Tilly 2007). The Ombudsman reported a doubling of hate crimes against national, ethnic, religious, and sexual minorities in 2017, with violence against LGBT individuals rising steadily through 2023 (Commissioner for Human Rights 2017, 2018, 2019, 2020, 2021, 2022, 2023).

The Prosecutor's Office documented an almost twofold rise in attacks motivated by xenophobia in 2017 compared to the previous year, with social studies showing a radicalization of public language and an increasing tolerance for hate speech (Commissioner for Human Rights 2017). Migrant rights were violated through pushback practices at the Polish–Belarusian border in 2021–23, in breach of asylum rights under the Geneva Convention and Charter of Fundamental Rights of the European Union, thereby reducing protection against arbitrary state action (Commissioner for Human Rights 2021, 2022, 2023; Tilly 2007). The introduction of a state of emergency at the Polish–Belarusian border in mid-2021 was assessed by the Ombudsman as incompatible with national and international human rights standards (Commissioner for Human Rights 2021).

While Ukrainian refugees in 2022 benefited from special legislation guaranteeing access to work, education, and health care, other migrant groups, including Roma or individuals from the Middle East, faced discrimination and pushbacks, highlighting double standards in state policy and undermining equality (Commissioner for Human Rights 2022). Access to humanitarian assistance was also unevenly applied, with some non-Ukrainian refugees and minorities encountering barriers when state services attempted to penalize the provision of aid, creating a chilling effect for civil society (Commissioner for Human Rights 2022).

People with disabilities faced persistent barriers, as the continued non-implementation of a 2014 CT ruling left caregivers without adequate support, while complaints about inaccessible detention facilities and delays in health care provision steadily increased, further reducing equality and protection (Commissioner for Human Rights 2016, 2017, 2018, 2019, 2020, 2021, 2022, 2023). Caregivers of adults with disabilities remained unable to secure effective protection of their rights despite a favourable 2014 CT ruling, with the health care system grappling with staff shortages, long waiting times, and bureaucratization (Commissioner for Human Rights 2019).

During demonstrations by caregivers and people with disabilities in the Sejm in 2018 and 2021, government officials repeatedly promised reforms that were not implemented. The Ombudsman attributed the stagnation in care and the failure to integrate policies to systemic underfunding, bureaucratic complexity, and communication failures between ministries (Commissioner for Human Rights 2018, 2021).

These policies deepened social divisions, undermined democratic cohesion, and aligned with Tilly's de-democratization framework, prioritizing state control over inclusive governance (Tilly 2007). They also fostered a political environment in which loyalty to the state and its ideological narrative prevailed over pluralism and open public debate. As a result, mechanisms of accountability weakened, and social trust in democratic institutions declined further, reinforcing a cycle of limited participation and growing polarization.

State control and delegitimization of civil society

Civil society faced severe repression through state mechanisms designed to control and marginalize independent initiatives, reducing the breadth and mutual obligations within Tilly's framework (Tilly 2007). The establishment in 2017 of the Narodowy Instytut Wolności – Centrum Rozwoju Społeczeństwa Obywatelskiego (National Institute of Freedom – Civil Society Development Centre) centralized the distribution of non-governmental organization (NGO) funding. Restructuring resource allocation processes in ways that excluded organizations critical of the government, particularly those focused on women's, migrant, and minority rights, while also subjecting them to financial audits and public delegitimization through smear campaigns (Commissioner for Human Rights 2017, 2018, 2019, 2020, 2021, 2022, 2023).

The restriction of NGO activities led to diminished capacity to monitor state actions and provide social services. International partners, including the European Commission and United Nations agencies, expressed formal concern, noting that Poland's ranking in global civil society freedom indices significantly declined since 2016 (Freedom House 2025).

NGOs monitoring judicial reforms or advocating for refugee rights were systematically stripped of funding, while pro-government entities received preferential treatment, thereby undermining equality in civic participation. Meanwhile, the state sought to construct an alternative form of 'state--sponsored civil society' by redirecting financial resources towards affiliated or newly created organizations loyal to the government. This parallel network of organizations served to legitimize state policies and to neutralize independent voices, transforming financial capital into an instrument of political influence and symbolic dominance over the opposition and the broader citizenry.

Legislative changes further restricted freedom of association by introducing numerous formal and practical obstacles to civic activity, including tightened regulations on public assemblies, complex procedures for obtaining public benefit status, and increased financial audits of NGOs (Commissioner for Human Rights 2017, 2018, 2019). These measures systematically narrowed the space for social engagement, discouraging spontaneous civic initiatives and undermining trust between the state and citizens. Consequently, independent organizations and grassroots movements increasingly retreated from public visibility, further reducing the breadth of civic participation as defined by Tilly's framework and consolidating state dominance in the sphere of collective action (Tilly 2007; Commissioner for Human Rights 2022).

A concerning phenomenon was the growing financial and political pressure on the Ombudsman's institution, with its independence systematically undermined through budget cuts, recruitment obstacles, and blocking the appointment of a new Ombudsman (Commissioner for Human Rights 2020, 2021). These measures systematically weakened civil society's role in democratic governance, consistent with Tilly's de-democratization framework, marginalizing citizen consultations and civic engagement (Tilly 2007).

From 2022, proposals and public debates concerning additional transparency obligations for NGOs, particularly with regard to the disclosure of funding sources and programme partners, together with intensified audits and reporting burdens, created additional pressure on civil society organisations, especially smaller ones, and contributed to a chilling effect that limited their capacity for innovation and risk-taking in the civic sector (Commissioner for Human Rights 2022). For example, NGOs supporting women's reproductive rights or monitoring border policies were bypassed in funding competitions, while state-aligned organizations received significant grants, undermining equality in civic participation.

Smear campaigns publicly stigmatized NGOs, portraying them as threats to national interests, with notable examples including organizations monitoring government actions or supporting refugees, further reducing their breadth of influence (Commissioner for Human Rights 2017, 2018, 2019, 2020, 2021, 2022, 2023). The Ombudsman's independence was undermined by budget cuts, recruitment obstacles, and political pressures, with attempts to block new appointments in 2020–21 violating institutional standards and weakening protection against state abuses (Commissioner for Human Rights 2020, 2021).

Conclusion

The process of de-democratization in Poland from 2015 to 2023, analysed through the Ombudsman's annual reports and supported by Charles Tilly's theoretical framework, is a clear example of systemic human rights restrictions through the instrumentalization of law, the politicization of the judiciary, and the marginalization of societal oversight mechanisms.

Legislative and institutional changes undermined the fundamental principle of the separation of powers, directly impacting the protection of individual rights. The politicization of the CT, the NCJ, and the SC turned the judiciary into a tool for advancing political interests, while restricting individuals' right to a fair trial and equality before the law.

The right to assembly and protest was systematically curtailed through the prioritization of pro-government gatherings and repressive responses to protesters. Freedom of speech was undermined by political control over the public media and the marginalization of independent voices, reducing informational pluralism and limiting societal access to comprehensive information. The independence of the local media was also severely compromised. Simultaneously, the right to privacy was systematically violated through widespread surveillance practices, often conducted without effective oversight mechanisms.

De-democratization processes particularly affected the rights of women, as well as ethnic, national, and sexual minorities, in addition to migrants and refugees. The introduction of restrictive reproductive policies and limited access to health care services, alongside discriminatory rhetoric against the LGBT community, rising violence against minorities, and pushback practices directed at migrants, constituted violations of the principles of equality and non-discrimination. These phenomena deepened social divisions, weakening democratic cohesion.

Repression of NGOs and activists limited the space for democratic oversight of power. Centralized funding, stigmatization, smear campaigns, and formal administrative barriers effectively curtailed the autonomy of independent social movements and their participation in public life.

Human rights violations and systemic institutional restrictions led to a decline in public trust in the state and its institutions. This process fuelled social polarization, heightened tensions and societal divisions, and reduced the potential for civic activity and democratic participation. During this period Poland was classified by numerous international organizations as a country experiencing democratic regression.

The de-democratization processes under study require urgent diagnosis and remedial action. The future of Polish democracy depends on rebuilding judicial independence, restoring civil liberties and media pluralism, protecting the rights of marginalized groups, and ensuring state openness to social consultations and oversight. This also necessitates the full implementation of international obligations and dialogue with European institutions.

The period 2015–23 witnessed systemic de-democratization in Poland, characterized by the instrumentalization of law, the restriction of civil rights and freedoms, and the repression of civil society. These processes led to a lasting weakening of the rule of law and the protection of human rights. The restoration of democratic mechanisms will require comprehensive reforms, civic engagement, and effective legal and political oversight.

A key challenge in this process lies in strengthening societal understanding of human rights and democratic principles. An important step includes the introduction of mechanisms to counter further social polarization through the promotion of dialogue between different social groups and support for independent institutions monitoring adherence to the rule of law. International pressure and support, including from the EU, can play a significant role in motivating the Polish authorities to implement reforms. Without such measures, there is a risk that the democratic crisis will become further entrenched, which could lead to even greater social alienation and the weakening of rule of law structures. These challenges are further complicated by the legacy of a post-1989 model of socialization that prioritized consumerism over active citizenship. The predominance of market-oriented values over civic participation has hindered the development of a culture of responsibility, solidarity, and engagement – conditions necessary for democratic resilience.

References

Freedom House. 2025. *Freedom in the World 2025: Poland*. https://freedomhouse.org/country/poland/freedom-world/2025.

International IDEA. n.d. *Poland: Democracy Tracker*. https://www.idea.int/democracytracker/country/poland.

Kulesza, M. 1991. 'Zagrożenia reformy (w sprawie zadań i kompetencji samorządu terytorialnego)'. *Samorząd Terytorialny* 1–2: 86–90.

Kulesza, M. 1993. 'Stan prac nad reformą administracji publicznej'. *Samorząd Terytorialny* 10: 42–47.

Kulesza, M. 2006. 'Konsolidacja zarządzania w samorządzie – wybrane zagadnienia. Uwagi do dyskusji'. *Samorząd Terytorialny* 7–8: 5–17.

Mieńkowska-Norkiene, R., Szymański, A., and Zamęcki, Ł. 2024. 'The Deteriorating Legislative Role of the Legislature in Multilevel Democracies. Case of Poland'. *The Theory and Practice of Legislation* 12(2), 109–134. doi:10.1080/20508840.2024.2338500.

Rzecznika Praw Obywatelskich (Commissioner for Human Rights). 2016. *Report on the Activities of the Commissioner for Human Rights in 2016 and on the State of Observance of Human and Civil Rights and Freedoms*. https://bip.brpo.gov.pl/pl/content/informacja-o-dzia%C5%82alno%C5%9Bci-rzecznika-praw-obywatelskich-w-roku-2016-oraz-o-stanie-przestrzegania.

Rzecznika Praw Obywatelskich (Commissioner for Human Rights). 2017. *Report on the Activities of the Commissioner for Human Rights in 2017 and on the State of Observance of Human and Civil Rights and Freedoms*. https://bip.brpo.gov.pl/pl/content/informacja-o-stanie-przestrzegania-wolnosci-i-praw-czlowieka-i-obywatela-w-2017-r-oraz-o.

Rzecznika Praw Obywatelskich (Commissioner for Human Rights). 2018. *Report on the Activities of the Commissioner for Human Rights in 2018 and on the State of Observance of Human and Civil Rights and Freedoms.* https://bip.brpo.gov.pl/pl/content/informacja-o-dzialalnosci-rzecznika-praw-obywatelskich-oraz-o-stanie-przestrzegania-wolnosci-i-praw.

Rzecznika Praw Obywatelskich (Commissioner for Human Rights). 2019. *Report on the Activities of the Commissioner for Human Rights in 2019 and on the State of Observance of Human and Civil Rights and Freedoms.* https://bip.brpo.gov.pl/pl/content/informacja-roczna-rpo-2019.

Rzecznika Praw Obywatelskich (Commissioner for Human Rights). 2020. *Report on the Activities of the Commissioner for Human Rights in 2020 and on the State of Observance of Human and Civil Rights and Freedoms.* https://bip.brpo.gov.pl/pl/content/informacja-o-dzialalnosci-rzecznika-praw-obywatelskich-w-roku-2020-oraz-o-stanie-praw.

Rzecznika Praw Obywatelskich (Commissioner for Human Rights). 2021. *Report on the Activities of the Commissioner for Human Rights in 2021 and on the State of Observance of Human and Civil Rights and Freedoms.* https://bip.brpo.gov.pl/pl/content/rpo-informacja-roczna-2021.

Rzecznika Praw Obywatelskich (Commissioner for Human Rights). 2022. *Report on the Activities of the Commissioner for Human Rights in 2022 and on the State of Observance of Human and Civil Rights and Freedoms.* https://bip.brpo.gov.pl/pl/content/rpo-informacja-roczna-2022.

Rzecznika Praw Obywatelskich (Commissioner for Human Rights). 2023. *Report on the Activities of the Commissioner for Human Rights in 2023 and on the State of Observance of Human and Civil Rights and Freedoms.* https://bip.brpo.gov.pl/pl/content/rpo-informacja-roczna-2023.

Tilly, C. 2007. *Democracy.* Cambridge: Cambridge University Press.

V-Dem Institute. 2023. *Democracy Report 2023. Defiance in the Face of Autocratization*, https://www.v-dem.net/documents/29/V-dem_democracyreport2023_lowres.pdf.

10 Post-2015 Changes in Migration Law as an Element of the De-democratization Phenomenon in Poland[1]

Anna Magdalena Kosińska

Introduction

Following changes in migration procedures triggered by the so-called 2015 migration crisis, Poland ceased to be a country of emigration or transit and became a receiving country, which marked a significant shift compared to the period after World War II (Okólski 2012). Following the rise to power of the Prawo i Sprawiedliwość (Law and Justice Party) in Poland in 2015, migration became a polarizing argument in the public discourse. As a result, certain legal measures were put in place that affected the level of human rights protection and Poland's compliance with its international obligations. This chapter aims to present the most important legal instruments in migration law adopted after 2015 and to show how they have contributed to the deepening the process of de-democratization in Poland. National legislation will be analysed, including the 'border regulation' and other legislative changes concerning crisis management at the Polish–Belarusian border. Moreover, the chapter will examine legal omissions in connection with the 2015 migration crisis and the lack of solidarity in migration management. This analysis will provide a springboard for a discussion of proceedings pending before European courts concerning Poland's alleged violations of migrants' rights. In line with the research thesis, the de-democratization process in the context of migration began after 2015 and remains ongoing due to legal instruments employed at the national level as well as actions undertaken by the European Union (EU). This discussion is based on an investigation of the law in force and a critical source analysis.

Shaping Polish migration law within the framework of shared competence with the EU

Migration law at the national level is a result of the sharing of competences in the Area of Freedom, Security and Justice (AFSJ) between the member states and the EU (Article 4 of the Treaty on the Functioning of the European Union – TFEU). As noted by Costello, the Union creates within the AFSJ a 'secure migration status that takes precedence over national law'

DOI: 10.4324/9781042002030-11

(Costello 2016, 14). Although the AFSJ was originally established under the Amsterdam Treaty, today its treaty-based foundations for the co-creation of EU member states are set out in Article 67 and subsequent provisions of the TFEU (Dickson 2022). Accordingly, at the domestic level, national authorities enjoy certain flexibility in engaging legal instruments.

Pursuant to Article 9 of the Konstytucja Rzeczypospolitej Polskiej z dnia 2 kwietnia 1997 r. (Constitution of the Republic of Poland of 2 April 1997), 'the Republic of Poland shall respect international law binding upon it'. Accordingly, Poland is obliged to observe treaty regulations, including the co-creation of migration policy. Article 9 thus also provides an obligation to respect EU axiology (Dynia 2018).

The fundamental values on which the political and law-making actions of the EU and its member states are based are enshrined in Article 2 of the Treaty on European Union (TEU). It provides that:

> The Union is founded on the values of respect for human dignity, freedom, democracy, equality, rule of law as well as respect for human rights, including rights of persons belonging to minorities. These values are common to the member states in a society in which pluralism, non-discrimination, tolerance, justice, solidarity and equality between women and men prevail.

Bodnar and Grzelak argue that this provision, together with Article 6 of the TEU, should serve as a basis for any actions in migration policy (Bodnar and Grzelak 2023), constituting the democratic legitimization of the EU as a community of values (Dynia 2018). Therefore, following the universal recognition of democracy as a fundamental value of international law, the EU is tasked with safeguarding member states' implementation of democratic principles within Union policies, including migration and asylum policy. In this context, Article 80 of the TFEU cannot be overlooked. It establishes that the policies of the Union are governed by the principle of solidarity and fair sharing of responsibility between the member states. However, in practice, this obligation has not always been observed in migration law, as evidenced by the refusal of Poland, the Czech Republic, and Hungary to participate in the relocation process (Judgment of the Court of Justice of 2 April 2020).

However, as Klaus critically observes, attempts to identify the values enshrined in the TEU within Union policies adopted since the migration crisis, often characterized as 'security first', have been to no avail (Klaus 2020). One of such example is the Proposal for a Regulation of the European Parliament and of the Council Addressing Situations of Instrumentalisation in the Field of Migration and Asylum (COM/2021/890 final). Ultimately, the proposal was incorporated into Regulation (EU) 2024/1359 of the European Parliament and of the Council of 14 May 2024 addressing situations of crisis and force majeure in the field of migration and asylum. This development has a tremendous impact on the human rights dimension of EU migration policy and arguably blurs member states' democratic efforts in the realm of asylum and migration.

The migration situation in Poland after 2015

Domestic determinants, policies, and relevant legislative acts have contributed to the process of de-democratization in migration law. In practice, the legal and political strata overlap and are difficult to separate. The design of the Polish post-2015 migration law and policies has been influenced by the following phenomena, resulting in regulated and non-regulated migration flows:

1 Russia's 2014 annexation of Crimea has had an impact, albeit a modest one, on attitudes towards migration from Ukraine (Mikołajczyk and Jagielski 2022);
2 The 2015 EU migration crisis, following which Poland refused to participate in the relocation and resettlement mechanism (Pacek 2020);
3 The COVID-19 pandemic, which led to border closures and restrictions on the right to asylum (Sobczak-Szelc et al. 2023);
4 Attempts at illegal crossings of the Polish–Belarusian border have played a significant role. In Poland, refusals to accept applications for international protection at the Terespol border crossing point have taken place for years (Bodnar and Grzelȧk 2023). In mid-2021 there was an escalation of the crisis at the border due to organized cooperation between Belarus and other actors to facilitate the influx of migrants with irregular status through the Polish–Belarusian border. According to statistics from the Polish Border Guard, in 2021 alone almost 40,000 attempts were made to cross the EU's external border illegally (Grześkowiak 2023). This situation has been described as a 'hybrid war' on the one hand, and as the phenomenon of 'instrumentalization of migration' on the other. According to the Proposal for a Regulation of the European Parliament and of the Council addressing situations of instrumentalisation in the field of migration and asylum, this is understood as 'a situation where a third country instigates irregular migratory flows into the Union by actively encouraging or facilitating the movement of third-country nationals to the external borders, onto or from within its territory and then onwards to those external borders, where such actions are indicative of an intention of a third country to destabilise the Union or a Member State';
5 Finally, the Russian Federation's military invasion of Ukraine in February 2022 was the binding factor in the formation of the migration policy. The influx of migrants that followed and the reception policy showed that culturally close groups may more readily benefit from Poland's hospitality policy.

In managing migration, the role of the state is to guarantee social order, which requires an effective migration policy (Świeca 2024). Poland's first such strategic migration policy document was adopted in 2012 and was defined as 'apolitical' (Klaus 2020). Following the rise to power of the Law and Justice Party in 2015, work on a new migration policy began. The draft was ultimately presented in 2019 (Polityka migracyjna Polski 2019). It assumed that '[the policy] must be subject to the principles of state security and effectively prevent emerging violations and irregularities accompanying migration processes and combat them'. Thus, security concerns as well as the 'concept of leading culture' became key issues (Mikołajczyk and Jagielski 2022). The draft law was criticized by leading Polish non-governmental organizations (NGOs), such as the Helsinki Foundation for Human Rights, and was ultimately not adopted (Szulecka 2019).

After 2015, government policy and discourse were dominated primarily by security concerns, particularly those related to threats associated with migration inflows, although labour market concerns have also been raised (Pacek 2020). As noted by legal scholars and commentators, a new migration discourse appeared in which migrants were increasingly framed as 'security issues', while the widespread use of terms such as a 'wave of migrants' or the 'mass influx' of migrants triggered a sense of threat (Sobczak-Szelc et al. 2023). This was accompanied by the portrayal of migrants as a 'suitable enemy', alongside actions to criminalize migration and the adoption of a 'closed door' policy (Klaus 2017). At the same time, migration from ethnically similar countries was supported (Gruszczak 2022). The Polish government's Sustainable Development Strategy 2020–30 noted that 'solving demographic problems and labour market needs solely by immigration of groups that are religiously and culturally different may in the long run exceed potential benefits and threaten the cohesion of social structures' (Ministry of Funds and Regional Policy 2017).

In the international arena, a sign of de-democratization was Poland's rejection of the so-called Global Compact on Refugees, a framework document adopted in December 2018 by United Nations (UN) member states, as well as the Global Compact for Safe, Orderly and Regular Migration adopted in Marrakech, Morocco, also in 2018 (Ministry of the Interior and Administration 2018). The Polish government also expressed opposition to the relocation and resettlement programme implemented at the EU level following the 2015 migration crisis, proposing instead a 'flexible solidarity' concept together with other Visegrad Group states. Such solidarity 'should enable member states to decide on specific forms of contribution taking into account their experience and potential. Furthermore, any distribution mechanism should be voluntary' (Kotzur 2016).

Main legal changes as instruments for governing the migration crisis at Poland's external borders

De-democratization is particularly noticeable in legal instruments adopted after 2015. Migrants' fundamental rights, including those of non-voluntary migrants, are guaranteed in international legal instruments addressing human rights protection that are binding on Poland, as well as in the Polish Constitution. The most important provisions from the point of view of the subject matter analysed here include:

1 Article 18 and 19 of the Charter of Fundamental Rights of the European Union, which guarantee the right to asylum and prohibit collective expulsions;
2 Article 33 of the 1951 Geneva Convention Relating to the Status of Refugees, which enshrines the principle of non-refoulement, i.e. protection against removal in the event of a risk of inhumane treatment;
3 Article 56 of the Constitution of the Republic of Poland of 2 April 1997, which guarantees the right to asylum and international protection.

The selection of legislative acts presented in this chapter, whether adopted or amended, is cross-sectional to show readers the nature of the legislative changes introduced and the ways in which migration law is being shaped.

The first foundational legal instrument that should be noted is the Act on Anti-Terrorist Activities passed on 10 June 2016; its adoption was a response to the terrorist attacks in Brussels, Belgium, and Paris, France. Although this regulation aimed to strengthen security, in effect it permitted actions to be taken against all non-Polish citizens where there is a concern that they may carry out terrorist activities (see Article 9 of the Act on Anti-Terrorist Activities). The catalogue of actors is very broad and in consequence each third-country national may potentially be suspected of such activities (Klaus 2020). Without questioning the validity of the regulations introduced for the implementation of security policy, they contribute to the public discourse on the perceived harmfulness of migration processes and the threats associated with them. As a result, the human rights framework that should go hand in hand with the reception of third-country nationals gets blurred.

The Regulation of the President of the Republic of Poland of 2 September 2021 introducing a state of emergency in parts of the Podlaskie and Lubelskie provinces has affected the social perception of migration. The adoption of this Act was justified by threats to the security of citizens and public order arising from the situation at the Polish–Belarusian border. Consequently, the Regulation also limited the possibility of implementing certain constitutional rights and freedoms of Polish citizens, such as the organization of and participation in mass events or public assemblies. The next step, justified as actions to strengthen security at the border, was the passing on 29 October 2021 of the Act on the Construction of State Border Security, namely the so-called border fence. Following amendments to the Act on 17 November 2021, Article1(1) made it possible to introduce a temporary ban on being in the border zone in situations of

> having to ensure security and public order in the border zone due to a threat to life or health of persons and to property resulting from crossing

> the Polish border against the law or attempts to do so, or justified risk of commission of other prohibited acts.

Thus, further legislative measures restricting the freedom of movement were introduced.

The most controversial issue in amending migration law was the 'legalization' of pushbacks. The latter may be defined

> as various measures taken by States, sometimes involving third countries or non-State actors, which result in migrants, including asylum seekers, being summarily forced back, without an individual assessment of their human rights protection needs, to the country or territory, or to sea, whether it be territorial waters or international waters, from where they attempted to cross or crossed an international border.
>
> (González Morales 2021, 4)

On 20 August 2021, the Polish government passed a Regulation that allowed the immediate return of migrants with unregulated status to the national border. Human rights activists argued that such a regulation was in contravention to the Polish Constitution (Grześkowiak 2023) and could not be upheld. Consequently, the Act of 14 October 2021 on amending the Foreigners Act and Certain Other Acts came into force, and introduced a provision stipulating that, in the event of an illegal crossing of the Polish border by a third-country national, the Chief Officer of a Border Guard Post 'shall draft a border crossing protocol and shall issue a decision ordering the third-country national to leave the territory of the Republic of Poland' (see Article 1(3)). Grześkowiak notes that this Act introduced a new form of administrative Act previously unknown in the Code of Administrative Procedure (Grześkowiak 2023). Moreover, Article 3 of the Act provided that an application submitted by a third-country national immediately after crossing the border contrary to the law could be left unexamined. In effect, it needs to be stated that the Regulation of 20 August 2021, as well as the subsequent Act, were incompatible with the non-refoulement principle. The non-refoulement principle is recognized as the 'common ground of protection' (Chetail 2014), and states parties to the Geneva Convention are absolutely obliged to respect it. Pursuant to Article 33 of the Convention, protection should be granted to all persons seeking asylum in good faith even if they do not hold any travel documents. Thus, an individual assessment must be carried out in each case concerning an application for protection, and the forced removal of such persons constitutes a violation of the non-refoulement principle as well as the procedural obligations under the Convention relating to granting international protection (Goodwin-Gill and McAdam 2007). There is no doubt that the Regulation entailed a restriction on the right to protection guaranteed under Article 56 of the Constitution. According to the jurisprudence of the Polish Trybunał Konstytucyjny (Constitutional Tribunal – CT), limitations on constitutional rights and freedoms, based on the principle of proportionality under Article 31(3) of the Constitution, may only be introduced by statute (Walczak-Kowalik 2019; see too the Judgment of the CT of 29 September 2009). A Regulation, as an Act of lower rank, therefore does not meet the constitutional requirements for limiting the rights of the individual.

The de-democratic nature of legal instruments adopted in response to the crisis at the Polish–Belarusian border becomes particularly noticeable when compared with Poland's response to the exodus of Ukrainians from their homeland following the outbreak of the war in 2022. According to UN High Commissioner for Refugees (UNHCR) statistics, approximately 5.5 million people fled Ukraine within the first two months of the conflict (Gerlach and Ryndzak 2022). A key turning point allowing the provision of assistance to war refugees was the EU's introduction of temporary protection under Directive 2001/55/EC (Macková et al. 2024). It was an important step, particularly as the Council of the EU decided not to resort to it during the Syrian conflict, and for many years the Directive remained dormant. Poland subsequently implemented a wide-ranging programme of assistance to migrants from Ukraine, the basis of which was provided for in the Act of 12 March 2022 on Assistance to Citizens of Ukraine in Connection with Armed Conflict on the Territory of that Country.

Human rights response: proceedings against Poland before the European courts

The ongoing process of de-democratization in EU law and migration policy has elicited a response from both European and national courts. Key proceedings concerning Poland's alleged violations of the guarantees of the 1953 European Convention on Human Rights (ECHR) continue to be adjudicated before the European Court of Human Rights. In *M.K. and Others* v. *Poland*, the applicant were Russian nationals who had appeared at the border crossing point in Terespol approximately 30 times seeking asylum but were repeatedly refused. The Court held that Poland had violated Article 3 of the ECHR, *inter alia*, due to restriction of access to the asylum procedure and the risk of inhumane and degrading treatment in the event of the applicants being removed to their country of origin. In another judgment, *D.A. and Others* v. *Poland*, the Court reached a similar decision. It held that Article 3 of the ECHR had been violated due to the return of third-country nationals to Belarus, the lack of access to the asylum procedure, and a risk of inhumane treatment in the event of a return to their country of origin, the Syrian Arab Republic. To date, the major case of *R.A. and Others* v. *Poland* remains pending. The complaint was submitted by third-country nationals in the border zone near the village of Usnarz Górny on the Polish–Belarusian border, in respect of whom the Court implemented provisional measures. Despite these measures, these individuals were not given assistance, while arguments on the Polish side were based on the belief that these third-country nationals were subject to Belarusian jurisdiction. At the time of writing, the case was pending before the Grand Chamber.

The proceedings before the Court of Justice of the European Union (CJEU) against Poland were in turn initiated by the European Commission. They were brought under Article 258 of the TFEU as 'infringement proceedings' on the grounds that Poland had failed to meet its obligations under the Treaty. The complaint concerned Poland's refusal to cooperate in the relocation of migrants who had arrived in Italy and Greece during the 2015 migration crisis. Ultimately, the CJEU ruled on 2 April 2020 that Poland had violated its obligations resulting from Council Decision (EU) 2015/1523 of 14 September 2015 establishing provisional measures in the area of international protection for the benefit of Italy and of Greece.

In the context of the migration crisis, Polish national courts in their judgments have also addressed violations relating to the situation at the external border. For example, following the Polish Commissioner for Human Rights' appeal against the Order Regulation no. 1/2023 of the Governor of the Podlaskie Province dated 16 February 2023 concerning the regulations in force in the border zone adjacent to the external national border in the territory of the Podlaskie Province, the Provincial Administrative Court in Białystok declared the measure invalid in its judgement of 13 July 2023. It is worth noting that the activities of the Commissioner's Office were particularly significant in signalling violations of migrants' rights at the border. At the same time, these actions have contributed to real protective outcomes, including interventions resulting in the deportation of third-country nationals (Kosińska 2025).

International organizations have not remained indifferent to the situation in Poland and the anti-migration narration. Notably, the Committee on the Elimination of Racial Discrimination issued recommendations for Poland on combating hate speech and hate crime, while the Human Rights Committee addressed issues such as access to asylum (Mikołajczyk and Jagielski 2022). Polish NGOs have also presented clear messages on Poland's violations of the right to asylum and the principle of non-refoulement (Mikulska 2021; Stowarzyszenie Interwencji Prawnej 2022).

Conclusion

In line with the research thesis advance in this chapter, the process of de-democratization in law and migration policy initiated after 2015 remains ongoing. Notably, Mikołajczyk and Jagielski claimed that an anti-immigration policy does not need to be actively pursued; rather, it may manifest in a country's passive attitude/indifference in the context of protection of migrants' rights and of creating a system of effective protection (Mikołajczyk and Jagielski 2022). It appears that public opinion has become accustomed to so-called non-entrée policies (Grześkowiak 2022) and to framing irregular migration primarily as a 'threat' (Świeca 2024). This was demonstrated by the introduction in March 2025 of a temporary restriction of the right to apply for international protection, the duration and effect of which was extended to May 2026 so far.

Migrants are therefore portrayed in public discourse as posing a threat to the existing public order and security, often without due consideration of the need for an individual analysis of the legal situation of each third-country national entering the country. This narrative also complements actions focused on antagonizing various social groups, which is achieved through the populist use of the figure of the ‘other’ as a threat to the existing cultural order and national identity of the state. The list of entities that fit the definition of the ‘other’ remains broad, and often they are individuals from so-called vulnerable groups, such as LGBT+ persons, Roma, and members of national minorities. Therefore, the de-democratization of migration remains a dangerous tool, potentially contributing not only to the creation of harmful stereotypes but also to discriminatory actions. A low level of education within civil society may further undermine this phenomenon.

At the same time, a systemic shift in attitudes towards migration to the EU can be observed, often described by legal scholars and commentators as characteristic of the post-Cold War period (Caballero-Velez et al. 2024). This shift is facilitated by the growing securitization of migration and the tendency to frame migration policy in the context of problems of individual countries, a phenomenon referred to as de-Europeanization (Klaus 2020), compounded by a crisis of solidarity and the application of ‘flexible solidarity’ (Pacek 2020). In this context, it appears that addressing de-democratization requires action at the EU level, in particular to detect deficiencies in domestic law, assess their incompatibility with EU fundamental rights standards, and strengthen solidarity among member states.

Note

1 This chapter is based on a research project entitled ‘The Ombudsman as a Guarantor of Protection of Fundamental Rights of Migrants’ (no. 2020/39/B/HS5/01424), funded by the National Science Centre in Kraków, Poland.

References

Bodnar, Adam and Agnieszka Grzelak. 2023. “The Polish–Belarusian Crisis and the (Lack) of European Response’, *Białostok Legal Studies* 28(1): 57–86. doi:10.15290/bsp.2023.28.01.04.

Caballero-Velez, Diego, Magge Lee, and Matthew Lights. 2024. ‘Beyond Fortress Europe: Instrumentalised Migration Management in Central and Eastern Europe’. In Mary Bosworth, Katja Franko, Maggy Lee, and Rimple Mehta (eds), *Handbook on Border Criminology*. Cheltenham: Edward Elgar Publishing, pp. 155–170.

Chetail, Vincent. 2014. ‘Are Refugee Rights Human Rights? An Unorthodox Questioning of the Relations between Refugee Law and Human Rights Law’. In Ruth Rubio-Marin (ed.), *Human Rights and Immigration*. Oxford: Oxford University Press, pp. 19–72.

Costello, Cathryn. 2016. *The Human Rights of Migrants and Refugees in European Law*. Oxford: Oxford University Press.

Dickson, Rachael. 2022. *Migration Law, Policy and Human Rights*. London and New York: Routledge.

Dynia, Elżbieta. 2018. 'Unia Europejska jako wspólnota wartości'. In Ewelina Cała-Wacinkiewicz and Jerzy Menkes (eds), *Wspólne wartości prawa międzynarodowego, europejskiego i krajowego*. Warsaw: Wydawnictwo C.H. Beck, pp. 213–225.

Gerlach, Iryna and Olha Ryndzak. 2022. 'Ukrainian Migration Crisis Caused by the War'. *Studia Europejskie* (*Studies in European Affairs*) 26(2): 217–229. doi:10.33067/SE.2.2022.2.

Gonzales Morales, Felipe. 2021. 'Report on the Means to Address the Human Rights Impact of Pushbacks of Migrants on Land and at Sea'. Report of the Special Rapporteur on the Human Rights of Migrants, 47th Session of the Human Rights Council, 21 June–9 July, UN doc. A/HRC/47/30. https://docs.un.org/en/A/HRC/47/30 (accessed 25 September 2025).

Goodwin-Gill, Guy S. and Jane McAdam. 2007. *The Refugee in International Law*. Oxford: Oxford University Press.

Gruszczak, Artur. 2022. 'The Problem of Otherness: Poland's Immigration Policy and the Virtues of Parochialism'. *Studia Europejskie* (*Studies in European Affairs*) 26(2): 107–122. doi:10.33067/SE.2.2022.7.

Grześkowiak, Maciej. 2023. 'The "Guardian of the Treaties" is No More? The European Commission and the 2021 Humanitarian Crisis on Poland–Belarus Border'. *Refugee Survey Quaterly* 42(1): 81–102. doi:10.1093/rsq/hdac025.

Klaus, Witold. 2020. "Between Closing Borders to Refugees and Welcoming Ukrainian Workers'. In Elżbieta M. Goździak, Izabella Main, and Brigitte Suter (eds), *Europe and the Refugee Response: A Crisis of Values?*London and New York: Routledge, pp. 74–90.

Klaus, Witold. 2017. 'Security First: New Right-Wing Government in Poland and its Policy Towards Immigrants and Refugees'. *Surveillance and Society* 15(3/4): 523–528. doi:10.24908/SS.V15I3/4.6627.

Kosińska, Anna. 2025. 'The Ombudsman's Role in Protecting the Rights of Refugees and Irregular Migrants: Poland's Experience in Comparison to Sweden and Greece Law and Practice'. *Review of European and Comparative Law* 62(3): 1–20.

Kotzur, Markus. 2016. *Flexible Solidarity – Effective Solidarity?* (Blog). Flexible solidarity – effective solidarity? - Völkerrechtsblog (accessed 25 September 2025).

Macková, Lucie, Agnieszka Zogata-Kusz, Ondřej Filipec, and Nikola Medová. 2024. 'Temporary Protection for Ukrainian Refugees in the Czech Republic and Poland'. *Nationalities Papers: The Journal of Nationalism and Ethnicity* (Online), 1–20. doi:10.1017/nps.2024.61.

Mikołajczyk, Barbara and Mariusz Jagielski. 2022. "'Good Change' and Migration Policy in Poland." In Vladislava Stoyanova and Stijn Smet (eds), *Migrants' Rights, Populism and Legal Resilience in Europe*. Cambridge: Cambridge University Press, pp. 23–258.

Mikulska, Anna. 2021. 'Każda noc to perspektywa kolejnych ofiar'. *Grupa Granica opublikowała raport o kryzysie humanitarnym*. Raport Grupy Granica: każda noc to persp ektywa kolejnych ofiar OKO.press - OKO.press (accessed 22 September 2025).

Ministerstwo Spraw Wewnętrznych i Administracji (Ministry of the Interior and Administration). 2018. *Polska nie wyraziła poparcia dla Globalnego Paktu ws. Uchodźców*. Warsaw: Ministerstwo Spraw Wewnętrznych i Administracji. Polska nie wyraziła poparcia dla Globalnego Paktu ws. Uchodźców - Ministerstwo Spraw Wewnętrznych i Administracji - Portal Gov.pl (accessed 22 September 2025).

Okólski, Marek. 2012. 'Transition from Emigration to Immigration. Is It the Destiny of Modern European Countries?' In Marek Okólski (ed.), *European Immigration: Trends, Structures and Policy Implications.* Amsterdam: Amsterdam University Press, pp. 23–44.

Pacek, Małgorzata. 2020. 'Polish Migration Policy in the Context of the Migration Crisis'. *Studia Europejskie* (*Studies in European Affairs*) 24(3): 85–107.

Departament Analiz i Polityki Migracyjnej MSWiA. 2019. *Polityka Migracyjna Polski: Projekt z dnia 10 czerwca 2019 r.* Warsaw: Departament Analiz i Polityki Migracyjnej MSWiA. https://interwencjaprawna.pl/wp-content/uploads/2019/06/Polityka-migracyjna-Polski-wersja-ostateczna.pdf (accessed 22 September 2025).

Stowarzyszenie Interwencji Prawnej. 2022. *Wywózki (push-backi) są niehumanitarne, niezgodne z prawem i opierają się na nielegalnym rozporządzeniu*, 31 March. Wywózki (push-backi) są niehumanitarne, niezgodne z prawem i opierają się na nielegalnym rozporządzeniu - Stowarzyszenie Interwencji Prawnej (accessed 22 September 2025).

Sobczak-Szelc, Karolina, Marta Pachocka, Konrad Pędziwiatr, Justyna Szałańska, and Monika Szulecka. 2023. *From Reception to Integration of Asylum Seekers and Refugees in Poland.* London and New York: Routledge.

Ministerstwo Funduszy i Polityki Regionalnej (Ministry of Funds and Regional Policy). 2017. *Strategy for Responsible Development until 2020 (with a Perspective to 2030).* Warsaw: Ministerstwo Funduszy i Polityki Regionalnej. https://www.gov.pl/web/fundusze-regiony/informacje-o-strategii-na-rzecz-odpowiedzialnego-rozwoju (accessed 25 September 2025).

Szulecka. Monika. 2019. 'Border Management and Migration Controls in Poland'. Global Migration: Consequences and Responses. Working Paper 2019/24, August. https://respondmigration.com/wp-blog?offset=1573543355904.

Świeca, Karolina. 2024. 'The Role of the State Towards External Migration in the Aspect of Security Analysis of the Republic of Poland'. *Annales Universitatis Maria Curie-Skłodowska Lublin Polonia* 71(1): 145–154. doi:10.17951/g.2024.71.1.145-154.

Walczak-Kowalik, Beata. 2019. 'Bezpieczeństwo publiczne a prawa i wolności jednostki'. In Daria Bieńskowska and Ryszard Kozłowski (eds), *Prawa człowieka i ludzkie bezpieczeństwo. Osiągnięcia i wyzwania w 70. Rocznicę ogłoszenia Powszechnej Deklaracji Praw Człowieka.* Warsaw: Wydawnictwo C.H. Beck, pp. 109–120.

Primary Legal Sources

Act of 10 June 2016 on Anti-Terrorist Activities, *Dziennik Ustaw* (*Journal of Laws*) 2025, item 194, consolidated text of 14 February 2025.

Act of 29 October 2021 on Construction of State Border Security, *Dziennik Ustaw* (*Journal of Laws*) 2023, item 1390, consolidated text of 21 July 2023.

Act of 14 October 2021 on amending the Foreigners Act and Certain Other Acts, *Dziennik Ustaw* (*Journal of Laws*) 2021, item 1918, consolidated text of 25 October 2021.

Act of 17 November 2021 on amending the Act on the Protection of the State Border and Certain Other Acts, *Dziennik Ustaw* (*Journal of Laws*) 2021, item 2191, consolidated text of 30 November 2021.

Act of 12 March 2022 on Assistance to Ukrainian Citizens in Connection with the Armed Conflict on the Territory of the Country, *Dziennik Ustaw* (*Journal of Laws*) 2025, item 337, consolidated text of 18 March 2025.

Charter of Fundamental Rights of the European Union, OJ C 202, 7 June 2016, p. 389–407.

Constitution of the Republic of Poland of 2 April 1997, *Dziennik Ustaw* (*Journal of Laws*) 1997 no. 78, item 483 as amended.

Convention for the Protection of Human Rights and Fundamental Freedoms as amended by Protocols No. 13, 5, and 8 and supplemented by Protocol No. 2, Rome, 4 November 1950, ETS No. 5.

Convention Relating to the Status of Refugees, Geneva, 28 July 1951, UNTS vol. 189, p. 137.

Council Decision (EU) 2015/1523 *of 14 September 2015 establishing provisional measures in the area of international protection for the benefit of Italy and Greece*, OJ EU L 239 of 15 September 2015, p. 246.

R.A. and Others v. *Poland*, application no. 42120/21, European Court of Human Rights.

D.A. and Others v. *Poland*, application no. 51246/17, judgment of the European Court of Human Rights.

Judgment of the Constitutional Tribunal of 29 September 2009, SK 52/05, OTK-A 2008, no. 7, item 125.

Judgment of the Court of Justice of 2 April 2020. European Commission v. *Poland*, C 715/17, ECLI:EU:C:2020:257.

Judgment of the Provincial Administrative Court in Białystok of 13 July 2023, II SA/Bk 365/23.

M.K. and Others v. *Poland*, application nos 40503/17, 42902/17, and 43643/17, judgment of the European Court of Human Rights.

Order Regulation of the Governor of the Podlaskie Province No. 1/2023 of 16 February 2023 on the rules of order in force in the border zone adjacent to the external state border in the Podlaskie Province. https://edziennik.bialystok.uw.gov.pl/WDU_B/2023/934/oryginal/akt.pdf (accessed 22 September 2025).

Proposal for a Regulation of the European Parliament and of the Council Addressing Situations of Instrumentalisation in the Field of Migration and Asylum, COM/2021/890 final.

Protocol Integrating the Schengen Acquis into the Framework of the European Union; Treaty of Amsterdam Amending the Treaty on European Union, the Treaties Establishing the European Communities and Certain Related Acts, OJ C 340, 10 November 1997, p. S1–S6.

Regulation (EU) 2024/1359 of the European Parliament and of the Council of 14 May 2024 addressing situations of crisis and force majeure in the field of migration and asylum and amending Regulation (EU) 2021/1147, OJ L, 22 May 2024, p. 1-24.

Regulation of the Council of Ministers of 27 March 2025 on the temporary limitation of the right to submit requests for international protection, Dziennik Ustaw (*Journal of Laws*) 2025, item 390, consolidated text of 27 March 2025.

Regulation of the Minister of the Interior and Administration of 20 August 2021 amending the Regulation on temporary suspension or restriction of border traffic at certain border crossing points, Dziennik Ustaw (*Journal of Laws*) 2021, item 1536, consolidated text of 20 August 2021.

Regulation of the President of the Republic of Poland on 2 September 2021 on introducing the state of emergency in the area of part of the Podlaskie Province and part

of the Lubelskie Province, Dziennik Ustaw (*Journal of Laws*) 2021, item 1612, consolidated text of 2 September 2021.
Treaty on European Union, consolidated version, OJ C 202, 7 June 2016, p. 13–46.
Treaty on the Functioning of the European Union, consolidated version, OJ C 202, 7 June 2016, p. 47–199.

11 De-democratization Processes in Local Government

Małgorzata Kmak

Introduction

Processes of de-democratization in local government constitute a significant area of scholarly research, particularly in the context of the dynamic political and systemic changes that have taken place in Poland over the past decade. The period of Zjednoczona Prawica (United Right) governance from 2015 to 2023 was marked by phenomena such as the centralization of power and the restriction of the autonomy of local government units, raising fundamental questions regarding the effective implementation of the constitutional principle of decentralization and the democratic functions of local government.

The chapter aims to identify and critically analyse processes of de-democratization in Polish local government. The research hypothesis posits that from 2015 to 2023 there was a systematic weakening of local self-governance, manifested, *inter alia*, through the transfer of competences and financial resources to central government entities, increased dependence of local governments on partisan instruments, and limitations on local communities' participation in decision-making processes. The objective of the research is to identify the mechanisms, manifestations, and consequences of the de-democratization of local government in Poland from 2015 to 2023. The analysis focuses on four key dimensions. First, the centralization of competences, particularly evident in the areas of water resource management, spatial policy, and the education system; second, the reduction of civic participation and the weakening of the agency of local communities in shaping public policy; third, the growth of partisan mechanisms in the process of allocating financial resources, which curtails the independence of local governments; and fourth, the effects of a lack of financial transparency, leading to the destabilization of the functioning of local government units and a decline in public trust.

Decentralization of local government: an example of disintegration

The principle of decentralization, set out in Article 15 of the Konstytucja Rzeczypospolitej Polskiej z dnia 2 kwietnia 1997 r. (Constitution of the

DOI: 10.4324/9781042002030-12

Republic of Poland of 2 April 1997), constitutes a fundamental pillar of the state's territorial structure. According to Article 15,

> the territorial structure of the Republic of Poland shall ensure the decentralization of public power. The basic territorial division of the state shall be determined by statute, allowing for the social, economic, and cultural ties which ensure to the territorial units the capacity to perform their public duties.

In Chapter VII, which is crucial to the system of local government, the Constitution stipulates that 'local government shall perform public tasks not reserved by the Constitution or statutes to the organs of other public authorities' (Constitution of the Republic of Poland 1997, Art. 163). In this way, the Constitution provides for an organizational structure of the state based on the dispersal of competences and the autonomy of local governments, which is conducive to the effective management of local affairs and enhances civic participation (cf. Dolnicki 2016, 24–25).

The concept of decentralization refers to the process of transferring not only tasks, competences, and financial resources, but also responsibility from higher to lower levels of public authority, with the aim of broadening their powers and autonomy. Local government is part of the executive branch and employs administrative measures in its activities. It operates on the basis of statutes and is subject to supervision by state executive authorities (Skrzydło 2004, 225). The principle of decentralization of public power, as a practical implementation of the principle of subsidiarity, strengthens the rights of citizens and their communities, paving the way for a rational division of public tasks between the state apparatus and local government (Izdebski 2007, 64). This is not a one-off undertaking, but a process aimed at increasing the efficiency of administration, tailoring decisions to local needs, and strengthening local democracy. Decentralization is therefore a permanent feature of the political culture of a democratic state (Judgment of the Constitutional Tribunal 2003). The actions undertaken by the United Right government during the period 2015–23 at times constrained the decentralization processes.

The changes introduced by the Water Law Act of 20 July 2017 provide an example of the centralization of competences previously exercised by local governments. Not all of these changes can be attributed to the transposition of European Union legislation (Kruś 2019, 615). A significant proportion reflect the intentions of the Polish legislator (Kruś 2019, 616). An example is the establishment of the State Water Holding 'Polish Waters', which functions as a body fully subordinate to the minister responsible for water management within the central government administration. Such a solution should be interpreted as a manifestation of actions that violate the principle of decentralization of local government. This entity has taken over a substantial part of the previous duties and competences of local government units.

'Polish Waters' manages water resources at the national level, acting as a steward of the entire territory of the state, rather than of its constituent components. It has assumed the competences of both the National Water Management Authority (the central organizational unit for national water management) and the seven regional water management boards, as well as those of previously exercised by local government units. This phenomenon should be viewed as an example of centralization within the water management system. Furthermore, the Water Law Act has limited the competences of the voivodeship marshals (the elected heads of regional self-government units at the provincial level), who, prior to the amendment, were responsible for issuing water permits and for managing the programming, planning, and supervision of water treatment facilities. As a result of the statutory changes, the marshals have been deprived of their authority in decisions concerning, among other things, ensuring the integrity and stability of flood embankments (Kruś 2019, 623). Such a reduction in the competences of local authorities is a symptom of the violation of the principle of decentralization.

Another manifestation of centralization in the area of water law, this time of a financial nature, is reflected in the changes that have deprived voivodeship self-governments of part of their financial resources in favour of central government bodies. Fees for water services, including environmental charges related to the discharge of rainwater and meltwater, which previously constituted the revenues of voivodeship self-governments prior to the amendment of the Water Law Act, are now transferred directly to the State Water Holding 'Polish Waters' (Water Law 2017, Art. 255).

The centralization of duties and competences has also affected the reporting process. The water management boards operating in individual regions, while carrying out the tasks of 'Polish Waters', are responsible, *inter alia*, for analysing reports on the implementation of the 'National Programme for Municipal Wastewater Treatment', a programme approved by the Polish Council of Ministers. In the event that substantive or formal deficiencies are identified, the municipalities are obliged by 'Polish Waters' to submit revised or supplementary reports. Prior to these changes, such documentation was submitted to the voivodeship marshals (Kruś 2019, 624). Similarly, until 2017, supervision of water companies' associations was the responsibility of the voivodeship marshals. These changes indicate a systematic reduction of the role of voivodeship self-governments in the management of water resources.

A further indication of the violation of the decentralization principle in local government is the changes made in 2023 to the Programme of Actions to Reduce Water Pollution by Nitrates from Agricultural Sources and to Prevent Further Pollution by the Polish Council of Ministers. In accordance with the Act of 20 July 2017 – the Water Law – the minister responsible for water management was obliged to develop a programme aimed primarily at limiting water pollution caused by the fertilization of agricultural land with natural fertilizers (Water Law 2017, Art. 103(1)). Thereafter, this programme was adopted in the form of a regulation by the Council of Ministers and was applied uniformly across the country. Previously, similar programmes were issued by the directors of regional water management boards in the form of regulations applicable to specific areas. In addition to nationwide environmental monitoring to assess the programme's effectiveness, supervision of its implementation is exercised by the minister responsible for water management, representing the central administration (Water Law 2017, Art. 356).

As a result of the amendments to the Water Law Act, the competences and duties previously exercised by local government administration bodies have been transferred to 'Polish Waters'. Despite the formal preservation of a decentralized structure, the real shift of power and responsibility to an entity subordinate to the central administration significantly curtails the autonomy and agency of local government units. This phenomenon should be interpreted as a manifestation of a de-democratization process within the sphere of local government, which permanently and systematically weakens the role of local authorities by concentrating executive power at the central level.

Another significant manifestation of the weakening position of local government in Poland is the centralizing tendency observed in the area of spatial planning, which is of crucial importance from the perspective of self-governance. An example of such interference is the amendment to the Act of 20 May 2016 on Investments in Wind Power Plants. The legislature did not provide for the transfer of powers to local government units in relation to decisions concerning the location of such investments within municipal territories.

On 13 March 2023, the President of the Republic of Poland signed an Act amending the Wind Energy Investments Act and certain other legal acts. The amendment maintained the minimum distance between wind power plants and residential buildings at 700 metres (retaining the provision set out in Article 4 of the Wind Energy Investments Act of 20 May 2016). This decision was taken despite opposition from industry representatives, producers, and a significant number of local governments, which had called for the distance to be reduced to 500 metres. The original government bill had provided for reducing the distance to 500 metres; however, during the proceedings of the parliamentary Committee for Energy, an amendment was tabled, initiated by members of the Prawo i Sprawiedliwość (Law and Justice Party), increasing the distance to 700 metres. The amendment was subsequently accepted by the Committee and the Sejm (Assembly, the lower house of the Polish parliament) (TVN24 Biznes 2023).

Prior to the adoption of the Act in question, representatives of local governments addressed an appeal to the prime minister and members of parliament, drawing attention to the potential threats arising from the proposed legislative solutions.

> It is we, the local authorities, who are closest to the citizens and best understand their expectations and the social mood towards this type of

> investment. Therefore, we do not understand why the central government wants to impose rules that deprive us of the ability to decide for ourselves … By changing the minimum distance from 500 metres to 700 metres, you will destroy a compromise that has been worked on for nearly three years.
>
> (Association of Polish Cities 2023)

The appeal emphasized that the need to readapt to the new requirements introduced by the amendment to the Act would entail significant investments of time and financial resources.

Consultations constitute an important democratic mechanism through which citizens express their collective preferences regarding state policy (Tilly 1997, 25). The appeal was signed by a total of 15 local government organizations, representing various levels and communities of local government. Despite the emphasis on fundamental principles of local government, such as constitutional independence and autonomy in the management of local affairs, the legislature decided to adopt the bill in its original wording and did not take the proposed changes into account. The cases described illustrate the phenomenon of the marginalization of the role of local governments in key decisions concerning local spatial policy, constituting a significant constraint on the principles of decentralization and public participation in the Polish local government system.

Limiting the autonomy of local governments in the implementation of local educational policy

Another key area of activity for local government units is their participation in shaping and implementing the state's educational policy. Local governments perform an important coordinating function in the operation of educational institutions, adapting their activities to the diverse needs of local communities. The legislature has equipped local governments with a range of legal instruments that enable the effective management of this area (Educational Law 2016, Art. 11, Art. 29).

In 2009, local government units gained the right to independently shape the network of schools in their area, which was intended to ensure universal access to education for all children residing in a given district. A significant change at that time was the abolition of the requirement to obtain a positive opinion from the education superintendent, representing the central government administration, on matters of modifying the school network (Ministry of National Education 2024). This opinion became non-binding, which underscored the autonomy of local governments in implementing local educational policy.

In 2015, the situation changed with the reinstatement of the requirement to obtain a binding opinion from the education superintendent in decisions concerning the school network (Educational Law 2016, Art. 89 § 3). From a legal perspective, this grants the superintendent a de facto right of veto over key decisions of local government, which in practice constitutes an interference by a central government administrative body in a sphere of competence traditionally assigned to the local community (Sześciło 2018, 12). As Dawid Sześciło notes, such a change effectively precludes local public debate on the organization of the school network, transferring decision-making to the central level (Sześciło 2018, 12). The obligation to obtain a positive opinion from the education superintendent applies, *inter alia*, to the establishment of a public school network plan by the municipality, the founding of public schools or institutions by entities other than local governments, and the liquidation of educational units run by local governments. The lack of precise criteria for the superintendent's decisions in these matters significantly restricts the independence and autonomy of local government units in their own affairs, thereby weakening the principle of decentralization of public authority (Pietrasik 2024, 35).

On 13 January 2022, the Sejm of the Republic of Poland passed an amendment to the Educational Law Act and other legal Acts. The changes once again sparked a debate on the role and powers of the education superintendent. The aforementioned amendment establishes the education superintendent as a supervisory body over local government units, implying a restriction of their independence in carrying out their own tasks (Supreme Administrative Court 2022), while at the same time not providing for any financial compensation for the extension of the superintendent's powers in the area of liquidating schools and educational institutions. According to experts, such a solution is in conflict with Article 171 of the Constitution of the Republic of Poland (Frankiewicz 2022, 3).

The scope of supervisory powers granted to the education superintendent interferes with the performance of the local government's own tasks, particularly in the sphere of appointing and dismissing the heads of the municipality's organizational units and decisions concerning the structure of the public school network within the territory of a given unit. Such practice departs from the constitutionally permissible standard of supervision, which is limited to that of legal compliance. Article 171 § 2 of the Constitution of the Republic of Poland unequivocally states that supervision over local government units should be exercised by the prime minister, voivodes and, in financial matters, the Najwyższa Izba Kontroli (Supreme Audit Office – SAO). The education superintendent is not included in this rigorously defined catalogue; consequently, there is no basis for the exercise of supervisory powers by this body, particularly so as it does not bear responsibility for the decisions made in this regard.

In the opinion of Ryszard Piotrowski, an expert in constitutional law in Poland, the provisions of the amendment to the Educational Law Act violate the principle of the independence of local government, which reflects the principle of subsidiarity set out in the Preamble to the Constitution of the Republic of Poland (Local Government and State Administration

Committee 2022, 3). In the expert's view, they also violate other fundamental principles of the rule of law and the decentralization of public authority specified, *inter alia*, in Articles 15 and 166 of the Constitution of the Republic of Poland, and undermine citizens' trust in state bodies and the legal order established by them (Local Government and State Administration Committee 2022, 3). A lack of respect for the principle of subsidiarity limits citizens' participation in a community-based public debate that is independent of state bodies.

As early as the legislative process for the amendment in 2021, the Commissioner for Human Rights pointed to the risk of violating self-governance and the principle of decentralization of public authority, as well as the possibility of restricting the right to education guaranteed under Article 70 of the Constitution of the Republic of Poland. He emphasized that the decisive role of the education superintendent in giving opinions on the activities of social organizations and associations operating in schools could weaken parental involvement in school life, and would contravene the model of social participation declared by the public authorities. The 2022 amendment to the Educational Law expanded the powers of the education superintendent, thereby limiting the independence of local governments and violating the constitutional principles of decentralization and subsidiarity. This change can be seen as weakening local dialogue and citizen participation in school life.

The restriction of the right to self-government, exemplified by the centralization of education management

The 2016 education system reform significantly restructured the organization of schooling, directly affecting the scope and form of tasks carried out by local government units (Sześciło 2018, 14). Although local governments retained formal responsibility, the legislative process was characterized by a significant deficit in their participation in shaping the reform's principles, which may be interpreted as a manifestation of de-democratizing mechanisms. Education, as one of the most crucial areas of local government activity, was reshaped without due consideration of their substantive input or meaningful involvement in developing the changes (Sześciło 2018, 14).

As early as October 2016, the government's draft amendment to the Educational Law Act was met with a negative opinion from the Joint Commission of the Government and Local Government, which stressed the need to analyse the justification for many of the planned changes, such as the lack of substantive grounds for the closure of *gimnazja* (middle schools) and the reintroduction of an eight-year primary school system (Joint Commission of the Government and Local Government 2016). In August 2016, key local government organizations operating within the Commission expressed their joint opposition to the changes proposed by the Ministry of National Education, arguing that no reliable analyses, reports, or expert opinions had been presented to confirm the need for restructuring the middle school system.

They emphasized that international studies, such as the Programme for International Student Assessment (PISA) conducted under the auspices of the Organisation for Economic Co-operation and Development (OECD), demonstrated a high level of achievement among Polish lower secondary pupils and significant progress in educational outcomes at this stage.

> We believe there are no serious arguments for this change. No analyses, reports, or expert opinions have been presented to justify the need to close the middle schools … The results of Polish 15-year-olds place them among the top pupils in Europe and the rest of the world. Other studies, conducted between 2008 and 2013 on safety in middle schools with the participation of 31,000 respondents (21,500 pupils and 9,500 parents), also confirm a positive assessment in this regard.
>
> (Association of Rural Municipalities of the Republic of Poland 2016)

The arguments raised by local government representatives were not taken into account. Critical comments made during the legislative process were not incorporated into the draft Act. Attempts to organize a public hearing on the draft Act in the Sejm, aimed at facilitating a broader parliamentary debate, were rejected by the parliamentary committees. In response to this lack of dialogue, local government organizations and non-governmental entities active in the field of education took the initiative to organize a civic public hearing; however, representatives of the Ministry of National Education failed to attend (Sześciło 2018, 15). Following the publication of the draft Act, both the Ombudsman and local government bodies began to receive complaints concerning troubling aspects of the proposed changes. The implementation of the newly enacted regulations posed a serious organizational and technical challenge for local governments. The Act was adopted on 14 December 2016, and was implemented in Polish schools in 2017 (Rondalska 2017, 301).

According to data obtained from local government units, the Association of Polish Cities estimated that the additional costs associated with the introduction of the new education system amounted to over 1 billion złoty in 2017, significantly exceeding the funds allocated for this purpose in the state budget (Association of Polish Cities 2025, 2–3). The most significant expenditures included the adaptation of school infrastructure and severance payments for dismissed teachers. In a letter addressed to Prime Minister Mateusz Morawiecki dated 26 January 2018, the President of the Association of Polish Cities, Zygmunt Frankiewicz, pointed to the underestimation of the reform's costs, which, he stressed, was creating serious problems for pupils, parents, and teachers, and was imposing significant financial burdens on local governments that were almost entirely uncompensated in practice (Association of Polish Cities 2018). In the letter to the prime minister, he observed that the funds declared by the Ministry of National Education to finance the reform, estimated at 53 billion złoty and sourced from the reserve of the educational part of the general subsidy, were in fact funds already allocated to local governments for carrying out routine educational tasks. This reserve, which is solidarity-based in nature, is part of the general subsidy and does not constitute additional state budget funding, thereby limiting the scope for increasing external financing (Association of Polish Cities 2018).

Furthermore, an analysis by the SAO indicates that expenditure by all local government units on educational tasks between 1 January 2017 and 30 September 2021 totalled over 382 billion złoty, accounting for 29.8% of total local government expenditure during that period (SAO 2022, 7). These figures illustrate the scale and complexity of the financial burdens associated with the reform that were transferred to local government units, highlighting the underestimation of financial needs in the implementation process.

The lack of consistent and clear communication from government bodies, as well as the ambiguity of the information provided, intensified the information chaos, making it difficult for both teachers and local governments to prepare effectively for the reform's implementation and to adapt to the new organizational conditions. Sławomir Broniarz, president of the Polish Teachers' Union, stated at a press conference on 9 October 2017 that, as a result of the reform, 6,500 teachers had lost their jobs, while over 18,500 had been working on reduced-hour contracts, in multiple institutions, or had been placed on inactive status (Portalsamorządowy 2017). At the same time, however, the Ministry of National Education claimed that 10,000 new teaching positions had been created (Radwan 2017).

The subordination of schools to the central administration and the reduction of the role of local authorities in the field of education to an almost exclusively financing function constitute a significant restriction of the right to self-government. The changes introduced in the Educational Law Act have led to a clear weakening of the self-governance of local educational communities and a limitation of the competences of local governments, without adequate consideration of local educational needs.

The rise of partisanship through the increased financial dependence of local governments on earmarked grants from the central administration

An analysis of the functioning of local government in Poland between 2015 and 2023 reveals a progressive process of de-democratization, which significantly affects the principle of decentralization and the autonomy of local government units. From the beginning of this period, representatives of local governments and experts highlighted the gradual weakening of the position of local authorities. Despite denials from the central government, which pointed to the supposed strengthening of local self-governance, there was a lack of reliable indicators allowing for an unequivocal assessment of these processes (Bendyk 2024, 5).

In response, a team of experts at the non-governmental organization, the Fundacja im. Stefana Batorego (Stefan Batory Foundation), including Marta

Lackowska, Radomir Matczak, Paweł Swianiewicz, Dawid Sześciło, and Katarzyna Wojnar, created the Local Government Index, a tool measuring the level of local autonomy in Poland in the context of relations between central and local government. The Index analyses three key dimensions: the financial and functional capacity; the political strength; and the institutional strength of local governments. The research findings indicate a systematic decline in the value of the Local Government Index during the period of United Right governance, from 73.58 points in 2014, to 55.74 points in 2021, to 51.91 points in 2022, and to 47.79 points in 2023 (Lackowska et al. 2024). The value of the indicator is interpreted as a telling assessment of the relationship between central and local government, confirming a sustained process of recentralization (Lackowska et al. 2024) and de-democratization. It may be assumed that one of the factors affecting the financial and functional capacity of local governments is their growing dependence on earmarked grants allocated by the central administration.

Systematic and unfavourable changes were observed in the revenue structure of local government unit budgets from 2015 to 2023. These were reflected in a declining share of own-source revenues in favour of the growing importance of earmarked grants, over which local governments had limited control. This shift facilitated the political distortion of resource allocation, as local governments increasingly acted as implementers of government policies, leading to an erosion of their independence and a rise in the level of partisanship in local management (cf. Olejnik and Grygo 2024).

An example of the politicization of decision-making processes is the functioning of the Local Government Road Fund established in 2018 (later renamed the Government Road Construction Fund), which was intended to support infrastructure investments at the local level. Funds were distributed on the basis of general criteria, including the income level of the local government unit, and their allocation was controlled by a commission appointed by the voivode (see the Act on the Government Road Construction Fund 2018, Art. 24), which encouraged subjective assessments that took political preferences into account. According to Paweł Swianiewicz, there is evidence to suggest that the political orientation of local authorities influenced decisions regarding the allocation of funds under this programme (Swianiewicz 2020, 2). This gave rise to what he calls *skrzywienie polityczne* (political bias), whereby a grant is used as a tool to enhance the electoral prospects of a political group, as well as to reward those units where the ruling group has significant support (Swianiewicz 2020, 2). At the same time, the grant becomes a tool for discriminating against units where the opposition has support. Analyses have shown that the greatest support was received by local governments affiliated with the ruling Law and Justice Party, while more than half of all the opposition-led municipalities received no support (Swianiewicz 2020). Although the phenomenon of using grants to support ruling parties also exists in other countries, in Poland its scale was significantly more pronounced during the period 2015–20 (cf. Czepil 2022, 76).

Similar mechanisms can be observed in the operation of the Government Fund for Local Investments, a programme initiated by the government using non-repayable funds from sources such as the COVID-19 Counteracting Fund. While the first tranche of funding was distributed according to a top-down algorithm, subsequent tranches were made dependent on the decisions of the Commission for the Support of Local Government Units, thereby increasing the risk of partisan allocation (Springer 2023, 35). Municipalities governed by leaders recommended by the Law and Justice Party received significantly higher rates of support per capita compared to neutral or opposition-affiliated municipalities (Springer 2023, 35).

An analysis of the distribution of funds from the second tranche, disbursed to municipalities in December 2020, reveals a clear correlation between the political alignment of local authorities and the scale of support received. The average grant per capita in municipalities governed by Law and Justice Party representatives amounted to 253 złoty, compared with 134 złoty in politically neutral municipalities, 60 złoty in municipalities opposed to the ruling party, and a mere 25 złoty in municipalities associated with authorities from the the Platforma Obywatelska (Civic Coalition) (Flis and Swianiewicz 2021, 5). For the country as a whole, the average grant amounted to 83 złoty (Flis and Swianiewicz 2021, 5). Thus, municipalities governed by leaders affiliated with the Law and Justice Party received support at approximately three times the national average, whereas municipalities associated with the Civic Coalition received support at around one-third of that level, with an overall tenfold disparity in per capita allocations (Flis and Swianiewicz 2021, 5). Jacek Flis and Paweł Swianiewicz define such a significant divergance from the national average in per capita grant allocation – dependent on who is in power – as the *czynnik 'przegięcia partyjnego'* (partisan skew factor) (Flis and Swianiewicz 2021, 5). The results of their analysis indicate that 86% municipalities governed by the ruling party received support from the fund, whereas only 19% of municipalities associated with the Civic Coalition were granted funding. Furthermore, 44% of politically neutral municipalities and 61% of municipalities in which the Law and Justice Party had lost power received no funds at all (Flis and Swianiewicz 2021, 9). The data presented unequivocally point to the application of partisan criteria in the process of allocating financial resources to local governments.

The legality of the distribution of funds from the Government Fund for Local Investments in 2020 was also questioned by the SAO. In its audit report, the SAO identified three main irregularities. First, excessive support was granted to units planning controversial investment expenditures or to those that had already benefited from investment grants. Second, the imposition of a cap on funding limited the level of support received by the largest cities, such including Kraków, Łódź, Poznań, Szczecin, and Warsaw, as well as counties such as Poznań County. Third, voivodeship-level self-government units were excluded from the distribution of funds (SAO 2024, 14). The audit also revealed that, of the 331 local government units whose revenues during the period 2020–22 were lower than in 2019, as many as 118 received no financial support from this fund, despite having submitted the relevant applications (SAO 2024, 14).

Thus, an analysis of the political allocation of public funds within the Government Fund for Local Investments demonstrates that this instrument was used to consolidate the ruling party's influence at the local level, leading to a reduction in the independence of local government and an increase in partisanship. Such phenomena pose a significant threat to the implementation of the constitutional principle of decentralization and to the democratic character of local government, which further deepens the process of de-democratization and weakens the principle of subsidiarity. Consequently, institutional and financial changes are polarizing the relationship between central and local authorities, limiting citizen participation in decision-making at the local level, and reinforcing partisan dominance within the local government structure. The analysis suggests that the rise of partisanship through the instrumentalization of earmarked grants has contributed significantly to the erosion of local government autonomy, intensifying the processes of de-democratization and recentralization in Poland from 2015 to 2023.

The consequences of limiting the financial transparency of local government activities

Local government units operate within the general legal framework of the state, which often uses them as instruments for implementing its own policies, while simultaneously burdening them with additional responsibilities and restricting their access to financial resources (Skarzyński 2012, 328). This operational model leads to the systematic depletion of assets and the financial independence of local governments. Despite the negative trends affecting the own-source revenues of local government units, no systemic compensatory mechanisms were developed from 2015 to 2023 to safeguard their financial stability against tax changes and economic crises, including the COVID-19 pandemic.

Tax changes in Poland, including the reduction of the Personal Income Tax (PIT) rate from 18% to 17% in 2019 and subsequently to 12% in 2022, adversely affected the revenue base of local government units. These reforms also included the introduction of tax exemptions for young people, large families, and working seniors, as well as the increase of the tax-free allowance to 30,000 złoty under the 'Polish Deal', a major fiscal and socio-economic reform programme introduced by the government led by the Law and Justice Party (Ministry of Finance – National Revenue Administration 2022). Hanna Zdanowska, mayor of Łódź since December 2010, noted in an interview that systemic opacity and a lack of trust between local and central government hinder effective crisis management, particularly in the face of challenges posed by the war in Ukraine and high inflation. Zdanowska emphasized: 'We want to support local communities, but we are not met with understanding, because the government constantly claims that local government budgets are at an all-time high' (Theus 2023).

According to a 2021 report by the SAO, an additional 12 billion złoty was allocated in the state budget for local governments. Of this sum, 8 billion złoty was intended to compensate for losses resulting from tax revenue reductions caused by the 'Polish Deal', while the remaining 4 billion złoty was allocated to water and sewage infrastructure investments (SAO 2024, 14). The distribution of these funds proved to be non-transparent and inconsistent. The criteria applied did not adequately reflect actual needs; for example they relied on a wealth index rather than estimated PIT losses in allocating funds to municipalities. Furthermore, the introduction of minimum and maximum support thresholds discriminated against large metropolitan areas, particularly Warsaw, which was significantly more exposed than other municipalities to a decrease in PIT revenues following the implementation of the 'Polish Deal' programme (SAO 2024, 14).

In 2022, due to the need for additional financial support for local government units, the Ministry of Finance decided to grant them an additional share of the PIT revenue (Act on the Revenues of Local Government Units 2003, Art. 70j). Once again, the distribution was non-proportional; instead, the funds were allocated according to an algorithm whereby the rural municipality of Chojnice received additional support equivalent to 3.8% of its PIT share, whereas the municipality of Przytuły received support equivalent to almost 236% of its PIT share (SAO 2024, 15). In total, in 70 municipalities, the amount of additional support exceeded 100% of their projected PIT revenues (SAO 2024, 15).

Identical mechanisms and irrational distribution criteria were maintained in 2023, when over half of the 14.1 billion złoty in additional funds was distributed on the basis of projected PIT revenues (Act on the Revenues of Local Government Units 2003, Art. 70o § 2(1)). The correction coefficients applied distorted the proportionality of allocations, resulting in significant discrimination against large cities such as Warsaw, Kraków, and Wrocław. Warsaw received additional support equivalent to just 0.8% of its PIT share (SAO 2024, 15). In the case of the municipality of Przytuły, as in the previous year, the planned support was 142 times greater relative to its PIT revenues than that allocated to Warsaw (SAO 2024, 15). In total, 195 municipalities received additional support that was greater than their projected PIT revenues.

The analysis reveals that the distribution criteria were often non-transparent, inconsistent, and discriminatory towards selected local governments. During the COVID-19 pandemic and in the aftermath of the 'Polish Deal', large cities suffered the most, as they were unable to obtain support commensurate with the scale of their lost revenues. The funding caps and differentiation coefficients introduced by the Ministry of Finance resulted in a de facto unjustified restriction of financial support. According to the SAO,

> in 2021, the leadership of the Ministry of Finance, in consultation with the leadership of the Chancellery of the Prime Minister and the Prime Minister himself, established a support limit for municipalities at such a level that only Warsaw would lose a portion of its revenues … As a result of the introduction of these financial caps alone, Warsaw lost over 790 million złoty between 2020 and 2023.
>
> (SAO 2024, 13)

Other large cities, including Kraków, Łódź, Poznań, Szczecin, and Wrocław, also incurred losses.

The growing arbitrariness in the process of financing local government units from 2015 to 2023 significantly curtailed their independence and freedom of action. Grant-based transfers gradually replaced own-source revenues, making local governments dependent on the decisions of central authorities. The criteria for awarding grants were unclear and imprecise, with some decisions being made on a discretionary basis. This lack of transparency in resource allocation led to a significant reduction in the transparency of local government activities, which in turn weakened public sway and the potential for civic participation. Disparities in the level of financial support rarely correlated with the actual needs of local government units, and the preferential treatment of selected units violated the principles of equality and administrative justice. The solutions adopted by central authorities were characterized by their temporary, inconsistent, and discretionary nature (SAO 2024, 10), which introduced further uncertainty and hampered effective financial management at the local level. This policy resulted in the erosion of the strategic autonomy of local governments and impeded the effective delivery of public services. Despite the shortcomings identified by the SAO, the Ministry of Finance has not undertaken any steps to reform the local government revenue system (SAO 2024, 10).

Conclusion

The balance of power between the state and the nation is a key determinant of whether political development is characterized by democratization or de-democratization. An analysis of the functioning of local government in Poland from 2015 to 2023, a period corresponding to the governance of the United Right alliance, reveals a progressive process of de-democratization that has significantly affected the principles of decentralization and the autonomy of local government units. Democratization refers to the dominance of the will of the people, while de-democratization denotes its weakening in favour of the power of the state, which is breaking free from the control of its citizens. During the period under study, a shift of competences and financial resources from local government units to bodies subordinate to the central administration was observed. For instance, legislative changes concerning water management – consolidating control within the State Water

Holding 'Polish Waters' – as well as increased supervision by education superintendents over local education policy resulted in a marked weakening of the independence and decision-making capacity of local authorities.

The process of de-democratization also manifested itself in the restriction of citizen participation in public life and increasing partisanship in the functioning of local governments. Financial mechanisms for supporting local infrastructure, such as the Local Government Road Fund and the Government Fund for Local Investments, were used as political instruments for the preferential allocation of funds, favouring units affiliated with the ruling party. Such practices undermine the democratic principles of equality and administrative justice, and also limit public oversight of local governance. Furthermore, the lack of transparency and consistency in the financing systems for local governments, especially in the context of the effects of the tax changes implemented under the 'Polish Deal', deepened the dependence of local government units on central authority, thereby restricting their strategic autonomy. Under the United Right's governance, local government was not a partner but rather an executor of decisions made at the central level. The role of local government was denigrated, as evidenced by the statement from the head of the Ministry of the Interior and Administration, Mariusz Błaszczak, following the catastrophic windstorm that struck parts of Poland in August 2017: 'You can rely on the state services, especially the fire brigade, but not on local governments' (Mikowski 2017).

During the period 2015–23, the United Right government focused on key areas of local government, such as water management, spatial planning, and education, justifying this with security considerations, the need to regulate local development, and the shaping of public awareness. These actions are part of the de-democratization mechanism described by Charles Tilly, in which the power relationship between the state and its citizens shifts in favour of central state authorities, thereby limiting local government and autonomy. The centralization of powers in key areas of local life can be interpreted as an indicator of a broader process of de-democratization, characterized by the strengthening of state control at the expense of local governments. This leads to a weakening of self-government and a reduction in decentralization, undermining local democracy and the autonomy of citizens in local decision-making. In 2024, the government led by Donald Tusk initiated efforts to reverse reforms that had diminished the competences and financial resources of local governments (Chancellery of the Prime Minister of the Republic of Poland 2024a). The aim of the proposed changes is to restore decision-making authority to the local level, enabling municipalities, counties, and provinces to make relevant decisions directly. In addition, the new regulations are intended to enhance the quality of public services and improve the effectiveness of local government units (Serwis Samorządowy PAP 2024).

References

Bendyk, Edwin. 2024. 'Słowo od Fundacji Batorego'. In Marta Lackowska, Radomir Matczak, Paweł Swianiewicz, Dawid Sześciło, and Katarzyna Wojnar (eds), *Indeks Samorządności 2024: Bilans dekady 2014–2023*. Warsaw: Fundacja im. Stefana Batorego, p. 5. https://www.batory.org.pl/wp-content/uploads/2024/06/Indeks-samorzadnosci_edycja-3.pdf.

Bukowski, Stanisław. 2024. 'NIK potwierdza: Rząd PiS skroił samorządy'. *Wspólnota* 7. https://wspolnota.org.pl/newsletter/nik-potwierdza-rzad-pis-skroil-samorzady.

Czepil, Bartosz. 2022. 'Wykorzystanie II transzy Rządowego Funduszu Inwestycji Lokalnych jako instrument polityki klientelistycznej rządu wobec samorządu w perspektywie doświadczeń z województwa opolskiego'. *Studia Regionalne i Lokalne* 2(88): 74–93. https://studreg.uw.edu.pl/dane/web_sril_files/1850/2022_2_czepil.pdf.

Dolnicki, Bogdan. 2016. *Samorząd terytorialny*. Warsaw: Wolters Kluwer.

Flis, Jarosław and Paweł Swianiewicz. 2021. *Rządowy Fundusz Inwestycji Lokalnych - reguły podziału.*, Warsaw: Fundacja im. Stefana Batorego. https://www.batory.org.pl/wp-content/uploads/2021/01/Rzadowy-Fundusz-Inwestycji-Lokalnych-regu%C5%82y-podzia%C5%82u.pdf.

Frankiewicz, Zygmunt. 2022. 'Wprowadzenie'. In Senate Committee for Local Government and State Administration of the Republic of Poland (ed.), *Materiały i stanowiska eksperckie ws. ustawy z 13 stycznia 2022 r. o zmianie ustawy – Prawo oświatowe i innych*. Warsaw: Komisja Samorządu Terytorialnego i Administracji Państwowej Senatu RP, pp. 3–4. https://www.senat.gov.pl/download/gfx/senat/pl/senatinicjatywypliki/10706/4/613_mat.-_publikacja_kstap.pdf.

Izdebski, Hubert. 2007. *Fundamenty współczesnych państw*. Warsaw: Wydawnictwo Prawnicze LexisNexis.

Kancelaria Prezesa Rady Ministrów (Chancellery of the Prime Minister). 2024a. *Renesans idei samorządu*. Warsaw: Kancelaria Prezesa Rady Ministrów. https://www.gov.pl/web/premier/renesans-idei-samorzadu.

Kancelaria Prezesa Rady Ministrów (Chancellery of the Prime Minister). 2024b. *Rządowy Fundusz Inwestycji Lokalnych*. Warsaw: Kancelaria Prezesa Rady Ministrów. https://www.gov.pl/web/premier/rzadowy-fundusz-inwestycji-lokalnych.

Komisja Samorządu Terytorialnego i Administracji Państwowej (Committee for Local Government and State Administration Committee). 2022. *Materiały i stanowiska eksperckie w sprawie ustawy z dnia 13 stycznia 2022 r. o zmianie ustawy – Prawo oświatowe i niektórych innych ustaw (druk senacki 613)*. Warsaw: Komisja Samorządu Terytorialnego i Administracji Państwowej. https://www.miasta.pl/uploads/document/content_file/1088/KSTAP_-_materialy_dot._druku_613_-_1.2.2022.pdf.

Komisja Wspólna Rządu i Samorządu Terytorialnego (Joint Commission of the Government and Local Government). 2016. *Opinia Komisji Wspólnej do rządowego projektu nowelizacji Prawa oświatowego*. Warsaw: Komisja Wspólna Rządu i Samorządu Terytorialnego. https://www.miasta.pl/aktualnosci/z-komisji-wspolnej-rzadu-i-samorzadu-terytorialnego-1778c6e1-484d-4ade-a4a6-1e6b6b367f67.

Kruś, Maciej. 2019. 'Wody Polskie – nowy podmiot w Prawie wodnym'. *Studia Prawa Publicznego* 3(27): 615–629. https://dspace.uni.lodz.pl/bitstream/handle/11089/39885/615-629_Kru%C5%9B.pdf?sequence=1&isAllowed=y.

Lackowska, Marta, Radomir Matczak, Paweł Swianiewicz, Dawid Sześciło, and Katarzyna Wojnar. 2024. *Indeks Samorządności 2024: Bilans dekady 2014–2023*. Warsaw: Fundacja im. Stefana Batorego. https://www.batory.org.pl/wp-content/uploads/2024/06/Indeks-samorzadnosci_edycja-3.pdf.

Mikowski, Marcin. 2017. *Bez zaufania. Błaszczak: brak profesjonalizmu w samorządach.* Warsaw: Serwis Samorządowy PAP. https://samorzad.pap.pl/kategoria/archiwum/bez-zaufania-blaszczak-brak-profesjonalizmu-w-samorzadach.

Ministerstwo Edukacji Narodowej (Ministry of National Education). 2024. *Odpowiedź podsekretarza stanu w Ministerstwie Edukacji Narodowej – z upoważnienia ministra – na interpelację nr 1558 w sprawie likwidacji szkół.* Warsaw: Ministerstwo Edukacji Narodowej. https://www.sejm.gov.pl/sejm7.nsf/InterpelacjaTresc.xsp?key=1481D591.

Ministerstwo Finansów – Krajowa Administracja Skarbowa (Ministry of Finance – National Revenue Administration). 2022. *Podatki 2015–2022. Korzystne zmiany dla Polaków.* Warsaw: Ministerstwo Finansów – Krajowa Administracja Skarbowa. https://www.gov.pl/web/kas/podatki-2015–2022-korzystne-zmiany-dla-polakow.

Ministerstwo Infrastruktury (Ministry of Infrastructure). 2023. *Program azotanowy.* Warsaw: Ministerstwo Infrastruktury. https://www.gov.pl/web/infrastruktura/program-azotanowy.

Naczelny Sąd Administracyjny (Supreme Administrative Court). 2022. *Wyrok z dnia 20 października 2022 r. sygn. III OSK 5503/21.* Warsaw: Naczelny Sąd Administracyjny. https://www.inforlex.pl/dok/tresc,NSA.2022.001.300025797,Wyrok-NSA-z-dnia-20-pazdziernika-2022-r-sygn-III-OSK-5503-21.html.

Najwyższa Izba Kontroli (Supreme Audit Office– SAO). 2022. *Finansowanie zadań oświatowych realizowanych przez jednostki samorządu terytorialnego. Informacja o kontroli. KAP.430.001.2022 Nr ewid. 21/2022/P/21/006/KAP.* Warsaw: Najwyższa Izba Kontroli, pp. 1–92. https://www.nik.gov.pl/plik/id,27115,vp,29915.pdf.

Najwyższa Izba Kontroli (Supreme Audit Office– SAO). 2024. *Wsparcie finansowe samorządów przez państwo w okresie reform podatkowych i odbudowy gospodarki po epidemii COVID-19. Informacja o wynikach kontroli, KBF 430.5.2024 Nr ewid. 83/2024/P/23/009/KBF.* Warsaw: Najwyższa Izba Kontroli. https://www.nik.gov.pl/kontrole/wyniki-kontroli-nik/pobierz,P-23-009-wsparcie-finansowe-samorzadow-COVID,typ,kk.pdf.

Olejnik, Łukasz W. and Marcin Grygo. 2024. *Dotacje dla swoich? Analiza rządowych dotacji inwestycyjnych dla samorządów w latach 2019–2023.* Warsaw: Instytut Finansów Publicznych. https://www.ifp.org.pl/wp-content/uploads/2024/04/Dotacje_dla_swoich-raport-Instytutu-Finansow-Publicznych.pdf.

Pietrasik, Ewelina. 2024. *Zagrożenia dla konstytucyjnej zasady decentralizacji władzy publicznej.* Wrocław: University of Wrocławpp, pp. 27–38. https://repozytorium.uni.wroc.pl/dlibra/publication/150568.

Portalsamorzadowy. 2017. *Likwidacja gimnazjów. ZNP wylicza ilu nauczycieli straciło pracę. MEN: Będzie 10 tys. nowych etatów.* https://www.portalsamorzadowy.pl/edukacja/likwidacja-gimnazjow-znp-wylicza-ilu-nauczycieli-stracilo-prace-men-bedzie-10-tys-nowych-etatow,98876.html.

Radwan, Artur. 2017. 'Reforma oświaty: Ilu nauczycieli straciło pracę? Są już najnowsze dane'. *Gazeta Prawna.* https://serwisy.gazetaprawna.pl/edukacja/artykuly/1076804,ilu-nauczycieli-stracilo-prace-po-reformie-oswiaty.html.

Rondalska, Dorota. 2017. 'Reforma szkolna z roku 2016 – troska o ucznia czy innowacja na zamówienie polityczne'. *Studia Edukacyjne* 45: 291–310. http://cejsh.icm.edu.pl/cejsh/element/bwmeta1.element.ojs-doi-10_14746_se_2017_45_20/c/22805-21592.pdf.

Rzecznik Praw Obywatelskich (Commissioner for Human Rights). 2021. *Stanowisko RPO w sprawie wyrażone w piśmie do Przemysława Czarnka Ministra Edukacji i*

Nauki. VII.7037.73.2021.AT. Warsaw: Rzecznik Praw Obywatelskich. https://bip.brpo.gov.pl/sites/default/files/RPO_do_MEiN_kuratorzy_22.06.2021.pdf.

Serwis Samorządowy PAP. 2024. *Ruszyły prace nad przepisami przywracającymi kompetencje samorządom.* https://samorzad.pap.pl/kategoria/aktualnosci/ruszyly-prace-nad-przepisami-przywracajacymi-kompetencje-samorzadom.

Skarzyński, Ryszard. 2012. *Podstawowy dylemat politologii: Dyscyplina nauki czy potoczna wiedza o społeczeństwie. O tradycji uniwersytetu i demarkacji wiedzy.* Białystok: Wydawnictwo Temida.

Skrzydło, Wiesław. 2004. *Ustrój polityczny RP w świetle Konstytucji z 1997 roku.* Kraków: Zakamycze.

Springer, Beata. 2023. 'Kluczowe zmiany w samodzielności i ustrojowej niezależności JST kadencji 2018–2023'. *Studia Politologiczne* 67: 24–42. doi:10.33896/SPolit.2023.67.2.

Swianiewicz, Paweł. 2020. *Raport: Wpływ polityki partyjnej na rozdział dotacji celowych na przykładzie Funduszu Dróg Samorządowych.* Warsaw: Wspolnota. https://wspolnota.org.pl/fileadmin/Raport_FDS.pdf.

Sześciło, Dawid. 2018. *Recydywa centralizmu? Zmiany w polityce państwa wobec samorządu po 2015 roku.* Warsaw: Fundacja im. Stefana Batorego, pp. 12–15. https://www.batory.org.pl/upload/files/Programy%20operacyjne/Masz%20Glos/D_Szesc ilo%20Recydywa%20centralizmu.pdf.

Theus, Jan. 2023. *Samorządowcy stracą 30 mld na Polskim Ładzie. Nie mamy na bieżące wydatki, inflacja nas wykańcza.* Warsaw: OKO.Press. https://oko.press/samorzadowcy-30-mld-polski-lad-biezace-wydatki.

Tilly, Charles. 1997. *Rewolucje europejskie 1492–1992* (*European Revolutions, 1492–1992*). Warsaw: Wydawnictwo Krąg, Oficyna Wydawnicza Volumen.

TVN24 Biznes. 2023. *Apel do premiera i Sejmu. Zniszczą Państwo kompromis wypracowywany przez niemal 3 lata.* https://tvn24.pl/biznes/z-kraju/ustawa-wiatrakowa-sejm-zdecyduje-o-poprawkach-senatu-apel-organizacji-samorzadowych-do-premiera-mateusza-morawieckiego-i-sejmu-st6809760.

Związek Gmin Wiejskich RP (Association of Rural Communities of the Republic of Poland). 2016. *Stanowisko polskich samorządów dotyczące zmian w systemie oświaty.* Warsaw: Związek Gmin Wiejskich RP. https://www.zgwrp.pl/wp-content/uploads/2016/09/stanowisko-samorzadow-ws-zapowiadanych-zmian-w-oswiacie.pdf.

Związek Miast Polskich (Association of Polish Cities). 2018. *List z 26 stycznia 2018 r. Zygmunta Frankiewicza, w imieniu Zarządu Związku Miast Polskich, do Premiera Mateusza Morawieckiego z prośbą o przeanalizowanie sytuacji związanej z finansowaniem oświaty samorządowej, w perspektywie wyzwań dotyczących potrzeb inwestycyjnych, związanych ze Strategią na rzecz Odpowiedzialnego Rozwoju.* Wałbrzych: Związek Miast Polskich. https://www.miasta.pl/uploads/document/content_file/568/Stanowisko_Zarz_du_ZMP_finansowanie_o_wiaty_-_list_do_Premiera_DO_PUBLIKACJI.pdf.

Związek Miast Polskich (Association of Polish Cities). 2023. *Apel samorządów do Premiera Mateusza Morawieckiego i Sejmu RP.* Wałbrzych: Związek Miast Polskich. https://www.miasta.pl/aktualnosci/apel-samorzadow-do-premiera-mateusza-morawieckiego-i-sejmu-rp.

Związek Miast Polskich (Association of Polish Cities). 2025. *Raport dotyczący kosztów wprowadzenia nowego systemu edukacji.* Wałbrzych: Związek Miast Polskich. https://prod-zmp.s3.plwaw.scw.cloud/uploads/attachment/file/2638/Raport_final_wysy_ka_i_www.pdf.

Primary Legal Sources

Act of 9 March 2023 amending the Wind Energy Investments Act and certain other legal acts. *Dziennik Ustaw (Journal of Laws)* 2024 item 859.
Act of 13 November 2003on the revenues of local government units. *Dziennik Ustaw* (*Journal of Laws*) 2024, item 356.
Act of 20 May 2016on investments in wind farms. *Dziennik Ustaw* (*Journal of Laws*) 2024, item 317.
Act of 23 October 2018on the Government Fund for Road Development. *Dziennik Ustaw* (*Journal of Laws*) 2022, item 1846.
Act of 31 March 2020amending the Act on specific solutions related to the prevention, counteraction and combating of COVID-19, other infectious diseases and the crisis situations caused by them, and certain other acts. *Dziennik Ustaw* (*Journal of Laws*) 2024, item 1831.
Constitutional Tribunal (Poland). Judgment of 18 February 2003, case no. K 24/02, (OTK ZU) No. 2A/2003, item 11. https://isap.sejm.gov.pl/isap.nsf/download.xsp/WDU20030380334/T/D20030334TK.pdf.
Constitution of the Republic of Poland of 2 April 1997, *Dziennik Ustaw* (*Journal of Laws*) 2009, No. 114, item 946.
Educational Law of 14 December 2016. *Dziennik Ustaw* (*Journal of Laws*) 2024, item 737.
Regulation of the Council of Ministers of 31 January2023. *Dziennik Ustaw* (*Journal of Laws*) 2023, item 244. https://dziennikustaw.gov.pl/D2023000024401.pdf.
Water Law of 20 July 2017. *Dziennik Ustaw* (*Journal of Laws*) 2025, item 960.

12 Civil Society's Responses to Democratic Erosion

Dorota Pietrzyk-Reeves

Introduction[1]

This chapter examines the growing potential and resilience of civil society in Poland in response to processes of de-democratization under the Prawo i Sprawiedliwość (Law and Justice Party) coalition government in power from 2015 to 2023. Despite government imposed polarization and attempts to close the public space to the independent voices of civic actors, civil society organizations (CSOs) and social movements have not only acted as a firewall against further constitutional backsliding, but have also consolidated their own missions, resources, and social support. As interviews with CSOs show, these unintended consequences have had both chilling and transformative effects on the independent civil society sector. Findings from surveys and focus groups suggest that an increasing number of Poles have been mobilized in recent years, with many expressing the view that active civic engagement matters, particularly in relation to issues that people care about. This empirical evidence makes it possible to theorize the relationship between civil society and democratic erosion, and to draw some important lessons from the case in question. De-democratization changes the relationship between civil society and the state as the government no longer tries to consult citizens and CSOs whose advocacy role is questioned and undermined when the channels of communication with those in power are closed. This suggests that weak, underperforming democracies generate a need for a strong civil society to counteract democratic erosion, which in itself creates a dual challenge. First, civil society is now assessed in terms of its capacity to react, to organize and mobilize collective action, and to influence public life and those in power. Second, civil society actors face worsening conditions for their action and obstacles that are created to weaken their voice and impact. This second challenge, described by scholars as the 'closing of public space' phenomenon provides the context for an analysis of the first challenge: the capacity, resilience, and overall responses of civil society actors to the impact of de-democratization.

Comparative research conducted not only in Poland but also in other Central and Eastern European countries (Pietrzyk-Reeves and McMahon 2022; McMahon et al. 2024) suggests that, more than three decades after the

DOI: 10.4324/9781042002030-13

fall of communism, Polish civil society, despite persistent ideological divisions, is not weak, but rather is dynamic, self-sufficient, and consistent in maintaining its independence while pursuing its goals. Its activism focuses on a wide variety of socially significant issues, from the natural environment, through social and humanitarian assistance, to the rights and freedoms of individuals and groups. This activism addresses not only everyday concerns, but also more abstract issues, such as specific civil rights or the quality of democracy, which drive civic engagement and mobilization (Pietrzyk-Reeves and Pickering 2025). This chapter focuses on these new dynamics in civil society development, prompted by processes of de-democratization. Beginning with the evolution of civil society after 1989, it examines the responses of CSOs and citizens to the challenges and obstacles created by democratic erosion and constitutional backsliding, which have had a profound effect not only on the functioning of the judiciary, but also on civil society and its role as a check on power, the arena of social accountability.

The evolution of civil society and changing opportunity structures

Civil society is not only a sphere for the articulation of various group interests, but also a necessary arena for political education and the shaping of political preferences. It represents the space of voluntary civic activity that enriches a democracy. The liberal principle of autonomy can be fulfilled through the system of decision-making that includes the involvement of citizens and their associations who can deliberate on the public issues that affect them. They must have adequate opportunities to form their preferences and to place issues on the public agenda (Rothstein et al. 2004). It is the liberal and constitutional components of the democratic order that provide the necessary framework for associational life, which lies at the core of civil society and structures its relationship with the state.

Following the collapse of communist rule in Poland, civil society undoubtedly played an important role in the processes of transformation and democratization after 1989. This role has been perceived by researchers primarily in relation to the consolidation of democracy, to which a vibrant civil society was expected to contribute considerably (Linz and Stepan 1996). To understand the current condition of civil society in Poland, it is important to discuss briefly the evolution it has undergone over the past three decades, which encompasses four stages: (1) the institutionalization and development of non-governmental organizations (NGOs) in the 1990s; (2) the weakness of civil society and processes of 'NGOization' from 2000 to 2015); (3) the erosion of democracy and the shrinking of public and civic space after 2015; and (4) increased civic activism and resilience from 2017 onwards.

The first stage was primarily related to the shaping of the institutional conditions for the functioning of civil society in a democratic state, and it coincided with the most difficult period of democratization, particularly in the economic sphere. On the one hand, this period witnessed the dynamic growth of registered CSOs actively engaged in the implementation of various social goals in the new political and economic reality, as well as in staging of numerous protests (Ekiert and Kubik 1999). On the other hand, it led to the alienation and discouragement of many citizens affected by the consequences of economic transformation (Kurczewski and Kurczewska 2001; Gliński 2011). This discouragement, coupled with civic experiences of the previous system, was reflected in low levels of social capital and membership of organizations, contributing to the perception of civil society in Poland as weak (Howard 2003; Ekiert and Foa 2017). During the 1990s and 2000s (stage 2), Polish civil society may have appeared weak compared to other societies in stable Western democracies, if its strength or weakness is measured solely in terms of membership of organizations. However, this indicator is difficult to consider as having explanatory value (Pietrzyk-Reeves and Samonek 2023). In fact, the number of registered organizations steadily increased in the 2000s (Klon/Jawor 2021), as did other forms of activism and civic engagement not captured in quantitative research, often ad hoc and spontaneous, such as protests, grassroots-level local activities, urban movements, climate movements, and charity work. Civil society development was characterized by the professionalization of NGOs (Lang 2012, 62) and the expectation that it would become a panacea for various social and political problems did not materialize. Civic actors were also unable to prevent the erosion of democracy after 2015.

The third and fourth stages in the presented typology clearly overlap, as the legal solutions and policies that led to the erosion of liberal democracy and the shrinking of the public space for civil society after 2015 ultimately produced the opposite of the intended effect: an increase in civic activism and a shift in CSOs' strategies in response to new threats, thereby strengthening, not weakening, the independent civic sector, despite limited opportunities for advocacy (McMahon and Niparko 2022; Pospieszna and Pietrzyk-Reeves 2022). From 2015 to 2016, there was greater scepticism among activists, but it was soon replaced by renewed optimism and strategy change. As a feminist activist pointed out:

> In 2015 and 2016, I was very sceptical, but now I have emotional peace, which does not mean the situation has radically improved, but there is so much social and civic activity that my heart is filled with joy. And I think that even if we don't survive in the current format and aren't able to meet women's needs as thoroughly as we do now, we will exist in a different format. It is fantastic that these different forms of protest are spreading, that there are so many of them and that they concern such important issues.
>
> (Interview conducted by the author in 2019)

The liberal perspective assumes that civil society develops spontaneously through the efforts of citizens who are free to associate with one another. In other words, it is not the role of government to initiate, animate, or strengthen civil society development. This logic was, however, reversed during the process of democratization in Central and Eastern Europe, where civil society's development was regarded as crucial for the consolidation of democracy and therefore required not only social but also governmental support. This took the form of institutional and legal provisions that established the formal legal and financial conditions under which CSOs could function. These provisions were embedded above all in the guarantee of freedom of association, freedom of assembly, and freedom of speech. Democratic erosion led to yet another different logic of governmental support for civil society development, which saw a need for wider social mobilization, especially at the local level, around certain shared values supported by the governing coalition. This strategy sought to secure an active role of 'value guardians' (McMahon and Niparko 2022, 1359) who would help to sustain voters' support for the Law and Justice Party (Ślarzyński 2018, 2022). The resulting 'pillarization' of civil society led some scholars to argue that this government-orchestrated civil society has become a threat to democracy (Ekiert 2021). Others raised the question of civil society's role as a firewall against autocratic power grabs (Bernhard 2020, 354), focusing on civil society actors' ability to defend democracy through monitoring the actions of state bureaucracy and protest, as well as providing social accountability.

Political systems may be relatively open or closed to different kinds of issues or groups. Political opportunity structure theory helps to explain how relatively open states encourage NGOs to participate in the political process. Although the theory takes into account the political environment for civil society advocacy there is also a broader socio-economic environment that matters. In essence, political opportunity structure research addresses institutional openness to social movements. It can, however, be extended to well-established NGOs whose impact varies depending on the issue-specific openness of the system (Mayer and Minkoff 2004; Kriesi 2004). In practice this means that certain issues will better resonate with the given political and ideological agenda of the government than other issues. NGOs' mobilization and impact will vary depending on certain aspects of system openness and closure (Koopmans et al. 2005). For example, female advocacy organizations will adopt different strategies depending on whether they operate under a liberal or left-leaning liberal coalition or a conservative government. In the latter case, influential policies might require a shift to cooperation with a wider social movement whose impact and visibility can be much higher, as demonstrated by the women's 'Black Strikes' that started in 2016 in Poland. In other words, the narrower the political opportunities for advocacy work, the greater the need there for groups to cooperate and form alliances, both among NGOs (including transnational cooperation) and, where possible, among NGOs and social movements (Schnyder 2015, 63–65).

In the literature on political opportunities, two aspects have been distinguished with regard to opportunities for mobilization. The first concerns an institutional dimension and the access social actors have to the institutionalized political system, the configuration of power, and the system's responsiveness. The second aspect, equally important for this analysis, is a discursive component which concerns the public visibility, resonance, and political legitimacy of certain actors, identities, and claims (Koopmans et al. 2005). In both dimensions, the existing structure of political opportunities might prompt greater ties and connectivity between organizations of the same type or different types which has been the case in Poland in recent years. Environmental, women's, refugee inclusion, and human rights groups, for example, have established linkages, as they each share a common critique of the established political order and of government policies and legislation.

A shrinking public space and civic actors' strategy change

One of the consequences of democratic erosion or backsliding is the phenomenon described in the literature as the shrinking of the public space for civil society. This refers to strategies employed by public authorities aimed at limiting the impact of civic actors on political processes and decisions (Carothers and Brechenmacher 2014; Buyse 2018, 967) and is achieved by restricting the opportunities for civil society groups to engage in public activities (Ploszka 2020, 944). This has been a notable symptom of the Polish experience of democratic erosion under the coalition government led by the Law and Justice Party, which sought to shrink the space for dialogue between CSOs and the government (McMahon and Niparko 2022). Interestingly and paradoxically, this encouraged individuals and groups to mobilize in unique and important ways and to develop novel strategies not only to survive under the new circumstances, but to strengthen the mission and networks of civic actors. An open civic and public space is the bedrock of any open and democratic society, and is necessary for citizens to claim their rights and to influence the political and social structures around them. This is made possible through unobstructed exercise of three fundamental rights: freedom to associate, freedom to assemble peacefully, and freedom of expression. A public space, on the other hand, is necessary for the voices of citizens and groups (CSOs, social movements, and protests) to be expressed and heard by public authorities whether national or local, to interact, negotiate, and deliberate on matters that people care about.

For the Law and Justice Party, civil society has increasingly become an important sphere of social life requiring governmental support and, in certain areas of activity later described as conservative (Youngs 2018), even protection. This shift has been accompanied by the centralization of new funding strategies within a single governmental institution and by a redefinition of civil society's mission. According to the 2019 Law and Justice Party programme, which was introduced before its second parliamentary victory, one of priority areas for civil society development was the establishment of institutions that support 'civic activity in the province' (Law and Justice

Party 2019, 39), particularly when motivated by 'patriotism, traditional pro-social attitudes and activities deeply rooted in the history of Polish intellectual, worker and peasant elites as well as activity motivated by religion' (Law and Justice Party 2019, 187). This strategy, along with other reforms such as school reform, can be viewed as an attempt to shape a new citizen in accordance with the party's ideological principles, which openly contradict the norm of value pluralism characteristic of a liberal and open society. The government-orchestrated pushback against civil society started in 2016, targeting NGOs that worked in certain areas focused on promoting and defending liberal values such as anti-discrimination, human and minority rights, migration, the environment, and transparency in public life. Many organizations working to achieve these goals were denied public funding, which severely affected their operation and objectives. At the same time, the politicization of the public space negatively impacted private donors who were unwilling to support certain CSOs, while the polarization of the public media limited the voice of civil society actors in public debate or openly discredited them. The shrinking of the public space also took the form of a legislative amendment adopted in December 2016 that restricted the freedom of peaceful assembly and the right to counter-protest. Another strategy employed by the government was the establishment of the first government-organized NGO, the Polish National Foundation, which was responsible for the launch of a smear campaign against the judiciary in 2017, a prelude to the government's effort to undermine judicial independence (Ploszka 2020, 945). Consequently, as the result of these strategies, the space for dialogue between civil society and the authorities, as well as social consultations, have shrunk significantly, key freedoms such as freedom of assembly have been limited, and there was much less transparency in the process of legislation at the level of the national parliament, for which the key aspect is the requirement to hold public consultations on draft legislation (Szuleka 2019). At the outset of its term in office, the Law and Justice coalition government attacked NGOs associated with liberal values, minority rights, and open society, seeking to demobilize these groups, discredit them in the eyes of the public, or limit their influence (Korolczuk 2023).

Paradoxically, the new phenomenon of the shrinking public space for civic actors supports the thesis of civil society's impact on the quality and sustainability of democracy. When the public space for dialogue with public authorities becomes limited, the space for social mobilization becomes more crucial than before. A pertinent early example of this is the Akcja Demokracja (Action Democracy) movement, formed in 2015 by a group of people who believed that Polish NGOs were too distant from ordinary citizens and outdated in their views and operations. Instead of establishing another NGO, the founders sought to create a community of people who might meet and collaborate online to promote progressive causes across the country. Through its online platform and open network, it provided online and offline spaces for people with shared values and concerns about democratic erosion to work together. Similarly, the Komitet Obrony Demokracji (Committee for the Defence of Democracy), a social mobilization movement created in 2015 (and later registered as an NGO), was established to promote democracy, the rule of law, and human rights, to defend civil rights and media freedom, and to mobilize citizens to advocate for these principles. It organized public protests, demonstrations, and citizen-led projects such as 'Citizens' Election Control' to monitor elections. It has also engaged in educational activities aimed at promoting democratic knowledge.

These early responses indicated one possible direction in strategic reactions of civil society to de-democratization. Another necessary response was taken by CSOs affected by the new challenges. Drawing on over 30 semi-structured interviews conducted by the author during the period 2019–21 with representatives of CSOs engaged in the promotion of democracy, liberal norms, and transparency, it is possible to categorize the main areas of focus and strategic changes adopted by these organizations in response to the crisis. The selection included CSOs whose advocacy role was well established and which, either in their statutes or through their actions, declared support for democratic values, practices, and norms such as civil and political rights, transparency, non-violence, trust, tolerance, dialogue, and citizen participation. The interviews identified seven literature-driven themes: (1) the environment; (2) organizational capacity; (3) financial viability; (4) impact; (5) relations with state actors; (6) relations with non-state actors; and (7) support for domestic civil society. These semi-structured interviews aimed to examine how organized civic actors involved in advocacy and the protection of human rights, minority groups, and the environment (issues targeted by the Law and Justice Party-led government) continued their mission under conditions of a shrinking public space and how they responded to current challenges and the opportunity structures that exist and change over time. The overwhelming response of these organizations was to raise their voices as well as to build new strategies enabling them to survive and continue their mission in much more challenging conditions (Gerö 2020; Pospieszna and Pietrzyk-Reeves 2022).

According to the CSO representatives interviewed for this research, significant changes have occurred in the functioning of civil society at many different levels. These included a shift away from formal organizations in favour of grassroots structures such as urban movements, climate strikes, and local development campaigns. Fundraising and crowdfunding have become widespread, and support from individual donors has increased, including citizens willing to contribute to less obvious initiatives, such as the Civic Fund which collects funds for 're-granting'. Various unfunded initiatives have developed that offered support to individuals or organizations at risk. The professionalization of NGOs has also increased, due to the availability of local government, municipal, European, and corporate funding, which compels this professionalization and the achievement of declared goals. Professional NGOs do not mobilize citizens but often attract volunteers. Some activists even claimed in interviews that the shrinking of civic space was a myth that does not adequately describe the situation of Polish civil society. Activist movements, such as urban movements, the anti-smog movement, and the women's strike, have become more visible and more prominent in public debate. Some activists emphasized that the term 'activism' has gained renewed significance, and that the social potential for activism, which had been dormant for the past 20 years, can no longer be ignored, even by authoritarian governments. Mobilizing citizens seemed much easier thanks to the availability of social media and information, as well as various educational activities and the growing civic awareness of individuals and local communities.

Despite a widespread perception among scholars and practitioners that the public space has been shrinking since 2015, many activists emphasized that a much more significant process has been taking place in response to the new situation – a new social mobilization that to some extent undermines the static view of a shrinking civic space. Informal civic self-organization takes many different forms and in the new situation has come to be seen as a more spontaneous and practicable type of civic engagement. Examples of such engagement include participation in online consultations, signing online petitions, as well as supporting or criticizing certain policies through street protests. A wider mobilization has also taken place at the local level, where cooperation between local authorities and various advocacy groups has coalesced around certain widely supported goals, such as a clean natural environment or openness to civic activism.

Many CSOs in the sample collected for this research did not perceive the civic space to be shrinking; on the contrary, they viewed new challenges as opportunities to rethink and strengthen their mission wherever possible. They emphasized their search for innovative solutions, building closer relationships with target groups, seeking financial independence through the diversification of funding, as well as improving internal and external communication with people across the board. Advocacy organizations attempted to influence decision-makers and public policy either indirectly by impacting citizens' participation and awareness, or directly by mobilizing society to take public action including protest. In general, the CSOs interviewed for this study declared that they had improved their ability both to anticipate threats and to take advantage of new opportunities.

Two major changes in CSOs' strategies discussed by the interviewees were financial diversification and networking. The first strategy was prompted by shifting priorities, as governments were no longer willing to support progressive liberal CSOs. The goal was to reach independence from public funding through alternative mechanisms such as fundraising. The second strategy involved cooperation with other like-minded organizations in Poland and abroad. On the one hand, networking is necessary as achieving certain goals, particularly influencing decision-makers and engaging in joint advocacy and public awareness campaigns, requires collective effort. On the other hand, cooperation is driven by considerations of willingness and professionalism, as networks can facilitate the diffusion of information, the exchange of experience and best practices, the sharing of human resources, and fundraising. Building and joining networks is a strategy that pays off in the short and the long term as it provides access to resources such as information, support, communication, and opportunities for joint projects that can strengthen the mission of advocacy groups.

An important factor affecting the functioning and survival of interviewed organizations was their linkages with volunteer bases, beneficiaries, and local communities. An increase in volunteers and supporters of their activities enabled these CSOs to better understand community needs and priorities, and to address them in new, innovative ways. The emergence of new financial and institutional challenges also influenced the way in which CSOs operate and organize themselves by narrowing down the field of action to tailor it better to the needs of society, or by redefining the strategies of funding. For example, one of the organizations engaged in preventing the violation of human rights, particularly women's rights, organized a social media fundraising campaign that generated a larger sum than the subsidy that it had previously received from the Polish Ministry of Justice.

In general, the CSOs interviewed for this study provided insights indicating that they opted for voice rather than exit, and that legal solutions and policies leading to the erosion of liberal democracy and the shrinking of the public space for civil society after 2015 ultimately had the opposite effect, contrary to what was intended: an increase in civic activism, a shift in CSOs' strategies in response to new threats, and, consequently, a strengthening rather than a weakening of the independent civic sector, despite limited opportunities for advocacy.

Civil society actors, whether formal and institutionalized or informal and non-institutionalized, are embedded within society and gain their support from society. Depending on their mission and goals, some of them are also embedded in the public sphere, which provides an intermediary space between the political sphere of the state, the market, and the society/family. It is, however, their embeddedness in society and various communities that might play a particularly important role at times of crisis. Social trust in CSOs is the best indicator of such embeddedness and of the recognition of their role (Klon/Jawor 2017). In a nationwide opinion poll conducted in 2017, shortly after the smear campaign against NGOs in the public media, 56% of respondents declared trust in CSOs, compared to 50% in a similar survey conducted in 2014. Similarly, according to Edelman Trust Barometer, in 2018 the level of declared trust in NGOs in Poland reached 54%, placing the country second highest among other European countries. In the same survey, trust in government was declared by 25% of Polish respondents, while 34% expressed trust in the media (Edelman Trust Barometer 2018). This positive trend indicates that CSOs and activists had not been discredited in the eyes of the public; on the contrary, they had more supporters than before

2015. There is also growing awareness in society of the work done by CSOs and their contribution to the public good. Although this does not immediately translate into active involvement of citizens the number of those who are active has also been growing.

The growth of civic engagement

A survey of a representative sample of the Polish population (N = 1006)[2] contributed to a greater understanding of the dynamics and changes in civic engagement over several years, during a period marked by de-democratization. The compilation and comparison of these results provided new insights into the state of civil society in Poland. The survey measured individual participation in formally registered organizations, engagement in informal types of civic activity, as well as norms of citizenship such as support for democracy, the sense of political efficacy, and interpersonal trust. The comparison of results of the surveys shows higher engagement at the individual level across virtually all categories, both in terms of membership of organizations and civic activism.

In November 2019, 17.6% of respondents reported membership of at least one organization, with the highest share referring to affiliation with a church or other religious organization (7.7%), followed by sport and leisure organizations (4.0%), and trade unions (3.9%). Fewer than 1% of respondents reported membership of an online group related to their interests. The 2019 survey indicated low levels of membership of various types of organizations, which was particularly noticeable compared to other countries in the region where the same survey was conducted. For example, the percentage of people reporting membership of at least one organization in the Czech Republic was 38.8%, while in Bosnia and Herzegovina it was 18.7%. Results obtained from the March 2024 survey show an increase in membership of all types of organizations, with approximately 25% of respondents reporting membership of at least one organization. In this survey, cultural organizations ranked second after churches and religious organizations, while the proportion of respondents reporting membership of 'other associations' and online groups had doubled compared to 2019. In both surveys, the results are most strongly correlated with respondents'higher levels of education associated with higher rates of participation: in 2024, 34.5% of respondents with higher education reported membership of an organization, compared to 32.1% in 2019. Respondents aged 45–65 showed the greatest level of involvement, with approximately 30% reporting membership of an organization, while those aged 24 and under and those aged 65 and over reported the lowest level of participation. The decline in the share of respondents reporting no membership of an organization is consistent with researchers' assumptions (Dalton 2019) regarding the resources needed to engage in such activities (time, money, mobilization). In other words, higher levels of societal affluence are correlated with increased likelihood of associational membership. These results suggest that neither the erosion of democracy in Poland nor the negative rhetoric about the NGO sector has had a negative impact on membership of organizations regardless of their type; the increase applies to all types of organizations mentioned in the survey. Moreover, the COVID-19 pandemic does not appear to have constituted a barrier to this type of engagement.

Membership of an organization represents just one of the many forms of civic engagement. The second question posed to respondents in the survey concerned other forms of civic participation undertaken in the past 12 months. Respondents were asked about their participation in protests, social movements, public debates, petitions, and efforts to organize others to work together for a specific purpose. The results show an even greater increase in engagement than in the case of membership of organizations. In 2019, only 18% of respondents reported that they had engaged in various forms of civic activism; by 2024, the percentage of those involved in such activities had reached 27.1%. The slight decline in participation in protests and strikes, which had occurred frequently during the four-year study period, is surprising. By contrast, active membership of or involvement in civic associations and organizations, volunteering, and donating or financial support for organizations increased. Nearly twice as many respondents reported having engaged in 'organizing neighbours, the local community, co-workers, or other groups around a common goal or interest'. The significant increase in engagement is also explained by activism and volunteering related to helping refugees from Ukraine, reported by 8% of respondents. In this case, the study results are also significantly correlated with higher education; in this group, as many as 45.5% of respondents indicated that they had engaged in some form of civic activism in the past year. Engagement rates were very similar among women and men, with the most active respondents aged 25–34 and 45–54 living in medium-sized cities (50,000–200,000 inhabitants). The least active were Poles aged 18 or under and 65 or over, those with a primary school education, and those residing in rural areas.

In both surveys, respondents were also asked which issues or problems they believed should compel citizens to take action. This question was linked to a research hypothesis that most people engage in activities related to everyday problems, and less frequently in relation to abstract issues such as individual rights or judicial independence. The survey results show that, in 2019 and 2024, the largest share of respondents identified health care and social assistance as the most important unresolved problem (44% and 40%, respectively). The second most frequently cited issue in 2019 that should mobilize citizens in grassroots action was environmental protection (indicated by 26.7% of respondents), whereas in 2024 the rule of law and an independent judiciary proved more important (indicated by 26.1% of respondents), with environmental protection ranking lower, at 17.7%. In both 2019 and 2024, unemployment, poverty, and workers' rights were identified as the third most important issue (approximately 25% of respondents).

In 2024, the share of people citing women's rights increased significantly (21.4% compared to 12.7% in 2019), demonstrating increased public awareness of the importance of these rights, which was probably fuelled by women's activism between 2020 and 2022, manifested in numerous protests and strikes, primarily concerning reproductive rights.

The surveys also provided data on political efficacy, including preferences regarding democracy as a form of government, civic vigilance, and citizens' interest in politics. A particularly interesting finding is that, although the proportion of respondents who prefer democracy to all other forms of government remains stable, at 81% in 2019 and 2024, the share of those who 'strongly agree' increased in 2024 to 25.5% compared to 19.3% in 2019. This may signal satisfaction with the change of government in 2023 and renewed confidence that democracy remains the only viable form of governance, despite incidences of democratic backsliding. At the same time, the proportion of those who 'strongly disagree' with the proposition that non-democratic rule can sometimes be more desirable than democratic rule was almost 12% higher in 2024 than in 2019. Respondents overwhelmingly supported the view that citizens have a duty to monitor their government (84%), while 82.5% agree with the assertion that citizens should be actively engaged in social and public life. However, only 51% of respondents expressed an interest in politics in 2019; in 2024, this figure increased slightly, to 58%, with respondents reporting that they were interested or very interested in politics.

This increase can be correlated with a high level of civic and electoral mobilization during the October 2023 parliamentary election that led to a change of government and the defeat of the Law and Justice Party, opening yet another stage of civil society development. The new government promised to rebuild a 'healthy, friendly relationship between the central government and non-governmental organizations', a return to 'the reality of our public life', and to ensure that 'the status of non-governmental organizations and volunteering is the highest possible' (Sadlo 2025). However, at the time of writing, there was growing scepticism regarding this promise and about the way in which democratic quality might be restored (Bill and Stanley 2025).

Conclusion

De-democratization and the rise of illiberalism within electoral democracies are processes rather than singular events; they are dynamic and open-ended. A regime that appears to be deconsolidating may not ultimately deconsolidate, while a democracy that is backsliding may not collapse but instead recover and even thrive. Foa and Mounk's (2016) argument that nowadays citizens are less committed to democracy and more open to authoritarian alternatives than they once were is radical and cannot be substantiated with every case of democratic erosion. While respect for democratic norms and rules may have precipitously declined among some political elites, this does not necessarily extend to citizens accustomed to the rule of law and transparency as well as mechanisms that keep political corruption at bay. This civic awareness and civic culture can only be sustained and strengthened by a strong and autonomous civil society. Key lessons can certainly be drawn from the Polish case.

Scholars have argued that whether civil society actors have contributed to, abetted, or pushed back against recent de-democratization depends on the goals of CSOs and activists, as well as political opportunities. Civil society can be divided along political lines (Bernhard 2021; Ekiert 2021), with different groups being mobilized either to support illiberalism or to counter it. In Poland, it can be assumed that the reopening of the public space to civil society's influence will cause yet another evolution within it and contribute to further activation of groups, organizations, and movements that have become an integral part of Polish society and the democratic system. Qualitative research shows that there is significant civic potential within society, which is easy to mobilize (e.g. support for refugees from Ukraine or protests organized by women during the pandemic), but more difficult to translate into institutionalized forms of action. Therefore, it will be crucial to determine how civil society actors – organizations and movements – develop this potential and how dynamic individual awareness of the value of working towards common goals, needs, and values evolves over time. The role that civil society can play in the process of transition to a well-functioning democracy following a period of large-scale constitutional backsliding and polarization is an open and primarily empirical question.

Notes

1 This research was supported by a grant from the National Science Centre in Poland, project no. 2018/30/M/HS5/00437.

2 The survey, entitled 'Perceptions of Civil Society and Activism', was conducted on a representative sample of the Polish population in November 2019 by Kantar and in March 2024 by Ipsos using Computer-Assisted Personal Interviewing (CAPI) face-to-face interviews as part of their omnibus survey. It included seven questions on membership of organizations and other forms of civic engagement, perceptions of NGOs, and civic norms, such as trust, assessment of democracy, and perception of individual agency in the political sphere.

References

Bernhard, Michael. 2020. 'What Do We Know about Civil Society and Regime Change Thirty Years after 1989?' *East European Politics* 36(3): 341–362.

Bernhard, Michael. 2021. 'Democratic Backsliding in Poland and Hungary'. *Slavic Review* 80(3): 585–607.

Bill, Stanley and Ben Stanley. 2025. 'Democracy after Illiberalism: A Warning from Poland'. *Journal of Democracy* 36(3): 16–32.

Buyse, Antoine. 2018. 'Squeezing Civic Space: Restrictions on Civil Society Organizations and the Linkages with Human Rights'. *The International Journal of Human Rights* 22(8): 966–988.

Carothers, Thomas and Saskia Brechenmacher. 2014. *Closing Space: Democracy and Human Rights Support Under Fire.* Washington, DC: Carnegie Endowment for International.

Dalton, Russell J. 2019. *Citizen Politics: Public Opinion and Political Parties.* Thousand Oaks, CA: CQ Press.

Edelman Trust Barometer. 2018. *Global Report.* https://www.edelman.com/sites/g/files/aatuss191/files/2018-10/2018_Edelman_Trust_Barometer_Global_Report_FEB.pdf.

Ekiert, Grzegorz. 2021. 'Civil Society as a Threat to Democracy'. In Nathan Stoltzfus and Christopher Osmar (eds), *The Power of Populism and People: Resistance and Protest in the Modern World.* New York: Bloomsbury: 53–72.

Ekiert, Grzegorz and Roberto S. Foa. 2017. 'The Weakness of Postcommunist Civil Society Reassessed'. *European Journal of Political Research* 56(2): 419–439.

Ekiert, G. and J. Kubik. 1999. *Rebellious Civil Society: Popular Protest and Democratic Consolidation in Poland, 1989–1993.* Ann Arbor: University of Michigan Press.

Foa, Roberto and Yascha Mounk. 2016. 'The Democratic Disconnect'. *Journal of Democracy* 27(3): 5–17.

Gerö, Marton. 2020. 'Strategies for Survival: Human Rights Organizations' Responses to the Closing of Political Opportunity Structures in Hungary'. *Czech Journal of Political Science* 27(2): 119–139.

Gliński, Piotr. 2011. 'Twenty Years of Civil Society in Poland?' *Polish Sociological Review* 175(3): 271–300.

Howard, Marc Morje. 2003. *The Weakness of Civil Society in Post-Communist Europe.* Cambridge: Cambridge University Press.

Klon/Jawor. 2017. *Im bardziej nas znaja, tym bardziej nam ufaja.* Ngo.pl. https://publicystyka.ngo.pl/im-bardziej-nas-znaja-tym-bardziej-nam-ufaja.

Klon/Jawor. 2021. *Fakty o NGO w Polsce.* Ngo.pl. https://fakty.ngo.pl/fakt/liczba-ngo-w-polsce.

Koopmans, Ruud, Paul Statham, Marco Giugni, and Florence Passy. 2005. *Contested Citizenship: Immigration and Cultural Diversity in Europe.* Minneapolis: University of Minnesota Press.

Korolczuk, Elżbieta. 2023. 'Challenging Civil Society Elites in Poland: The Dynamics and Strategies of Civil Society Actors'. *East European Politics and Societies* 37(3).

Kriesi, Hanspeter. 2004. 'Political Context and Opportunity.' In David A. Snow, Sarah A. Soule, and Hanspeter Kriesi (eds), *Blackwell Companion to Social Movements.* Oxford: Blackwell: 67–90.

Kurczewski, Jacek and Janina Kurczewska. 2001. 'A Self-Governing Society Twenty Years after: Democracy and the Third Sector in Poland'. *Social Research* 68(4): 937–976.

Lang, Sabine. 2012. *NGOs, Civil Society, and the Public Sphere.* Cambridge: Cambridge University Press.

Linz, Juan J. and Alfred Stepan. 1996. *Problems of Democratic Transition and Consolidation Southern Europe, South America, and Post-Communist Europe.* Baltimore, MD: Johns Hopkins University Press.

Mayer, David S. and Debra C. Minkoff. 2004. 'Conceptualizing Political Opportunity'. *Social Forces* 82(4): 1457–1492.

McMahon, Patrice and Lukasz Niparko. 2022. 'Shrinking, Shifting, and Strengthening: The Dynamics and Diversity of Civic Activism in Poland'. *East European Politics and Societies* 36(4): 1355–1376.

McMahon, Patrice, Paula Pickering, and Dorota Pietrzyk-Reeves (eds). 2024. *Activism in Hard Times in Central and Eastern Europe: People Power*. London: Routledge.

Pietrzyk-Reeves, Dorota and Patrice McMahon. 2022. 'Introduction: Civic Activism in Central and Eastern Europe Thirty Years after Communism's Demise'. *East European Politics and Societies* 36(4): 1315–1334. https://doi.org/10.1177/08883254221089261.

Pietrzyk-Reeves, Dorota and Aleksandra Samonek. 2023. 'Measuring Civil Society: Lessons from Central and Eastern Europe'. *Communist and Post-Communist Studies* 56(1): 152–165.

Pietrzyk-Reeves, Dorota and Paula Pickering. 2025. 'Perceptions and Drivers of Civic Activism: The Cases of Bosnia Herzegovina and Poland'. *Communist and Post-Communist Studies58(4)*: 100-119.doi:10.1525/cpcs.2025.2461476.

Ploszka, Adam. 2020. 'Shrinking Space for Civil Society: A Case Study of Poland'. *European Public Law* 26(4): 941–960.

Pospieszna, Paulina and Dorota Pietrzyk-Reeves. 2022. 'Responses of Polish NGOs Engaged in Democracy Promotion to Shrinking Civic Space'. *Cambridge Review of International Affairs* 35(4): 523–544.

Prawo i Sprawiedliwość (Law and Justice Party). 2019. *Program Prawa i Sprawiedliwość*. Warsaw: Prawo i Sprawiedliwość. https://pis.org.pl/files/Program_PIS_2019.pdf.

Rothstein, Bo, Susan Rose-Ackerman, and Janos Kornai. 2004. *Creating Social Trust in Post-Socialist Transition*. Basingstoke: Palgrave Macmillan.

Sadlo, Katarzyna. 2025. 'Na półmetku rzadów'. Ngo.pl. https://publicystyka.ngo.pl/na-polmetku-rzadow-felieton-katarzyny-sadlo-tau.

Schnyder, Melissa. 2015. *Activism, NGOs and the State: Multilevel Responses to Immigration Politics in Europe*. London: Rowman & Littlefield.

Ślarzyński, Marcin. 2018. 'Rola klubów "Gazety Polskiej" w sukcesie politycznym Prawa i Sprawiedliwości w 2015 roku. Aktorzy lokalni czy aktor ogólnokrajowej sfery publicznej III RP?' *Przeglad Socjologiczny* 67(2): 139–158.

Ślarzyński, Marcin. 2022. 'Transformation of Civil Society in Poland under the United Right Government: From Compartmentalization to Political Division'. *Communist and Post-Communist Studies* 55(1): 131–154.

Szuleka, Malgorzata. 2019 'First Victims or Last Guardians? The Consequences of Rule of Law Backsliding for NGOs: Case Studies of Hungary and Poland'. CEPS. https://www.ceps.eu/system/files/MSzuleka_RoLandNGOs.pdf.

Youngs, Richard . 2018. *The Mobilization of Conservative Civil Society*. Washington, DC: Carnegie Endowment for International Peace.

13 Shrinking Civic Space

Legal and Political Strategies to Suppress Civil Society in Poland under Right-Wing Rule (2015–23)

Joanna Podgórska-Rykała

Introduction

The phenomenon of the 'shrinking', 'closing', or 'squeezing' of civic space is a trend that is becoming increasingly prevalent in many countries around the world (Buyse 2018; Płoszka 2020; Grabowska-Moroz and Śniadach 2021; Pospieszna and Pietrzyk-Reeves 2022). It encompasses actions taken by public authorities which, while framed as efforts to repair the state or increase its efficiency, introduce various legal and administrative measures aimed at restricting, harassing, or discrediting independent non-governmental organizations (NGOs) and, more broadly, civil society organizations (CSOs).[1] This process leads to the erosion of fundamental democratic principles such as freedom of speech and freedom of association. In practice, it takes the form of non-transparent financing mechanisms, unjustified cancellation of funding calls, and media campaigns slandering CSOs. The consequence of such actions is the systematic and effective restriction of their activities.

When analysing the scope and dynamics of this process, it should be emphasized that civic space is not solely the result of external pressures, but is shaped by interactions between CSOs and other political and institutional actors. As Buyse (2018: 969) notes, it is a 'moving target', created and transformed by the organizations that simultaneously remain dependent on it. Although threats and restrictions on civil society actors, stemming both from the state and from the internal mechanisms of the organizations themselves, have always existed, the past decade has ushered in a qualitatively new phenomenon. In many countries, civic space is being restricted in a structural, deliberate, and conscious manner.

Between 2015 and 2023, Poland, governed by the right-wing and populist Prawo i Sprawiedliwość (Law and Justice Party), was among the countries experiencing the most significant decline in civic space (Korolczuk 2022; Płoszka 2020; Ohlrich 2016; Marczewski 2025; Grabowska-Moroz and Śniadach 2021). Although in the parliamentary elections of 25 October 2015 the party gained only a narrow lead over the Platforma Obywatelska (Civic Platform), after the votes were counted, it secured, together with its

DOI: 10.4324/9781042002030-14

ideologically aligned coalition partners, a sufficient majority to take full control of government.

An analysis of the actions taken by the government in subsequent years reveals an increasing rate of reconstruction of state institutions. Both administrative and criminal law began to be used as tools to regulate or suppress the activities of CSOs. The introduction of anti-non-governmental organization (NGO) legislation, tighter control of public subsidies, arbitrary inspections, harassment, and instances of the criminalization of social activities undermined the foundations of civic space (Buyse 2018). As Bill and Stanley (2025) point out, the Law and Justice Party's rise to power in 2015 was almost immediately perceived, both domestically and abroad, as a significant threat to the democratic order in Poland. As early as 2016, leading international democracy indices, such as Freedom House and Varieties of Democracy (V-Dem Institute), noted a sharp decline in the quality of Polish democracy. According to a report published in that year, 'Poland [recorded] a steep drop from a relatively high level, down to a LDI score of 0.57, which is still above the world average of the LDI in 2016 (0.42)' (V-Dem Institute 2017, 13; see too Freedom House 2016). In 2017, the European Commission took unprecedented steps by launching Article 7 proceedings against Poland under the Treaty on European Union (TEU), which provides for the possibility of suspending membership rights for violations of the rule of law (COM/2017/0835 final). Poland's subsequent domestic actions provoked a sustained international response, including infringement proceedings before the Court of Justice of the European Union (CJEU), which led to many domestic disputes being reframed as part of a broader conflict over the rule of law in the Union.

However, this process did not go unnoticed, nor was it passively accepted by Polish society. On the contrary, it provoked a strong response from citizens and CSOs alike. These reactions were multifaceted and included institutional actions such as complaints, motions, and opinions addressed to international institutions, as well as grassroots forms of resistance, including street protests, social campaigns, and advocacy initiatives. All these actions, regardless of their scale and form, had a common goal: to uncover and halt the populist attack on the rule of law and the independence of Polish democratic institutions.

Paradoxically, the period of Law and Justice Party governance was characterized, on the one hand, by intense anti-democratic, right-wing populist government activity and, on the other, protests, social mobilization, self-organization, and the emergence of new forms of civic engagement. Although it should be noted that the longstanding systemic problems affecting the third sector intensified with the progressive regression of the rule of law, it was precisely during the period of restrictions and pressure under study that the activity of civil society became more visible to the general public. CSOs have become increasingly prominent both on social media and in the urban public space. Thanks to their somewhat forced increased involvement, they have gained a key role in defending and promoting fundamental democratic values such as the rule of law, equality, and civil liberties (Pospieszna and Pietrzyk-Reeves 2022).

The chapter addresses the following research question: to what extent, and through which mechanisms, did the Law and Justice Party that was in office between 2015 and 2023 restrict civic space in Poland, and how did civil society actors respond to these constraints? The aim of the analysis is to capture both the scope and nature of the restrictions introduced by the authorities and the ways in which civil society actors responded to them.

Due to the nature and scope of the study, a qualitative approach based on secondary data analysis (desk research) was employed. The empirical material includes a review of academic literature and an analysis of the content of documents produced by national and international organizations, reports from public and non-governmental institutions, as well as media materials and public announcements. This approach makes it possible not only to reconstruct the main trends in civil society policy during the period under analysis, but also to trace the evolution of resistance and civic mobilization strategies in the context of a progressive shrinking of democratic space. Although reliance on qualitative primary and secondary sources facilitates a broad reconstruction of trends and strategies, this approach has limited ability to capture organizational tactics at the micro level and the actual experiences of activists. Therefore, future research in this field should include interviews and ethnographic studies.

Money for the loyal: institutional mechanisms of shrinking civic space

One of the key factors shaping the condition of civic space is the practical ability of CSOs to obtain and maintain the financial resources necessary to operate publicly (Jenkins 2012; Buyse 2018). Restricting access to funding is one of the most effective forms of pressure, as it allows those in power to selectively strengthen organizations that support their policies and marginalize those that are critical of the government.

In Poland, a key moment in this regard was the adoption by the Sejm (Assembly, the lower house of the Polish parliament) on 15 September 2017 of the Act on the Narodowy Instytut Wolności – Centrum Rozwoju Społeczeństwa Obywatelskiego (National Institute of Freedom – Centre for the Development of Civil Society – NIF-CDCS). The Act, which came into force a month later, introduced the centralization of the allocation of public funds for various types of organizations (Day 2017; Bill 2020). The newly established Institute was given the power to decide which organizations would receive funding and which would be deprived of it. Concerns arose that such a legal structure would allow for the politicization of grant decisions and the subordination of funding mechanisms to government objectives (Pospieszna and Pietrzyk-Reeves 2022).

These concerns were particularly significant because the non-governmental sector in Poland is very large. The number of NGOs alone, including both associations and foundations officially listed in the Rejestr Gospodarki

Narodowej (REGON – National Official Register of Business Entities), amounted to 161,000 at the end of 2024, including 117,000 associations and 44,000 foundations. This figure also includes volunteer fire departments, which take the legal form of associations and numbered approximately 17,000 in 2024. According to data from Główny Urząd Statystyczny (Statistics Poland), even after deducting those entities which, despite being registered, are not in active operation, there are still around 75,000 active associations and foundations in the areas of social economy, volunteering, as reported by Statistics Poland. Of these organizations, 34% operate in the areas of sport, tourism, and recreation, 13% in culture and the arts, and 12% in education and childcare (Klon/Jawor 2025), although it should be emphasized that in the case of certain types of public tasks, it is precisely these organizations that are at the forefront of their implementation. Such areas include homeless shelters, support for the activation and integration of migrants into society and the labour market, and the provision of sports clubs. Tasks related to the protection of the rights of women, minorities, and marginalized groups are also mostly carried out by NGOs. According to estimates, the non-governmental sector in Poland receives approximately €1 billion annually from public funds from the state budget and local governments (Sieradzka 2016; Day 2017).

At the time the law was passed, the Organization for Security and Co-operation in Europe's Office for Democratic Institutions and Human Rights (OSCE/ODIHR 2017) pointed out that the provisions should include stronger guarantees of the Institute's independence and safeguards against government interference in the process of allocating funds. In subsequent years, numerous irregularities in funding calls confirmed the validity of these concerns, revealing cases of favouritism towards organizations affiliated with the ruling party at the expense of independent civil society actors. According to an audit conducted by the Najwyższa Izba Kontroli (Supreme Audit Office – SAO) (SAO 2024), the process of evaluating applications, selecting projects for funding, as well as their verification and settlement was unreliable and, in some cases, unlawful, inappropriate, or wasteful, and fraught with the risk of corruption. The audit covered the period from 1 January 2021 to 24 November 2023, taking into account facts and evidence beyond this period that were relevant to the audited activities. The control focused on two programmes managed by the NIF-CDCS, namely the Government Programme for Civic Initiatives Fund and the Government Programme for the Development of Civic Organizations. These two funds were selected because the NIF-CDCS allocated over 303 million złoty to their implementation in 2021–22. Eleven associations and foundations that received funding from programmes implemented by the Institute were also examined.[2] The audits carried out among NIF-CDCS beneficiaries covered the application process, implementation, and settlement of grant agreements for projects financed by the Institute, as well as the effects of the support provided.

The SAO (2024) highlighted a number of problems. These included the possibility of obtaining funding for identical activities from different priorities or programmes, as well as the multiple funding of projects by the same or related entities, creating a risk of double funding. Although the SAO was aware of these risks, it did not create a mechanism to prevent the risk of double funding for the same tasks. Furthermore, in some instances, applications were evaluated by experts associated with the applicants, and a lack of procedures for selecting experts and verifying conflicts of interest was pointed out. In addition, it was alleged that the competition committees arbitrarily changed the experts' assessments, which affected the ranking lists and resulted in the unjustified awarding of over 14 million złoty. The audit also revealed that project supervision and control were rudimentary, often limited to analysing statements without verifying source documents. The lack of transparent rules for selecting service providers and suppliers was highlighted, which made it possible to outsource them to persons associated with the beneficiaries. The SAO also pointed out that the agreements concluded with beneficiaries did not provide for safeguards against the sale of purchased real estate after five years from the date of purchase or other adequate solutions in this regard. One of the many examples of malpractice cited was the National Cybersecurity Institute Foundation, where approximately 50% of the project budget was allocated to the president and persons associated with him (e.g. his wife). The SAO noted that a significant part of the irregularities disclosed in 2024 were of a persistent nature, some of which had already been identified in its 2019 audit.

The Law and Justice Party advanced further proposals aimed at limiting the financial capacity of 'inconvenient' organizations. In August 2022, the government proposed another bill, which was quickly criticized, this time requiring NGOs to disclose their sources of foreign funding in a public register. Although this initiative was ultimately withdrawn, its content referred to solutions used in countries where restrictions on funding are used to exert systemic control over civil society. This trend is part of a broader global pattern of policies restricting access to foreign funding sources. As Buyse (2018) points out, more than 50 countries have introduced restrictions in this area in recent years. In Ethiopia, human rights organizations are prohibited from obtaining more than 10% of their funding from abroad; in Mauritania, such funding is banned entirely; and in Russia, since 2012, organizations supported by foreign funds and engaged in political activities are required to register as foreign agents. Similar regulations in Hungary (Gerö et al. 2020) have been found by the CJEU to be incompatible with EU law (Bretan 2020). In countries with limited internal resources, access to international funding is often crucial for the survival of CSOs, and blocking it can lead to the systemic weakening of the entire sector.

Discursive delegitimization and harassment of CSOs

The populist narrative of the Law and Justice Party, in office from 2015 to 2023, shaped the public debate in Poland in a way that significantly affected the functioning of CSOs. Control of public discourse and the delegitimization of organizations in the media is another important tool for restricting civic space, alongside financial constraints. As Buyse (2018) emphasizes, language and labelling play a key role in determining the scope of freedom and security of CSOs. The Law and Justice Party consistently combined institutional actions with political and media messaging, creating a climate of suspicion towards organizations dealing with issues considered 'inconvenient', particularly women's rights, LGBTIQ+ rights, refugee rights, and environmental protection (Follis 2019). The party's right-wing, populist ideological agenda not only limited the space for public discussion on equality, ecology, and human rights but also actively delegitimized entities defending these values.

This strategy was based on systematically ridiculing, accusing, and discrediting representatives of the civil sector through government-controlled public media, propaganda campaigns, and the rhetoric of high-ranking political actors. This message created a clear division between 'good organizations', i.e. those supporting the government narrative, often financed from public funds, and 'bad organizations', perceived as foreign agents, opponents of tradition or national values. These actions were part of a broader project to rebuild the axiological and social order. On the grounds of defending traditional values, women's rights were restricted (e.g. through the arbitrary application of restrictive abortion laws and the blocking of access to in vitro fertilization and contraception), freedom of expression was curtailed, protests were criminalized, and campaigns against the LGBTIQ+ community were framed as protecting the family and even children. At the same time, state-supported organizations were created to promote a conservative agenda and compete with existing NGOs in the public and financial spheres. In this way, the discrediting of independent CSOs became part of a broader government policy strategy aimed not only at neutralizing criticism, but also at taking control of public discourse and symbolically redefining concepts such as 'patriotism', 'democracy', 'freedom', 'family', and 'civic engagement'.

The campaign to discredit civil society was actively supported by public media, which is subordinate to the government's political authority. As early as 2016, Telewizja Polska (TVP – Polish Television) began to broadcast a series of reports portraying NGOs as corrupt and linked to the political elites of the previous government. As Day (2017) points out, in October of that year alone, at least seven such programmes were broadcast, suggesting that 10 leading NGOs were receiving funds as a result of fraud or nepotism. These allegations were not supported by any evidence, and their real purpose was to undermine public trust in the civil sector and limit its legitimacy in public debate (Grabowska-Moroz and Śniadach 2021). As a result, organizations critical of the government were not only marginalized in the media, but also exposed to symbolic violence and stigmatization.

In situations where CSOs are considered by the authorities to be too critical or too 'inconvenient', the state may also resort to a range of measures that are formally within the bounds of the law but in practice fall into a grey area between legal and non-legal actions (Buyse 2018). In the case of Poland after 2015, such actions included police raids and inspections of NGO offices, confiscation of computer equipment, and various forms of administrative harassment. Among the organizations that experienced such actions were women's rights organizations participating in mass protests against restrictive abortion laws, such as the Centrum Praw Kobiet (Centre for Women's Rights) (Day 2017). There were also reported acts of vandalism targeting organizations working for the rights of LGBTIQ+ people. In early 2016, the offices of the Campaign Against Homophobia and Lambda Warsaw were subject to a break-in, but the investigation was quickly dropped on the grounds that police were 'unable to identify the perpetrators' (The Express Tribune 2016). In the same year, unknown perpetrators ransacked the Poznań-based office of the Stonewall Group, and the actions of the authorities again appeared ineffective (Day 2017). The lack of response from law enforcement agencies in such cases can be interpreted as the state's tacit consent to symbolic and physical violence against groups and organizations perceived as incompatible with the government's ideological narrative.

Civil society responses and forms of resistance

Civil society responses to political moves after 2015 revealed both the resilience and deep diversity of this sector. In the face of growing authoritarianism and the shrinking of civic space, some organizations, especially watchdog, women, and legal movements, became the voice of social opposition to the dismantling of the rule of law and human rights violations (Pospieszna and Pietrzyk-Reeves 2022). Other entities, particularly those with a conservative profile, joined the project of ideological reconstruction of the state, becoming beneficiaries of the new system of power. This dynamic highlighted growing stratification within Polish civil society: from mobilization in defence of constitutional values to the instrumental use of NGO status to legitimize government actions. An analysis of these processes provides a better understanding of how civil society functions in conditions of democratic regression and how its various segments respond to the political challenges of illiberal transformation (Tilly 2003).

In November 2015, in direct response to the actions of the new Law and Justice Party-led government, the Komitet Obrony Demokracji (Committee for the Defence of Democracy – CDD) was formed, a mass civic movement that quickly became one of the most important symbols of social resistance to violations of the rule of law. The initiative arose from a grassroots impulse: on 18 November 2015, the writer and anti-communist opposition activist Krzysztof Łoziński published an article calling for the establishment of a committee to defend democracy, and one day later, journalist and social activist Mateusz Kijowski created a Facebook group with the same name. Within three days, over 30,000 users had joined the group, prompting the organizers to formalize their activities and create a social movement. On 2 December 2015, the CDD was officially registered as an association. In early December 2015, the CDD organized the first mass demonstrations against government decisions that violated the rulings of the Trybunał Konstytucyjny (Constitutional Tribunal). In their manifesto, the founders of the movement emphasized that its goal was to 'oppose violations of the law by those in power, remind citizens that they live in a democratic country, and that we should defend democracy with all our might' (Committee for the Defence of Democracy, 2015). The CDD's activities sparked a new wave of social mobilization in Poland. In the following years, the movement organized demonstrations in defence of the courts, free media, and civil rights, becoming an important element of the resurgent civil society (Grabowska-Moroz and Śniadach 2021).

In the face of growing political and economic pressure, some existing CSOs, particularly feminist movements, developed alternative strategies for action. Protests against the tightening of abortion laws in 2016, 2017, and 2020, which attracted more than 150,000 participants across the country, demonstrated the mobilizing capacity of these communities (Krizsán and Roggeband 2021; Szczygielska 2019; Graff and Korolczuk 2022). The collection of over half a million signatures for a citizens' initiative on safe access to abortion in 2017 confirmed that, despite repression, these organizations were able to create new forms of solidarity and grassroots resistance. A key moment was 3 October 2016, when approximately 100,000 people took to the streets in 118 Polish cities. They opposed a citizens' bill drafted by the Ordo Iuris Institute for Legal Culture Foundation, that would have introduced a total ban on abortion. The protest became known as the Czarny Protest (Black Protest). More than 50 solidarity demonstrations were also organized outside Poland, including in Europe, Canada, Kenya, and the People's Republic of China. Black Monday was not only the first mass action against the tightening of abortion laws, but also the largest mobilization of Polish women in defence of their rights. No previous *manifa* or demonstration had ever gathered so many participants. The protests were attended by women, men, and children from all over Poland, differing in age, education, socio-economic status, and worldview. Importantly, these mass protests enjoyed significant public support even during the preparatory phase. An IPSOS poll conducted on 28–30 September showed that the majority of Polish women (55%) and almost half of Polish men (45%) supported the women's rebellion (Chmielewska et al. 2017). The Black Protest and its subsequent iterations, including the Ogólnopolski Strajk Kobiet (All-Poland Women's Strike), became one of the most important social movements of the Law and Justice Party-led government's term in office, combining reproductive rights issues with broader opposition to authoritarian governance and the restriction of civil rights. Their characteristic features were decentralization, open structures, and the use of social media as the main channel for mobilization and communication (Korolczuk and Graff 2018). The women's movement in Poland underwent a significant transformation during this period, from organizations focused on expert and institutional work to more inclusive, street-level forms of resistance that brought together women from different classes, locations, and generations (Grzebalska and Petö 2018).

These protests also had a transnational dimension. Their symbols, slogans, and strategies spread across Central and Eastern Europe, inspiring mobilizations in other countries in the region, including Slovakia and Croatia (Krizsán and Roggeband 2021). In this way, the women's movement became one of the key regional actors in the fight for human rights and liberal democracy. Despite an intense campaign of discrediting by the authorities and pro-government media, women's civic initiatives managed to maintain a lasting presence in the public sphere, creating networks of support, education, and self-organization that went beyond narrowly defined activism. The feminist movement in Poland after 2016 can therefore be seen not only as a form of protest against the state, but also as a space for the development of new forms of citizenship and solidarity under conditions of restricted democratic freedoms (Graff and Korolczuk 2022; Grzebalska and Petö 2018).

During the Law and Justice Party's term in office, the judiciary was put in an exceptionally difficult situation. By criticizing judicial reforms, they exposed themselves to accusations of politicization and loss of impartiality, which in turn undermined public confidence in the justice system. These reforms, including changes in the functioning of the Krajowa Rada Sądownictwa (National Council of the Judiciary – NCJ), the Sąd Najwyższy (Supreme Court – SC), and the common courts, led to the effective blocking of constitutional review, one of the foundations of the rule of law. The legislative changes undermined the independence of the courts and thus contributed to the restriction of civic space in Poland (Grabowska-Moroz and Śniadach 2021; Pech 2023). In response to these processes, civil society, including the legal community, took action to limit the damage resulting from the dismantling of the independence of the courts. Their activity led to the Europeanization of the problem of the rule of law in Poland, resulting not only in the initiation of political procedures at the EU level (such as the procedure under Article 7 of the TEU, the rule of law framework, and debates and resolutions of the European Parliament), but also to interventions in proceedings before the CJEU (Grabowska-Moroz and Śniadach 2021).

One of the key moments of public resistance to the reforms was the wave of protests in July 2017 against draft laws on common courts, the SC, and the NCJ. At that time, a group of four lawyers initiated an informal movement called 'Free Courts', which quickly became a symbol of opposition to political control over the judiciary. Thanks to the active use of social media, this initiative effectively mobilized public opinion and contributed to maintaining public pressure on the government.

The two main judges' associations, the Polish Judges Association 'Iustitia' (founded in 1990) and the Judges Association 'Themis' (founded in 2010), have become the most recognizable institutional actors in this opposition.

Both have been the targets of propaganda and disciplinary attacks, being portrayed by the authorities as interest groups defending 'caste privileges' (Śledzińska-Simon 2018; Mastracci 2020). In fact, these associations played a significant role in organizing and coordinating protests in defence of judicial independence. Iustitia co-organized mass demonstrations in 2017, during which protesters lit candles and displayed banners bearing the slogan 'Constitution' – a symbol of civil resistance to the authoritarian tendencies of the government. In January 2020, the judicial community organized another internationally publicized protest, the 'March of a Thousand Robes', which aimed to oppose disciplinary proceedings against independent judges. The event was attended by representatives of the judiciary from many EU member states, dressed in official robes, which constituted a powerful symbol of European solidarity and the common defence of the values of the rule of law (Grabowska-Moroz and Śniadach 2021; Wyrzykowski 2019).

To strengthen its message and increase public understanding of the importance of judicial independence, Iustitia developed a specific public communication strategy that was previously unknown to organizations of this kind. Judges began to communicate with the wider public both through social media and by organizing open debates, educational events, and information campaigns. These activities enabled the establishment of lasting cooperation networks within the country, as well as with European and international entities. As a result, cases of harassment of Polish judges, including disciplinary proceedings, became the subject of international interest and sparked a wave of solidarity across the EU.

An analysis of data collected by Grzegorz Foryś (forthcoming) on all protests organized between 2015 and 2023 shows that a total of 133 protests took place in Poland during this period. In terms of geographical coverage, nationwide protests dominated, accounting for 70.7% of all such events in the period analysed. Digital tools and social media were central to rapid mobilization: Facebook groups, hashtags, and online networks helped to coordinate protests and disseminate information, compensating for limited access to mainstream media channels.

However, it should be remembered that civil society in Poland is not a homogeneous entity, and the reactions of its representatives to the government's actions after 2015 were varied and often uncoordinated. Not all organizations were affected by the restrictions on civic space. Some, particularly those with a conservative profile, benefited greatly from the new political configuration. They obtained significant public funds, greater access to decision-makers, and the opportunity to freely implement their own ideological programmes. In addition to organizations with personal ties to politicians or movements effectively taken over by the state, there was also a group of entities that consciously cooperated with the ruling coalition, recognizing this cooperation as a means of achieving common goals. Conservative think tanks played a particularly important role in this process, becoming partners of the ruling party in its efforts to reshape the ideological and symbolic landscape in Poland and promote a vision of society based on nationalist and fundamentalist values (Korolczuk 2022).

The most influential of these organizations was the Ordo Iuris Institute for Legal Culture Foundation, established in 2013. From the outset, it promoted an agenda of 'protecting life', 'family values', and Christian ethics, and from 2015 it became one of the key partners of the ruling camp in the non-governmental sphere (Korolczuk 2022; Graff and Korolczuk 2022). Ordo Iuris used its status as an NGO to legitimize state actions that restricted the rights of women, LGBTIQ+ people, and liberal organizations. In the public debate, representatives of the foundation often accused progressive organizations of pursuing 'foreign interests' and demanded that they disclose project documentation financed from public funds, which in practice had an intimidating effect and undermined their credibility (Korolczuk 2022; Graff and Korolczuk 2022; Dudkiewicz 2017). At the same time, right-wing political groups and associated social circles became increasingly involved in campaigns against the so-called gender ideology (Korolczuk and Graff 2018; Podgórska-Rykała 2016), presented as a threat to children, families, and national identity. Such narratives, reinforced by the Catholic Church and conservative media, served to mobilize the electorate by creating a moral threat and delegitimizing opposition circles as promoters of demoralization. Thanks to this alliance, conservative organizations gained not only stable funding and access to decision-makers, but also formal recognition in state institutions. A representative of Ordo Iuris was appointed to the NIF-CDCS in 2017, while the co-founder and first president of the foundation, Aleksander Stępkowski, took office as a judge of the SC in 2019. In 2020, the government recommended the co-director of Ordo Iuris as a member of the European Economic and Social Committee, an advisory body to the EU institutions that formally represent the voice of civil society (Korolczuk 2022). The latter example shows that, after 2015, civic space in Poland was not only narrowed, but also redefined and politicized, with some NGOs being incorporated into the process of legitimizing the government and its ideological project.

Conclusion

Eight years of Law and Justice Party governance represented a period of deep tension between liberal and illiberal visions of democracy in Poland. During the party's term in office, there was a gradual erosion of the principles that form the foundation of a modern constitutional state, in particular the separation of powers, judicial independence, and respect for minority rights (Wyrzykowski 2019). Poland has become one of the most striking examples of the global phenomenon of the shift towards an illiberal model of democracy – a system that retains democratic electoral procedures while systematically undermining their liberal content and institutional guarantees (Bill and Stanley 2025).

The success of the programme known as the 'Good Change' was made possible by a skilful combination of redistributive social promises with nationalist rhetoric and a conservative cultural shift (see Bill and Stanley 2025). While this policy responded to the sense of marginalization experienced by sections of society, at the same time it led to deep social divisions and the delegitimization of institutions previously considered pillars of liberal democracy (Bill and Stanley 2025). It was not until the October 2023 elections, which ended eight years of Law and Justice Party dominance, that the illiberal experiment in Poland was symbolically brought to a close, although its effects are likely to persist.

In this context, civil society played a particularly important role. Initially, watchdog and human rights organizations responded to the constitutional crisis through conventional means, including appeals, legal opinions, and statements appealing to the values of dialogue and institutional cooperation. However, these methods proved insufficient in the face of a government that rejected mechanisms of social control and ignored democratic standards. Over time, NGOs began to adapt their strategies, combining advocacy with street protests, international mobilization, and the building of new social coalitions (Pospieszna and Pietrzyk-Reeves 2022).

The processes taking place in Poland during the period 2015–23 were part of a broader international trend of de-democratization, including the weakening of independent institutions, the politicization of public media, and deepening political polarization (Tilly 2003; Coppedge 2017). The Polish case aligns with global trends of civic space restriction observed in several countries over the past decade, where legal and financial devices are combined with discursive delegitimization. In response to the controversial judicial 'reforms' in Poland, numerous international organizations, including the Venice Commission, the Parliamentary Assembly of the Council of Europe, the United Nations Special Rapporteur on the independence of judges and lawyers, the International Commission of Jurists, and the American Bar Association, have publicly condemned the Polish government's actions (Grabowska-Moroz and Śniadach 2021). Despite these interventions, CSOs bore the brunt of defending the rule of law and civil rights, often operating under conditions of political pressure, financial constraint, and discrediting campaigns.

During the process of social mobilization in 2015–17, several organizations were established which provided organizational support for protesters throughout the period under study. These included the CDD (2015), Obywatele RP (Citizens of Poland, 2016), Akcja Demokracja (Action for Democracy, 2015), the Ogólnopolski Strajk Kobiet (All-Poland Women's Strike, 2016), and the Stowarzyszenie Wolne Sądy (Free Courts Foundation, 2017). In order to maximize the effectiveness of their protest activities, these organizations, together with less prominent partners from the non-governmental sector, began cooperating almost from the outset, based on a shared set of pro-democratic values and concern for the public good. The most striking example of this cooperation was the involvement of the All-Poland Women's Strike in organizing protests in defence of the independence of the courts and the active support provided by activists of the CDD to the feminist movement (Foryś forthcoming). Importantly, the shrinking civic space was asymmetrical: while many independent NGOs were marginalized, pro-government organizations were empowered, a dynamic that institutionalized partisan pluralism rather than pluralism per se.

The analysis shows that, between 2015 and 2023, the Law and Justice Party-led government systematically redefined the boundaries of civic participation through legal, financial, and discursive instruments. Public funding became a tool of political control, while stigmatizing campaigns and administrative harassment eroded trust in independent organizations. Yet these pressures did not eliminate civil society; rather, they transformed it. New movements such as the CDD, the All-Poland Women's Strike, and judicial associations exemplified a bottom-up reconstruction of democratic agency. Paradoxically, the shrinking of civic space contributed to its politicization and reactivation, as Polish citizens and NGOs reasserted their role as defenders of the rule of law and fundamental rights. The Polish case thus highlights both the vulnerability and the adaptive strength of civil society in the face of populist authoritarianism. Civil society, although susceptible to pressure and divisions, can become a space not only of resistance to illiberal trends, but also a space for new forms of civic action and solidarity.

Based on the Polish experience, several recommendations can be made that address decision-makers at various levels of public administration, constituting a kind of policy-oriented conclusion. First, it is essential to prioritize transparent, multi-stakeholder grant allocation mechanisms and to support activities that strengthen the capacity of NGOs in order to reduce their vulnerability to political pressure and financial risks. Second, it is necessary to create a stable and pluralistic framework for cross-sectoral cooperation that guarantees the participation of organizations with diverse ideological profiles in consultation and decision-making processes. Finally, international actors, including EU institutions and grant-making networks, can play an important role by securing emergency funding channels, supporting advocacy initiatives, and developing transnational solidarity networks that strengthen the resilience of civil society in the context of democratic regression.

Notes

1 The latest data indicate that civil society is no longer dominated by the community of NGOs, but has become more nuanced. It also consists of diverse groups, both organized and unorganized, which transcend traditional definitions and divisions thanks to their new ways of thinking and acting (Cooper 2018). Research on civil society in this broad sense has shaped the understanding of distinctiveness, revealing the diversity of hybrid forms of organization, as well as the interpenetration of functions and networks between the state and civil society and between the market and civil society (Buyse 2018; Lilja 2015).

2 Audits conducted at the National Cybersecurity Institute Foundation, the asperIT Foundation, the SAPERE AUDE Social Initiatives Foundation, the e-fektywni.org Foundation, the Matecznik Pomocniczości i Dobroci Association, the Poznań Institute Foundation, the Centre for the Promotion and Development of Civic Initiatives 'PISOP', the Suwerenna Institute Foundation, the Association for the Development and Promotion of Podkarpacie PRO CARPATHIA, the Polska Wielki Projekt Foundation, and the Scytia Foundation.

References

Bill, Stanley. 2020. 'Counter-Elite Populism and Civil Society in Poland: PiS's Strategies of Elite Replacement'. *East European Politics and Societies* 36: 118–140.

Bill, Stanley and Ben Stanley. 2025a. 'Democracy after Illiberalism: A Warning from Poland'. *Journal of Democracy* 36(3): 16–32. doi:10.1353/jod.2025.a964585.

Bill, Stanley, and Ben Stanley. 2025b. *Good Change: The Rise and Fall of Poland's Illiberal Revolution*. Stanford, CA: Stanford University Press.

Bretan, Juliette. 2020. 'Polish Ministers Propose Law Making NGOs Declare Foreign Funding and Creating Public Register'. *Notes from Poland*, 9 August. https://notesfrompoland.com/2020/08/09/poland-seeks-to-make-ngos-declare-foreign-funding/.

Buyse, Antoine. 2018. 'Squeezing Civic Space: Restrictions on Civil Society Organizations and the Linkages with Human Rights'. *The International Journal of Human Rights* 22(8): 966–988. doi:10.1080/13642987.2018.1492916.

Chmielewska, Marta, Małgorzata Druciarek, and Izabela Przybysz. 2017. *Czarny protest – w stronę nowego 'kompromisu aborcyjnego?'* Warsaw: Instytut Spraw Publicznych.

Cooper, Rachel. 2018. 'What Is Civil Society? How Is the Term Used and What Is Seen to Be Its Role and Value (Internationally) in 2018?' K4D Helpdesk Report. Brighton: Institute of Development Studies. https://assets.publishing.service.gov.uk/media/5c6c2e74e5274a72bc45240e/488_What_is_Civil_Society.pdf.

Coppedge, Michael. 2017. 'Eroding Regimes: What, Where, and When?' Working Paper 57. V-Dem Institute. https://ssrn.com/abstract=3066677.

Day, Jonathan. 2017. 'Poland Seizes Control of Civil Society Funding'. Liberties. https://www.liberties.eu/en/news/poland-ngo-law-funding/13783.

Dudkiewicz, Ignacy. 2017. 'Gliński: W Polsce nie ma żadnego zagrożenia demokracji'. NGO.pl. https://publicystyka.ngo.pl/glinski-w-polsce-nie-ma-zadnego-zagrozenia-demokracji.

European Commission. 2017. 'Proposal for a Council Decision on the Determination of a Clear Risk of a Serious Breach by the Republic of Poland of the Rule of Law'. COM/2017/0835 final - 2017/0360 (NLE). Brussels: European Commission. https://eur-lex.europa.eu/legal-content/PL/TXT/?uri=CELEX:52017PC0835.

Follis, Karolina. 2019. 'Rejecting Refugees in Illiberal Poland: The Response from Civil Society'. *Journal of Civil Society* 15(4): 307–325. doi:10.1080/17448689.2019.1668626.

Foryś, Grzegorz. Forthcoming. *Social Movements and Democracy. Models of Democracy within Multi-Organizational Fields of Social Movements in Poland* (unpublished manuscript in the possession of the author).

Freedom House. 2016. *Score Changes in 2016*. https://freedomhouse.org/country/poland/nations-transit/2016.

Gerö, Marton, Pál Susánszky, Ákos Kopper, and Gergely Toth. 2020. 'Strategies for Survival: Human Rights Organisations' Responses to the Closing of Political

Opportunity Structures in Hungary'. *Politologickycasopis* (*Czech Journal of Political Science*) 2: 119–139.

Główny Urząd Statystyczny (Central Statistical Office of Poland). n.d. 'Social Economy, Volunteering'. https://stat.gov.pl/obszary-tematyczne/gospodarka-spoleczna-wolontariat/.

Grabowska-Moroz, Barbara and Olga Śniadach. 2021. 'The Role of Civil Society in Protecting Judicial Independence in Times of Rule of Law Backsliding in Poland'. *Utrecht Law Review* 17(2): 56–69.

Graff, Agnieszka and Elżbieta Korolczuk. 2022. *Anti-Gender Politics in the Populist Moment*. London: Routledge.

Grzebalska, Weronika and Andrea Petö. 2018. 'The Gendered Modus Operandi of the Illiberal Transformation in Hungary and Poland'. *Women's Studies International Forum* 68: 164–172. doi:10.1016/j.wsif.2017.12.001.

Jenkins, Garry W. 2012. 'Nongovernmental Organizations and the Forces Against Them: Lessons on the Anti-NGO Movement'. *Brooklyn Journal of International Law* 37(2): 459–553. https://brooklynworks.brooklaw.edu/bjil/vol37/iss2/4.

Klon/Jawor. 2025. 'Kondycja organizacji pozarządowych 2024'. May. https://kondycja.ngo.pl.

Komitet Obrony Demokracji (Committee for the Defence of Democracy). 2015. 'About the CDD – Who We Are'. https://ruchkod.pl/o-kod-zie/.

Korolczuk, Elżbieta. 2022. 'Challenging Civil Society Elites in Poland: The Dynamics and Strategies of Civil Society Actors'. *East European Politics and Societies* 37(3): 880–902. doi:10.1177/08883254221132282.

Korolczuk, Elżbieta and Agnieszka Graff. 2018. 'Gender as "Ebola from Brussels": The Anticolonial Frame and the Rise of Illiberal Populism'. *Signs: Journal of Women in Culture and Society* 43(4): 797–821.

Krizsán, Andrea and Conny Roggeband. 2021. 'Reconfiguring State-Movement Relations in the Context of De-democratization'. *Social Politics: International Studies in Gender, State & Society* 28(3): 604–628. doi:10.1093/sp/jxab027.

Lilja, Elisabeth. 2015. 'A New Ecology of Civil Society'. *Journal of Civil Society* 11 (2): 117–122.

Marczewski, Paweł. 2024. 'From Resistance to Action: Civic Mobilizations in Poland 2015–2023'. In Paweł Marczewski, Goran Forbici, and Fedor Blaščák (eds), *Resisting the Illiberal Turn in Poland, Slovenia and Slovakia*. Bratislava: Open Society Foundation Bratislava, pp. 15–45.

Marczewski, Paweł. 2025. *Demokracja obywateli: Mobilizacje społeczne w latach 2015–2023*. Warsaw: The Stefan Batory Foundation.

Mastracci, Matteo. 2020. 'Judiciary Saga in Poland: An Affair Torn Between European Standards and ECtHR Criteria'. *Polish Review of International and European Law* 9(2): 39–79. doi:10.21697/priel.2020.9.2.02.

Najwyższa Izba Kontroli (Supreme Audit Office). 2024. 'System dotacji dla organizacji pozarządowych potrzebuje uzdrowienia', 17 June. https://www.nik.gov.pl/najnowsze-informacje-o-wynikach-kontroli/narodowy-instytutu-wolnosci-niw-crso.html.

Ohlrich, Noreen. 2016. 'NGOs Fear the Forcible Shrinking of Civil Society in Poland'. *Nonprofit Quarterly*, 7 December. https://nonprofitquarterly.org/ngos-fear-forcible-shrinking-civil-society-poland/.

Organization for Security and Co-operation in Europe's Office for Democratic Institutions and Human Rights (OSCE/ODIHR). 2017. 'Opinion on the Draft Act of Poland on the National Freedom Institute – Centre for the Development of Civil

Society'. NGO-POL/303/2017[AIC], 22 August. Warsaw: Organization for Security and Co-operation in Europe.

Pech, Laurent. 2023. '7 Years Later: Poland as a Legal Black Hole'. Verfassungsblog, 17 January. doi:10.17176/20230118-001918-0.

Płoszka, Adam. 2020. 'Shrinking Space for Civil Society: A Case Study of Poland'. *European Public Law* 26(4): 941–960. doi:10.54648/euro2020072.

Podgórska-Rykała, Joanna. 2016. *Polityka równości płci na szczeblu lokalnym.* Sosnowiec: Humanitas.

Pospieszna, Paulina and Dorota Pietrzyk-Reeves. 2022. 'Responses of Polish NGOs Engaged in Democracy Promotion to Shrinking Civic Space'. *Cambridge Review of International Affairs* 35(4): 523–544. doi:10.1080/09557571.2022.202786.

Sieradzka, Monika. 2016. 'Polish NGOs Under Pressure'. *Deutsche Welle*, 12 January. https://www.dw.com/en/polands-government-wants-to-control-ngos/a-36609126.

Sledzińska-Simon, Anna. 2018. 'The Rise and Fall of Judicial Self-Government in Poland: On Judicial Reform Reversing Democratic Transition'. *German Law Journal* 19(7) (Special Issue). doi:10.2139/ssrn.3216482.

Szczygielska, Marianna. 2019. '"Good Change" and Better Activism: Feminist Responses to Backsliding Gender Policies in Poland'. In Andrea Krizsán and Conny Roggeband (eds), *Gendering Democratic Backsliding in Central and Eastern Europe: A Comparative Agenda*. Budapest: Central European University Press, pp. 120–160.

The Express Tribune. 2016. 'Growing Attacks on Polish Gay Rights Groups: Commissioner', 6 March. https://tribune.com.pk/story/1060258/growing-attacks-on-polish-gay-rights-groups-commissioner.

Tilly, Charles. 2003. 'Inequality, Democratization, and De-democratisation'. *Sociological Theory* 21(1): 37–43. http://www.jstor.org/stable/3108607.

V-Dem Institute. 2017. *Democracy at Dusk? V-Dem Annual Report 2017*. Chrome-extension://efaidnbmnnnibpcajpcglclefindmkaj/https://www.v-dem.net/documents/18/dr_2017.pdf.

Wyrzykowski, Mirosław. 2019. 'Experiencing the Unimaginable: The Collapse of the Rule of Law in Poland'. *Hague Journal on the Rule of Law* 11: 417–422. doi:10.1007/s40803-019-00124-z.

Conclusion

De-democratization Processes: Lessons from Poland

Grzegorz Foryś

The multifaceted nature of de-democratization processes

The theoretical framework for analysing the symptoms of de-democratization in Poland from 2015 to 2023, as discussed in this volume, was significantly influenced by Charles Tilly (2007). His approach to de-democratization made it possible to combine a general, universal model for analysing relations between the state and the *demos* with a certain degree of freedom in the selection of predominantly qualitative indicators of de-democratization processes. It provided an incentive for studying the various processes displaying symptoms of de-democratization across particular countries, for conducting comparative studies, and for attempting to establish to what extent some indicators are universal or specific. It was not possible to make such comparisons in this volume, as the analysis was confined to the Polish case; however, they may prove useful for further research on de-democratization processes affecting other countries. As this study primarily relies on qualitative research, its findings may also be applied to comparative studies in the future.

The research was conducted across three principal areas: the legal/judicial sphere, the economic dimension, and civil society and civil rights. First, key legislative problems originated in changes affecting judicial institutions and, more broadly, the courts and the judiciary as a whole. Second, the economic dimension was viewed from through the lens of renationalization processes, framed as the restoration of Polish ownership in crucial branches of the economy. The Zjednoczona Prawica (United Right) alliance employed its economic assets to secure electoral support, chiefly through the social transfers that were not always economically rational and that were dedicated to particular social categories. The third area of interest was devoted to civil rights and freedoms, as well as the reactions of civil society to the activities of the state described in the first part of this volume. Together, these three analytical perspectives facilitated the identification of a suitable set of indicators of de-democratization processes, as well as an assessment of the nature of relations between the state and society, which is key to an evaluation of the extent of democratic backsliding. In other words, the overall analysis is

DOI: 10.4324/9781042002030-15

closely tied to the chain of events that could be viewed as part of a cause and effect mechanism, an action-reaction sequence in which initiatives conducted by the state are met with societal responses. Examination of these matters led the contributors to formulate several conclusions addressing specific areas of analysis, such as law, economics, politics, and society, as well as those of a more universal character.

The neutralization of the oversight competences of the Trybunał Konstytucyjny (Constitutional Tribunal – CT) in Poland clearly facilitated the process of de-democratization in the legal area. As discussed in Chapter 3 in this volume, this development triggered the process of 'autocratic incrementalism', which was intended to manipulate public opinion by creating the impression that judiciary institutions were being strengthened, albeit that in reality this process led to their gradual decline as they became increasingly flawed and subordinated to political actors. The political capture of the CT gave state authorities a monopoly on determining the constitutionality of the effects caused by new legislative actions. In practice, this resulted in the rejection of legal solutions that did not meet the expectations of the government authorities and the acceptance of those that did. The consequences were twofold. First, the CT disregarded interpretations of the Constitution that were grounded in doctrine and constitutional jurisprudence. Second, fundamental political disputes shifted to the international level, resulting in the engagement of the Court of Justice of the European Union and the European Court for Human Rights. The process of the de-legalization of the CT led to the situation in which the Tribunal was not able to protect the constitutional axiology or to guarantee the proper functioning of the hierarchically organized system of norms, as had been the case after 1997 (Tuleja 2022, 269–70). The subordination of the CT was used as an instrument to further distort the justice system and weaken the autonomy of the judiciary branch, especially the Krajowa Rada Sądownictwa (National Council of the Judiciary – NCJ) and the Sąd Najwyższy (Supreme Court – SC) of Poland. While the manoeuvres involving the CT secured the eventual passage of the legislative initiatives proposed by the authorities, the struggle over the rule of law centred around the NCJ. The subordination of judges significantly affected everyday judicial practice, while the impunity of the state authorities of the United Right was ensured. In such a judicial system, citizens could easily find themselves at a disadvantage in potential disputes with the state. The legal area was crucial for constructing a new institutional order, departing from the norms of the democratic state of the law. The procedures for appointing the judges of the CT, which might have appeared to citizens as unobtrusive and a mere formality, could, in reality, equip the state with the instruments of power preservation and even become a cornerstone of the broader de-democratization process.

While state initiatives in the judiciary were of fundamental importance, and the democratic backsliding they caused was relatively visible, evaluation of the economic policies pursued by the United Right proved to be more difficult. There was considerable scope for favourable interpretations of the government's programmes, even the unsuccessful ones, as they could be presented as attempts to implement policies benefiting both the state and certain social groupings simultaneously. Other changes in the state's economic policy were harder to justify. These included renationalization processes, as well as the use of state assets to facilitate the takeover of private enterprises in order to ensure a competitive advantage of the state over society. State authorities increased funding of the public media, while non-governmental organizations (NGOs) were always ready to support the government and its right-wing agenda. To achieve these objectives, public finances were removed from parliamentary oversight and thus were put beyond citizens' control. The authorities constructed a narrative about the need to increase Polish ownership in key branches of the economy, leading to renationalization. This was followed by financial transfers to legally dubious initiatives in order to gain acceptance by certain parts of society and, finally, the financing of alternative forms of civil society. Consequently, the position of the state was strengthened and acquired a sense of agency that is typically associated with authoritarian regimes.

At the level of society, efforts to impose the state's will over the citizenry were observed in the restriction of the autonomy and empowerment of local communities, including a reduction of their competences and the selective allocation of funding to local governments. The symptoms of de-democratization were manifested in limitations on citizen participation in public life and the increased partisanship of local government, particularly its alignment with the United Right. Financial mechanisms supporting local infrastructure, such as the Local Government Road Fund and the Government Fund or Local Investments were used as political instruments for the preferential allocation of funds, favouring local governments connected with the Prawo i Sprawiedliwość (Law and Justice Party). Areas of developmental potential and strategic importance for local communities were placed under state control through surveying and water management practices. During the period under study, competences and financial resources were transferred from local governments to central state institutions.

The United Right's efforts to create a more subordinate society was also manifested in the curtailment of civil rights, particularly the freedom to assemble and the right to protest. This was not achieved through an explicit ban on protest, but rather by giving priority to pro-government rallies. Those who opposed such rallies could face repression. Freedom of speech was also undermined through political control over public media, as well as the marginalization of independent media. This significantly curbed citizens' access to a plurality of information sources, particularly as many local media outlets were acquired or financed by state-owned energy concerns. Furthermore, citizens' right to privacy was regularly violated by surveillance practices, often conducted without clear legal basis or appropriate oversight. Collectively, these measures contributed to a weakening of the rule of law, as well as to an erosion of human and civil rights in Poland. At the time of writing, these developments under investigation by the criminal justice system, and individuals involved in their initiation faced criminal charges.

The state activities directed at citizens were not imposed without any response from civil society. There were numerous protests against the changes that were introduced by the United Right which were perceived as posing a threat to democracy. Protests around issues related to the CT, judicial independence, media freedom, and women's rights were a clear indication that some processes of de-democratization had been set in motion and that civil society was engaged in defending its own position within the democratic order.

De-democratization indicators and theoretical perspectives

From 2015 to 2023, a number of multifaceted symptoms of de-democratization could be observed in the activities of the Polish state; nevertheless, it is possible to identify the key areas in which these processes occurred. Taken together, they formed a relatively cohesive and hierarchical 'de-democratization syndrome'. The hierarchical ordering within this syndrome was of secondary importance, as disconnecting the state from the will of the citizenry was prioritized, especially changes of a legislative and institutional nature. Constitutional provisions alone are insufficient to ensure that a given political system is democratic, as the rule of law and the everyday practice of the law may not fit together or meaningfully coexist with one another. However, it can be stated with certainty that legal changes that tamper with the foundations of democracy, such as the separation of government powers, the rule of law, judicial autonomy, and civil rights, all indicate democratic backsliding. In Poland, such measures led to a depiction of the legal infallibility of the state, in terms of legislation and its constitutionality being ensured by the subordinated CT and the judicature of the common courts. The latter was unsuccessful as the United Right was unable to fully subordinate the judiciary. The indicators of de-democratization employed in this volume pertain primarily to the key legal statutes regulating the functions of the most important judicial institutions. In sum, these changes significantly eroded the foundations of the separation of powers. According to the contributors to this volume, the reforms to the judicial system that negatively influenced the authority and independence of the courts should be treated as obvious, first-degree indicators of de-democratization of the utmost seriousness. Transformations of the judicial system from democratic to non-democratic forms can be effected with relative ease, but have far-reaching, or even radical, consequences.

The second-degree indicators of de-democratization described in the volume were directly linked to the relationship between the state and the citizenry. To some extent, they originated in legal changes that tampered with the foundations of democracy and civil rights. Following the outbreak of social protests, the state responded with repression. Some of them were self-evident and explicit, while others could be seen as more subtle legal 'innovations', constituting camouflaged threats to civil and human rights, usually enhanced by media activities. As noted earlier, public media were placed under state control and new pro-government media were established. This led to the monopolization of news resources and influenced the agenda in terms of selecting issues that were deemed worthy of attention. Thanks to these measures, the state was able to create a false narrative of the current situation and the intentions of the state. According to Sartori, 'free elections with unfree opinions express nothing. We say that the people must be sovereign. An empty sovereign who has nothing to say, without opinions of his own, is a mere ratifier, a sovereign of nothing' (Sartori 1987, 87). The state also engaged in creating alternative civil society organizations, which in practice became a reservoir of support for the United Right-led government. At the same time, pre-existing independent NGOs had experienced cuts in funding, thus restricting their activities, while the organizations supporting the government received disproportionate public funding. This facilitated the formation of a pro-government social base, while appearances of normalcy were maintained. Social polarization was encouraged, accompanied by symbolic exclusion from the national community. Although this did not entail physical exclusion, certain social groupings were labelled traitors or stigmatized as inferior members of Polish society. Symbolic exclusion also affected certain parts of society, such as opposition groups or sexual minorities, whose views did not align with the right-wing agenda. Indicators of de-democratization, including civil rights restrictions, repression of protesters, manipulation of institutional agency, and the diminished empowerment of local communities, closely corresponded to those proposed by Charles Tilly (2007). They may serve as a basis for constructing various indices measuring the quality of democracy in any given country. Indicators such as the number of citizen complaints, the frequency of protests, the extent of media freedom, or the level of dependence of local government on the state may be used to assess the extent to which a political system has slid towards de-democratization.

In the economic sphere, indicators of de-democratization are more difficult to capture than in the judicial system or the area of civil society/civil rights. The pursuit of democratic backsliding required the state to secure sufficient financial resources as well as relative social stability in order to be able to implement a carefully designed economic policy. It comprised a crucial part of a larger strategy that strengthened the role of the state in the economy, while responding to the needs of the moment. Consequently, the priorities of such a strategy might be opportunistic and prone to changes as decision-makers implemented them according to societal needs. In Poland, such measures were often adopted on an ad hoc basis and did not contribute to a coherent economic policy. The state treated the economy as an instrument for financing de-democratization processes while gaining more supporters and maintaining public order. Above all, these economic measures were used to enhance the strength and autonomy of the state, while the authorities consolidated their advantage over their political competitors. These developments were made possible by the aggregation of financial powers in the hands of the state (Innes 2014). As Fukuyama observes, 'state capture is the main institutional feature of democratic backsliding' (Fukuyama 2014, 54). In analysing de-democratization in the economic area, the contributors to this volume have focused on indicators pertaining to renationalization, centralization, and social transfers. At first glance, such measures may appear to reflect standard economic policies of the state, but when situated in a broader political context they reveal the true intentions of the state which seeks to gain strategic advantages over society and the ability to control it. It should be added here that state-owned companies served to implement state policies, while financial resources were transferred to loyal political groups, often without regard for the broader interests of society as a whole.

The indicators of de-democratization outlined in this volume do not constitute an exhaustive list of all the possible variables. Rather, this volume follows Charles Tilly's qualitative approach to de-democratization, enhancing it with less tangible context-specific characteristics. Certain similarities may be drawn with the critical observations of Viktor Orbán's regime in Hungary offered by Kim Lane Scheppele (2013, 562), who argued that 'forensic legal analysis can tell how such a system works, but political science supplies just such tools'. Although democratic backsliding in Poland has been less advanced than in Hungary, the two countries share comparable qualitative elements. Interestingly, the qualitative characteristics of Hungarian democracy described by Scheppele were also identified in Poland. The list of afflictions affecting Hungarian democracy closely resembles the problems facing Polish democracy during the period of governance by the United Right, as described in this volume. These include restrictions on practices of direct democracy; government control over public and other media; limitations on parliamentary and judicial control over the government; severe limitations on the independence of the CT; the use of veto powers to secure the interests of those in power (also practised in Poland thanks to presidential authority); the dominance of the governing party over the Państwowa Komisja Wyborcza (National Election Commission), nepotism, and corruption. Indicators of deepening social divisions may be added to this list. In Hungary, these divisions were ethnic in nature, while in Poland they originated in cultural issues and worldview preferences. Populist messages from the government to society also exacerbated these divisions. It would not be an exaggeration to state that the argument concerning the usefulness of qualitative approaches to diagnosing democracy has been confirmed. The qualitative indicators of de-democratization identified in this volume can also be found in the works of other authors (Sadurski 2018; Sata and Karolewski 2019).

Charles Tilly's approach to de-democratization is both descriptive and explanatory. Its wisdom can be found in the idea that the processes of democratization or de-democratization are a result of the rivalry between the state and the *demos*. Movements of these two entities along the dimensions of empowerment, agency, and mutual control reflect shifts between democratization and de-democratization. Tilly's approach is undoubtedly useful for detecting de-democratization based on quantitative characteristics, such as the number of demands made by citizens upon the state, the number of citizens facing repression, or the number of arrests made without warrants; however, it is insufficient for an in-depth analysis. Although it is possible to present quantitative values for derogations of the separation of powers, departures from the rule of law, restrictions on the free press and media freedom, civil rights violations, as well as examples of economic dependency of citizens on the state and similar quantifiable matters, it is still essential to address the populist narrative. The intentions of the state, as well as the variations of its message, can only be described in a qualitative manner. This type of analysis is particularly useful for studying changes in the rule of law. Autocratic incrementalism is not always measurable through standard indicators.

As noted earlier, the contributors to this volume acknowledge the universal logic of de-democratization processes, understood as changes enabling the state to achieve unquestionable dominance over the citizenry. However, each state arrives at this hegemonic position in its own way. The consequences of state actions, such as changes to the constitution, legal changes, media colonization, and control of NGOs, will often be replicated in particular countries. However, more specific decisions will stem from particular characteristics of the given political system, especially institutional and constitutional solutions and their practical applications. Moreover, the universal character of democratic backsliding that affects political systems in various parts of the globe does not preclude regional differentiation. As noted by the V-Dem Institute, 'India has continued on a path of steep decline, to the extent it has almost lost its status as a democracy. The United States – former vanguard of liberal democracy – has lost its way' (V-Dem Institute 2020). Such arguments concerning the decline of democracy are often ambitious, yet they are not suitable for building lasting explanations. They do not go beyond overplaying the importance of a single factor, such as the decline of political institutions (Norris and Inglehart 2019), the polarization of Western societies (Przeworski 2019), or authoritarian diffusion (Krastev and Holmes 2020). All these matters are important but do not provide a complete account of de-democratization. A more accurate perspective is offered by Karolewski (2021, 305), who argues that 'the democratic decline is to be found across the globe due to the fragility of liberal democracy itself'. As noted in Chapter 1 in this volume, the weaknesses of democracy render it susceptible to decline. In the contemporary context, these weaknesses are activated by factors that did not exist in the past, such as decline of the welfare state, globalization, and new media development. The interactions of these factors may be seen as a common denominator, although this does not provide a full explanation.

The specific conditions of every political system usually determine how quickly de-democratization factors may appear and how far de-democratization processes may go. No political system is exempt from being susceptible to de-democratization, as illustrated by the cases of Hungary and Poland, as well as Slovakia, the United States, and the United Kingdom. Political elites and their relationship with society comprise the common element of de-democratization processes in various countries. These elites have the propensity to instrumentalize the threats to democracy and state appropriation to their own advantage (see Karolewski 2021, 316). Societal acquiescence plays a role, particularly when resentment towards former corrupt elites that demanded sacrifices from society during regime changes in the late 1980s is employed (Lorenz and Anders 2021, 341). It should be added here that, in Poland, the model of regime transformation involved a strategy planned from above by the elites of the era. Therefore, the myth arose that 'anti-Polish liberal elites' allowed the right in Poland to shore up its political capital. The right-wing parties in Poland are responsible for inflating that myth, which exaggerated the costs of system transformation and presented them as an ongoing threat to democracy. Furthermore, 'changes in the nature of citizenship towards spectatorship, passivity and plebiscitary understanding of democracy favour democratic backsliding, even though they might not constitute democratic backsliding on their own' (Lorenz and Anders 2021, 316). Thankfully, the fate of democracy remains in our hands.

References

Fukuyama, Francis. 2014. *Political Order and Political Decay: From the Industrial Revolution to the Globalization of Democracy.* New York: Farrar, Straus and Giroux.

Innes, Abby. 2014. 'The Political Economy of State Capture in Central Europe'. *JCMS: Journal of Common Market Studies* 52(1): 88–104.

Karolewski, Ireneusz Paweł. 2021. 'Towards a Political Theory of Democratic Backsliding? Generalizing the East Central European Experience'. In Astrid Lorenz and Lisa H. Anders (eds), *Illiberal Trends and Anti-EU Politics in East Central Europe.* London: Palgrave Macmillan, pp. 301–322.

Krastev, Ivan and Stephen Holmes. 2020. *The Light That Failed: Why the West Is Losing the Fight for Democracy.* New York: Pegasus Books.

Lorenz, Astrid and Lisa H. Anders. 2021. 'Illiberal Trends and Anti-EU Politics in East Central Europe: Major Findings and Avenues for Future Research'. In Astrid Lorenz and Lisa H. Anders (eds), *Illiberal Trends and Anti-EU Politics in East Central Europe.* London: Palgrave Macmillan, pp. 323–347.

Norris, Pippa and Ronald Inglehart. 2019. *Cultural Backlash: Trump, Brexit, and Authoritarian Populism.* Cambridge: Cambridge University Press.

Przeworski, Adam. 2019. *Crises of Democracy.* Cambridge: Cambridge University Press.

Sadurski, Wojciech. 2018. 'How Democracy Dies (in Poland): A Case Study of Anti-constitutional Populist Backsliding'. *Revista Forumul Judecatorilor* 1: 104–178.

Sartori, Giovanni. 1987. *The Theory of Democracy. Revisited.* Chatham, NJ: Chatham House Publishers.

Sata, Robert and Ireneusz Paweł Karolewski. 2019. 'Caesarean Politics in Hungary and Poland'. *East European Politics*, 1–20.

Scheppele, Kim Lane. 2013. 'The Rule of Law and the Frankenstate: Why Governance Checklists Do Not Work'. *Governance* 26(4): 559–562.

Tilly, Charles. 2007. *Democracy.* Cambridge: Cambridge University Press.

Tuleja, Piotr. 2022. 'Geneza, rozwój i upadek sądownictwa konstytucyjnego w Polsce'. *Państwo i prawo* 10: 254–275.

V-Dem Institute. 2020. *Autocratization Surges: Resistance Grows. V-Dem Annual Democracy Report 2020*. Gothenburg: University of Gothenburg. https://www.v-dem.net/documents/14/dr_2020_dqumD5e.pdf (accessed 9 April 2020).

Index

Note: Locators in *italic* and **bold** refer figures and tables respectively, and locators followed by "n" refer end notes

www.ingramcontent.com/pod-product-compliance
Ingram Content Group UK Ltd.
Pitfield, Milton Keynes, MK11 3LW, UK
UKHW021308260926
475702UK00048B/860
* 9 7 8 1 0 4 1 3 6 3 1 2 5 *